Methods of Group Psychotherapy

Methods of
Group Psychotherapy

RAYMOND J. CORSINI, Ph. D.

Research Associate
Industrial Relations Center, University of Chicago

Counselor
Chicago Community Child Guidance Centers

The Blakiston Division
McGRAW-HILL BOOK COMPANY, INC.
New York Toronto London 1957

To Evelina Lavaggi Corsini,
group therapist extraordinary

Foreword

Twenty years ago, a few isolated experimenters in state hospitals, overwhelmed by the impossibility of seeing individually the vast number of psychotic patients in their care, called some of them together for group meetings. These meetings, called in desperation, burgeoned into the group therapy movement which today has a literature of nearly fifteen hundred items, hundreds of practitioners, two journals, and two societies.

Dr. Corsini has made a commendable effort to integrate and combine into a single volume the several dozen trends that merge into the concept of group psychotherapy. His fairness in giving their due to all the major schools of thought in this dynamically growing field is perhaps the greatest value of his book. That he has kept his head and has not become lost in the social presses that demand conformity and allegiance is a tribute to his sense of history in the widest sense of social movements. Unlike the practitioner who follows one line of thought, gives his soul to one master, and uses one set of jargon, he seems able to be in and yet not of any particular persuasion. Psychotherapy needs more eclectic thinking, more experimentation, simpler language, and more testing of hypotheses so that it will be free of the slavish, narrow, and stultifying loyalties with which it is now plagued, and these are the needs Dr. Corsini has met in this book.

I am amazed at the amount of material included in this volume and impressed by its scholarship and erudition, leavened with the author's sly sense of humor. Dr. Corsini is a careful, methodical workman, and he has tried to keep his own convictions from distorting the picture of group psychotherapy. This is difficult to do, since the more one works in an area, the more difficult it is to see outside the boundaries one has staked out.

I recommend this book as primary reading for all who want an impartial and comprehensive view of group psychotherapy. It should serve admirably as a text, and its extensive bibliography will guide the reader to more specialized areas in the field.

J. W. KLAPMAN, M.D.

Preface

During the preparation of "Methods of Group Psychotherapy," attention was fixed on the topic to the virtual exclusion of other matters in the sociocultural matrix in which group psychotherapy occurs. As a general orientation, it may be wise to attempt at this point a frame of reference.

Group psychotherapy is one of man's devices to meet his needs. It belongs within an area known as psychotherapy, and it is based on the premise that through controlled social interactions it is possible to attain personality and behavioral changes which will lead to greater subjective comfort and improved social behavior.

Two views exist about group psychotherapy. The first is that it is a diluted, more economical, less effective method than the individual procedure. This view is not usually shared by group therapists, who see the group method as a more complex, more difficult, more natural, and equally effective procedure.

Group psychotherapy evolves from religion, education, and the social sciences. It is therefore old and at the same time new. It is like a river, fed by old streams and penetrating into new territories.

From one point of view, group psychotherapy represents a procedure for the attainment of the ideal state wherein every individual maintains perfect harmony with others. The various goals sought by people who are involved in group psychotherapy may be summarized by the golden rule, and the particular means may be summarized by the admonitions "Love thy neighbor," "Know thyself," and "Do good works." Group psychotherapy may be said to be the application of ideal relationships between people in a temporary and artificial setting.

A considerable part of the material to be found within is a collection, an abstraction, and a summary of the work and ideas of others as interpreted and evaluated by the author. To a very real extent, the people cited in the index should receive credit as collaborators. An attempt has been made to give specific acknowledgments to those whose ideas have been restated.

"Methods of Group Psychotherapy" is directed primarily to practitioners and students of what Sanderson has called the "helping professions," to psychiatrists, psychologists, social workers, teachers, guidance workers, and others who deal with groups in therapeutic settings. It should be of interest to ministers, physicians, directors of social agencies, superintendents of institutions, and all who deal with people in need of psychological assistance. It may be of interest also to those who are concerned with social progress and mental health.

The material within, while the direct responsibility of the author, has nevertheless been influenced by many people from whom he obtained face-to-face information. The author has learned something of the mysterious processes known as psychotherapy in the classrooms of the following: Hubert Coffey and Walter Bromberg of the University of California at Berkeley; Carl Rogers and Thomas Gordon of the University of Chicago; Rudolf Dreikurs of the Adlerian Institute of Chicago; and J. L. Moreno of the Moreno Institute at Beacon, N.Y. The author was a member of a therapeutic group conducted by Dr. Rolland Tougas at the Counseling Center of the University of Chicago, and he was in individual therapy with Dr. Carl Rogers. In diverse manners, Drs. Peter Bell and George Meisinger of the Psychiatric Field Service of Wisconsin; J. W. Klapman of the Chicago State Hospital; Rudolf Lassner, David Schmidt and Norman Fenton of the California Department of Correction; Edgar Borgatta of the Russell Sage Foundation; and Stanley Lipkin and Stanley Standal of the University of Chicago have contributed to the author's growth and development in this field. Dr. Bina Rosenberg of the Adlerian Institute collaborated in the preparation of Chapter 4 when it was originally published in a somewhat different form in the *Journal of Abnormal and Social Psychology*.

The author is indebted also to his wife and daughter, who assisted him in many of the clerical tasks involved in the preparation of this book and in the clarification of the presentation, as well as by the forbearance required during the complicated and time-consuming work of writing a textbook.

The reader who finds errors of fact or interpretation or who discovers omissions of events or credits will do the author a service to so inform him.

RAYMOND J. CORSINI, PH.D.

Contents

PART ONE

History, Theory, and Procedures

CHAPTER 1 *Introduction*

In recent years a variety of group methods for treating individuals with psychological difficulties has been developed. Known under various names such as *group psychoanalysis, psychodrama, the class method, activity group therapy, guided group interaction,* etc., or generically as *group psychotherapy,* or more usually *group therapy,* these methods represent a revolution in psychotherapy and may well be the answer for some up-to-now unsolved problems, especially the economic issue of supplying professional services for the great number of persons who can not afford individual psychotherapy. Although the economic argument is compelling and may even be sufficient reason for their existence, group methods have unique characteristics which cause them to be considered independently of individual therapy; and moreover, they have demonstrated results superior to those obtained with individual therapy in some circumstances, so that the mere question of cost does not determine the value of group methods. Progress in the use of group methods, the variety of specific techniques, the clinical and experimental results reported, and a general growth of appreciation and understanding of the potentialities of these methods make it imperative that those concerned with the problem of psychotherapy, study and evaluate the possibilities of group therapy.

The purpose of this introductory chapter is to give the reader a definition of the subject of this book, to review reasons for the emergence and existence of group therapy, and to attempt to summarize its current status.

DEFINITION

Several writers have felt that the term *group psychotherapy* is ambiguous and not capable of being defined simply and inclusively. Renouvier, for example, states [313], "Group therapy is a collective name for various methods which often contradict each other." Ackerman comments [6], "Group therapy is as yet inadequately defined, encompassing a variety of material almost as different in concepts as the men who practise them." Hulse combines both ideas in stating [169], "Group therapy is a not too well defined method of treatment embracing a number of different procedures that often have little in common."

These somewhat pessimistic feelings about the definition of group psychotherapy may be dispelled by the view that there is a number of specific group procedures based on a variety of theories and philosophies and having varied objectives. What contributes to the confusion is that the term group psychotherapy may be used in two specific ways. It may be thought of as a generic term, encompassing a variety of procedures. It may also be thought of as a name for a single procedure. If by group psychotherapy therapist A means method X, and if therapist B understands that group psychotherapy means method Y, then it is obvious that the two are not communicating. The complexity of this problem becomes evident when it is realized that more than 25 specific methods have been described in the literature [88].

The term group psychotherapy was introduced in 1932 by J. L. Moreno [265]. By it Moreno meant a method of relocating people in a community by means of individual evaluations and placements into new groups, so that, as a result of the interactions of personalities, social and personal amelioration would occur. Moreno said [265], "group therapy... is a method of psychotherapy which combines the technique of assignments with the technique of spontaneous treatments." More recent definitions are offered by Abrahams and Slavson. Abrahams states [2] that group therapy is "... a group process led by someone significantly less involved in the pathology, to ameliorate the problems of group members in relations to themselves and society." Slavson [359] defines the subject as "... a special application of the principles of individual therapy to two or more persons simultaneously which also brings into the situation the phenomena and problems of interpersonal relations."

An Approach to a General Definition

A War Department bulletin states [396], "In a broad sense any procedure which tends to improve the mental health of more than one individual is group psychotherapy." This broad definition does not differentiate between ameliorative group situations which are therapy and those which are not therapy. For example, the superintendent of an institution once said, "We have a great deal of group therapy in this school. The boys march together, they attend movies; they listen to music; they go to school. As a matter of fact, everything they do is in groups."

Definitions can be too narrow. Cotton says [92], "I would define group therapy as an attempt to reinforce and strengthen the individual's defenses against anxiety by identification with, analysis by, and support from the group." A colleague once said about a particular method, "This is not group psychotherapy, because the members do not sit in a circle and talk."

It may be worthwhile to classify psychotherapy in terms of formats. There are four basic kinds: *autonomous, pair, small group,* and *large group.* Autonomous therapy, or "self-therapy," occurs whenever an individual establishes a planned system of self-treatment. By means of meditation, prayer, reading, work, exercise, etc., he may consciously attempt to attain certain goals, such as greater self-understanding, greater comfort with himself, and greater social adjustment. Reik [312] and Horney [168] have discussed autonomous therapy at length and have a great regard for its possibilities.

Pair psychotherapy, the kind which is best known and which goes under the name of *individual therapy,* consists of interviews between two people, one of whom is called the patient, the other, the therapist. The most familiar example is psychoanalysis. There are many varieties of individual therapy, such a hypnotherapy, dianetics, conditioned-reflex therapy, gestalt therapy, general semantics, nondirective therapy, direct analysis, as well as innumerable variations of Freud's psychoanalysis, as propounded by Adler, Jung, Ferenczi, Horney, Sullivan, Fromm, Rank, Weiss, Levy, Steckel, and others.

The third kind of psychotherapy, *group psychotherapy,* is the concern of this book. It may involve groups of from 3 to 50 but is confined mostly to groups ranging from 5 to 20.

The last general kind of psychotherapy is *milieu therapy,* in which an entire community is established as a beneficial organism. Jones [187], Bierer [41], Freeman and Schwartz [126], and Polansky, Miller, and White [289] have discussed this variety of psychotherapy.

The third kind of psychotherapy, the subject of this book, must be defined in such a way that only groups that are truly psychotherapeutic will be included. The following definition will be used in this book. *Group psychotherapy consists of processes occurring in formally organized, protected groups and calculated to attain rapid ameliorations in personality and behavior of individual members through specified and controlled group interactions.* The significant elements in this definition will now be examined.

Psychotherapy is a *formal,* not an incidental, process. It is not the resultant of other, primary activities. Psychotherapy is the primary activity. Although it may do one "good" to read, play gin rummy, or go to ball games, these activities are not examples of autonomous, individual, or group therapy—unless these processes are entered into with the explicit prior understanding that they are undertaken for the purpose of therapy. Nothing can be called psychotherapy unless there has been a formal prior intention to engage in the particular process for the amelioration of personal-social conditions or relations.

An essential concept in psychotherapy is that of *protection*. In psychotherapy there is always an understanding, whether implicit or explicit, that the individual members are freed from some of the usual responsibilities for their behavior. In a therapeutic situation a person can say and do things that the group would not permit under other circumstances. The member of a therapeutic group understands that, as a part of the process of self-exploration, he may safely operate in certain ways not generally acceptable in society. He expects that his communications will be regarded as privileged (i.e., confidential), and he understands that he is to respect the secrets of other members.

Psychotherapy is *calculated* to bring about desired results. Results can not be assured. No absolute standards of success can be applied. The therapist operates in ways that he *believes* may attain particular results, but he can give no assurance of satisfaction. He ventures into an area that remains in the realm of speculation. The nature of results attained, whether good or bad, has nothing to do with whether any process is to be called psychotherapy.

To deserve the name of psychotherapy, a process must aim at *rapidity* of results. Amelioration of personality or of behavior may occur in many ways—through accidental environmental happenings, through self-analysis, etc.—but formal psychotherapy necessarily has inherent in it the concept that through the procedure a hastening of processes will occur. For example, a procedure that will cure obsessions but takes 20 years to do so must be considered poor, solely because it takes too long. Therapy is a formal process believed to be more rapid in its results than life in general.

It is difficult to state with exactness what the final purpose of therapy is. We may call it *amelioration* or *improvement*, but of what? A patient may wish understanding or to be comfortable with himself; a therapist may desire insight or improved social capacity; those in the patient's environment may desire better social behavior on his part. It may be helpful to state that amelioration refers to changes of particular kinds within two contexts: subjective—i.e., within the patient's own phenomenological system; and objective—i.e., in terms of evident behavior. Different observers may work toward different changes, but usually there is agreement on the part of all concerned as to what "good" changes are.

The above definition will serve as the criterion for deciding what is and what is not group psychotherapy. The definition will be interpreted loosely; in fact, almost every procedure that has been called group therapy in the literature is acceptable.

WHY GROUP PSYCHOTHERAPY?

Twenty-five years ago the concept of group therapy was not in the air. Today every person in the field of applied social relations understands it. One may wonder why this particular procedure came about. Two kinds of explanations, differing only in viewpoint, not in substance, may be offered.

The first answer is economic and has been advanced by many persons. Statements such as the following indicate this line of thinking: "There is a lamentable lack of adequately trained psychotherapists now available to handle the large number of patients who seek treatment" [11]. "...the dearth of psychiatrists and the disproportionate number of psychotic subjects in large institutions has created a need for a group method" [37]. Put in terms of therapists, the argument goes somewhat as follows. Some individual therapists were faced with case loads that were impossibly large. Therefore, having heard about the group method, they tried it out, sometimes in desperation, with little belief in it or understanding of it. Thus, out of necessity, the method was developed. The following quotations tell their own story. Kline [207]: "...introduced at the V.A. because of a scarcity of psychiatrists." Cotton [92]: "Group psychotherapy grew out of social intuition and was fostered by expediency." Wender [403]: "The group approach was adopted because of its expediency."

However, the writer advances another argument, compatible with the economic argument but somewhat broader. This particular point of view is fostered by the observation that at least 20 different people, entirely independently of one another, have discovered group psychotherapy. This theory is based on the idea of a cultural demand. Riesman has presented us with the idea of the "lonely crowd" [315]. There seems to be no question that society in its development has isolated people from one another. Paradoxically, increases of communication and of transportation appear to decrease intimacy of relationships. It may be that group therapy represents a correction against social isolation engendered by technological improvements. In short, a strong need has developed for people to get closer together; it is met to some extent by group psychotherapy.

PRESENT STATUS OF GROUP PSYCHOTHERAPY

No accurate statistics exist in this field. However, by means of a variety of approaches and some speculation, a picture of the field is obtainable. Perhaps the best indicator of how group psychotherapy has developed and how it stands at present may be obtained from the statistics of publications. Table 1 is based on material taken from a bibliography of group psychotherapy.

Table 1.   Number of Books, Articles, and Dissertations in the Literature of Group Psychotherapy by 5-year Periods *

1906–1910	11
1911–1915	3
1916–1920	5
1921–1925	4
1926–1930	11
1931–1935	20
1936–1940	69
1941–1945	203
1946–1950	536
1951–1955	879

* From R. J. Corsini and L. J. Putzey. Bibliography of group psychotherapy. *Group Psychother.* vol. 9 (no. 3), 1956.

From Table 1 it appears that at least 1,700 articles, theses, and books have appeared in the literature. The rate of growth is geometric and reflects the growing interest in this field.

No one knows how many therapists or how many patients are taking part in group therapy. The two associations of group therapists have a total of approximately 1,000 members, and more than 1,000 people have contributed to the literature. From surveys such as those made by Geller [133], McCorkle [256], and Corsini and Lundin [89], it appears that in approximately one-half of mental hospitals and in one-quarter of correctional institutions, group psychotherapy is employed.

The group method has been used in schools, in outpatient clinics, in somatic and mental hospitals, in the military, in prisons and reformatories, in social agencies, in institutions for defectives and for the handicapped, in industry, and in guidance clinics. It has been used with a wide variety of individuals and for diverse problems. Every month one finds in the literature new and ingenious applications of group psychotherapy in specific institutions or to specific problems.

If one is interested in finding out whether or not group psychotherapy is really valuable, nothing takes the place of reading source material. One is struck by the consistently enthusiastic tone of those who report, mostly persons with experience in individual therapy. While one may well want to wait and see and may desire research reports and further evidence before coming to a conclusion, if these firsthand reports have any validity, the answer is in already: group psychotherapy is a significant factor in our cultural pattern. It is here to stay.

CHAPTER 2 *Historical Developments*

Hulse [169] and Dreikurs [105a] call Anton Mesmer the father of group psychotherapy; Klapman [199] assigns primary credit to Joseph H. Pratt; Bierer [39] feels the honors should be divided by Pratt and Alfred Adler; and Meiers [261] states that the earliest founders of true group psychotherapy were Pratt and Moreno. While all are correct in giving these individuals credit for their contributions, which differ considerably, none is correct in trying to establish primacy. Group psychotherapy is not a unidimensional entity, not an organic whole; it is instead a conglomerate of methods and theories having diverse multiple origins in the past, resulting inevitably from social demands, and developed in various forms by many persons. Each contributor has borrowed from the past and has made advances; but group psychotherapy is the product of many minds.

In attempting to write the history of group psychotherapy, three major divisions will be made: the *origins*, beginning in man's historic past and extending up to the beginning of the twentieth century; the *pioneer period*, running from about 1905 to 1930; and the *modern period*, beginning in 1931.

ORIGINS

Man has lived, worked, worshipped, and played in groups probably as long as he has existed. From group association he obtains something in addition to the evident benefits. These surplus consequences, such as feelings of good fellowship and of belonging, and identification with the group, while often not recognized as being of value in themselves, nevertheless are important in the psychological economy of individuals. We know today that man is a social creature and needs to belong, to be accepted, to be valued, to be wanted; and that unless he experiences these social feelings, he sickens and dies. Infants deprived of social stimulation are said to develop depressions accompanied by physical

9

and mental deteriorations which can be treated only through those emotional interchanges known as "mothering" [371].

While people worked and played in groups throughout history, there was not until recently an explicit understanding of the importance of group association for the psychological health of the individual. It is not fanciful to say that people who entered various social groups in which they found pleasure were participating in informal group psychotherapy. In a manner of speaking, every group into which one enters freely, in which one feels compatible, and from which one gets pleasure, is therapeutic.

Natural groups that serve the same purposes as artificial groups are certainly the more desirable; formal groups merely provided a substitute for whatever can be obtained from natural groups. It is when the latter do not exist for an individual that formal, artificial, or contrived groups have a place.

Historically we are able to find many examples of groups which seem to have given their members certain intangible benefits apparently quite similar to those obtained from formal group psychotherapy. An outstanding example was the healing temple that existed at Epidaurus from 600 B.C. to 200 A.D. [179]. People afflicted with mental and physical ailments repaired to this temple to obtain relief from symptoms. The procedures involved talks, lectures, rest, baths, and what appears to have been a kind of general suggestion therapy. The effects produced by philosophers and religious leaders on their audiences and congregations were no doubt quite like those obtained in group therapy. Although the intentions of early philosophers and religious leaders—to reach fuller knowledge of natural and divine law—were quite different from those of group therapists, who can deny that the feelings generated in those who listened to the Apology or the Sermon on the Mount were basically similar to those engendered in a therapeutic group? Jackson, a minister, explicitly states [174], "The sermon is the oldest form of group psychotherapy."

It is necessary to leap nearly 2,000 years to the time of the American Revolution to find an example of a group, therapeutic in intent, which may be considered the first example of formal group therapy.

Mesmer. Anton Mesmer, an Austrian physician, began to practice mental healing in Paris about 1776. He believed that he could cure physical ailments through certain emanations from his own body. Groups of afflicted persons sat around a wooden tub from which iron bars protruded, holding the affected parts of their bodies against these bars. Mesmer believed that a "magnetism" was thus sent into the bodies of his patients [13]. He obtained what appeared to be genuine cures. He was investigated by a number of scientific commissions, on one of which

Benjamin Franklin was a member. The reports of these commissions stated in effect that the cures were real but that the maladies were imaginary.

We have in this case a curious situation, not unusual in the history of science, of an individual successfully using certain methods but ascribing incorrect reasons for his results. Today more is known about hysteria, suggestion, hypnotism, and psychosomatic medicine than in the time of Mesmer. Nevertheless, those who have given Mesmer the title of the father of group psychotherapy do appear to have good reason.

De Sade. It will surprise those who think of the Marquis de Sade solely as a sexual degenerate from whose name originated the word "sadism" to learn that apparently he has been somewhat maligned. While there is no doubt that he was sexually perverse and that he deserved his many and long imprisonments, it also appears that at one time he was confined in a mental asylum by Napoleon as a political prisoner. While in the asylum of Charenton, De Sade, officially a patient, wrote and directed plays which were acted by other patients before the general public [141]. There was some opposition to de Sade's activities by the doctors of the asylum, but the superintendent supported these theatricals because of the good effects that they had on patients. And so, de Sade, even though he probably engaged in this activity for relief of boredom, deserves mention in the history of group psychotherapy.

Camus and Pagniez. Jean Camus and Paul Pagniez, two French psychiatrists, pupils of Déjérine, who were applying the Weir Mitchell rest-cure treatment for neurotics, made the observation that patients treated in wards improved more rapidly than those treated in solitude [67]. This information was neither understood nor followed up by anyone; it is an example, common in the history of science, of the observation of an important fact without the realization of its significance.

Freud. No method of psychotherapy can be considered apart from the influence of Freud, even if the theory and method are not in consonance with those of the great Viennese. Although Freud himself never used the group method and there seems to be no evidence that he even knew about it, he did establish certain now-common concepts about mental dynamics, especially the importance of the unconscious, for which all psychotherapists owe him a debt.

THE PIONEER PERIOD

The pioneer period of group psychotherapy extended about from 1906 through 1931, from Pratt's first description of his "class method" through Moreno's naming of the field. This crucial period has not as yet been clarified, especially because, although we know of considerable early

use of groups for therapeutic purposes, there have been relatively few
explicit published accounts. This is especially true of early European
efforts. Teirich [388] and Dreikurs [105a], who have summarized some of
the early developments, mention in passing such men as Ozertzovsky,
Rosenstein, Stransky, Metzl, Kauders, Spiel, Schultz, Hoff, Urban, Betz,
Hirschfeld, and Guilarowsky, but little is known of their specific theories
or procedures. Consequently, it is necessary to concentrate on the relatively few persons about whose efforts something is known. The importance of a man in any field depends not only on his insights and
operations but also on whether he communicated his ideas. Six men,
who did major work from 1906 to 1931, deserve to be called the pioneers
of group psychotherapy: Pratt, Lazell, Marsh, Adler, Moreno, and
Burrow.

Pratt. Joseph H. Pratt, an internist in the city of Boston, in the year
1906 presented a lecture at the Johns Hopkins Medical School on the
topic, "The Home Sanitarium Treatment of Consumption" [294, 295]. In
this paper, Dr. Pratt stated that he believed it possible to treat indigent
tuberculosis patients in their own homes. He believed that if those
afflicted with this dread disease would follow his rigid regimen, which
included rest, fresh air, and good food, they might survive the white
plague. He obtained funds from the Emmanuel Church of Boston, as
well as the assistance of the ministers of this church. To save his time he
gathered tuberculosis patients into groups to emphasize his strict hygienic
instructions. This group, gathered solely for the purpose of saving Dr.
Pratt's time by making it unnecessary to explain and exhort over and over
again, is often considered the beginning of scientific group psychotherapy [199].

Dr. Pratt's efforts were followed with great interest. Drs. David
Riesman of Philadelphia, F. J. Ripley of Brockton, D. Dencker of Boston,
and F. T. Fulton of Providence were among the physicians who employed the class method for the treatment of a variety of physical ailments. In addition, Elwood Worcester and Samuel McComb, ministers
of the Emmanuel Church, established the Emmanuel Church Health
Class and began to publish a series of pamphlets and a book [415] in
which they discussed the place of religion in medicine. Other physicians
did not obtain the same results. Medical societies did not take kindly
to the intrusion of the clergy into medicine [197], and as a result the
class method and the movement initiated by Pratt in 1906 appeared to
have died by the beginning of World War I.

One critic [61] wrote about the efforts of Worcester and McComb,
"Their efforts are ostensibly to aid legitimate medicine, as they proclaim,
but in reality are to usurp the doctor's functions in all disease."

Pratt's 1906 lecture was published in that year in two journals [294,

295]. In 1907 two more articles [296, 297] on the class method appeared. In 1908 [298] he reported further on results, and in 1911 [299], probably affected by some of the criticisms, in an article describing what the class method had accomplished, he said, "In this class . . . it seems to me that too much importance is attached to the class itself—the weekly meetings, the record books and the home visitations of the nurse—and too little importance to the three essentials of rest, fresh air, and good food." In 1917 [300] another article, describing the tuberculosis class, appeared. In 1922 [301] Pratt published a discussion of the principles of the class method to various chronic diseases. Twelve years later, in 1934 [302], he wrote an article on the emotions and their effects on psychoneuroses. Eleven years later, in 1945 [303], he summarized the group method in the treatment of psychosomatic disorders. In 1950, Pratt and Johnson [305] edited a booklet summarizing Pratt's work since 1930, and in 1953 [304] Pratt wrote another article concerning the use of Déjérine's methods in the treatment of the neuroses. It must be evident that Pratt's long and intimate association with the therapeutic group procedure requires that he be given primary consideration in any account of its history.

Pratt's career has two distinct phases. In 1906 he was interested in curing a purely somatic disease, tuberculosis, by the application of hygienic principles, and he called groups together to instruct members in a therapeutic regimen. In 1930 when he established a clinic at the Boston Dispensary, his concern was no longer with frank disease but, on the contrary, with persons who had nothing organically wrong with them but who nevertheless complained of physical symptoms. Now, instead of deprecating the class method, he made it the central therapeutic focus. In 1906 Pratt was an internist; in 1930 he had become a psychiatrist. What may have led to this change? We know that he had been in contact with the ministers Worcester and McComb, who were well versed in psychology and who preached psychosomatic medicine. We know that he read Ross's book on the common neuroses, published in 1924 [323], and that from this he apparently became interested in the theories of Déjérine, who had been translated into English by Dr. Smith Ely Jelliffe in 1913 [100]. Having achieved a psychological frame of reference, he changed both his approach and his purpose. It is of interest to note that up to 1953 Pratt was apparently not influenced to any extent by the dynamic psychotherapists who followed in the wake of Freud.

Marsh and Lazell. The proper place of these two psychiatrists in the history of psychotherapy is not easy to assess. The first to publish his views was Lazell, whose earliest paper appeared in 1921 [222], but by far the more important was Marsh, who did not begin to write until

1931 [247]. Marsh stated that he began to do group work as early as 1909 and that Lazell antedated him. Neither gives any answer to the question whether they were influenced by Pratt; the presumption is that both of them started their work independently of each other as well as of Pratt.

Marsh and Lazell used a procedure, quite similar to that employed by Pratt, which came to be known as the *repressive-inspirational* technique, still used in mental hospitals. Marsh had the idea of the therapeutic community, or *milieu therapy*, in which all the personnel of an institution would be involved in a common effort to develop themselves to the fullest extent [248]. He was a man well ahead of his time. His credo of group therapy, "By the crowd have they been broken; by the crowd shall they be healed," explains succinctly the essential message of group psychotherapy. However, neither Marsh nor Lazell appears to have had any great effect on other therapists; the statistics of the literature indicate that they did not fan the spark into life.

Adler. Alfred Adler, the first of Freud's followers to break away from him, began, about 1921, according to Seidler [342], to counsel children in front of groups. He carried out individual therapy in front of others. His first purpose, it appears, was instructional. He was not then interested in affecting the group: he wanted to treat his patient, and he wanted to demonstrate his procedures. However, it became evident to Adler that the group procedure was having effects on the doctors, the social workers, the teachers, and the psychologists who attended his demonstrations. More important, it appeared that the group instead of damaging the intimate doctor-patient relationship, as might have been expected, actually improved it. Nevertheless, it is not quite accurate to say that Adler actually carried out group psychotherapy; in reality he engaged in individual therapy in front of a group. If the group members participated, they did so as quasi therapists rather than as patients. The method that Alfred Adler developed has continued in use, with variation, to this day and may be said, with the above reservation in mind, to be the oldest form of group psychotherapy in existence.

Moreno. Probably the most important individual in the history of group psychotherapy is J. L. Moreno, also, like Freud, Mesmer, and Adler, a Viennese physician. Moreno has reported some diverting accounts of his early work, stating that even in his childhood he acted out elaborate improvised dramas. He took part in psychodramatic acting with children in the playgrounds of Vienna. He became interested in the Spontaneity Theatre, and tried, without success, to establish a new religion. While a medical student he attempted to help prostitutes rehabilitate themselves through group procedures [270]. At this time he became aware of the importance of "one individual becoming the therapeutic agent of the other." He experimented with a variety of action methods employing spontaneity and improvisations, became interested in psychotherapy, but violently rejected psychoanalysis.

In 1931 he suggested a new method of prison classification, arguing that if prisoners were grouped sociometrically the interactions would be beneficial. In a monograph on this thesis he used the magic words "group therapy" for the first time, although, as stated before, in a somewhat different sense from that currently employed [265]. Actually the group therapist did not even have to come into contact with the group members, since groups were to be constituted on paper in terms of analyses of their own strengths and weaknesses. In 1931 Moreno began to publish *Impromptu,* concerned for the most part with dramatics, not with psychotherapy. In 1937 appeared his journal *Sociometry,* and in 1947 *Sociatry,* later to be called *Group Psychotherapy.* He organized the first society of group therapists in 1942 and became its first president. His writings in the field of group therapy, especially in sociometry, a method of measuring social interactions, are voluminous. In addition, Moreno has gone up and down the breadth of this country and in Europe to expound his highly original doctrines. From the point of view of this book, Moreno's major accomplishments are three: first, he introduced a theory to account for group structure and operations; second, he introduced a new method of therapy in groups, which has been accepted by many people in a diversity of forms; and third, he has been the indefatigable exponent of the group therapeutic movement.

Burrow. Trigant Burrow was another of Freud's pupils who dissented. He developed an elaborate social theory of behavior known as *phyloanalysis,* which, probably because of the obscurity of his writing style, has not become popular [66]. In general, Burrow felt that the emphasis on the individual and his phenomenology, which was the essence of Freud's theory, was wrong and that there were no individuals in society, but rather members of groups. In different ways this seems also to be the message of Karen Horney, Harry Stack Sullivan, and Alfred Adler. Burrow abandoned classical psychoanalysis and for a time practiced "group analysis"[64]. In 1928 he wrote, "For several years I have, in association with others, been daily occupied with the practical observation of these interactions as they were found to occur in the experimental condition of actual group setting" [65].

However, Burrow had no influence on later therapeutic group work. He gave up such clinical groups and devoted himself in later years almost exclusively to the development of phyloanalysis.

Group Psychotherapy up to 1931

Pratt has his class method, Marsh and Lazell their repressive-inspirational technique, Adler his child guidance, Moreno his psychodrama, and Burrow his group analysis. In Europe, group workers called their procedures by a variety of names, including *Kollective Therapie*. Anyone looking at these several methods in 1931 would have seen little in common among them. In the way that words have of establishing concepts, it seems that Moreno's term *group therapy*, which he used to indicate a sociometric method of reclassifying prisoners, actually helped establish the concept of psychotherapy of individuals in groups. This term became the generic name for all methods of therapeutic group work. The modern period of group psychotherapy began with the introduction of the new term; it established a common conceptual frame of reference.

THE MODERN PERIOD

In discussing historical developments from 1932 on, we are dealing with the work of contemporaries, which is with difficulty surveyed objectively. Although the past of group psychotherapy is old, its history is new. So much has been done so recently that to obtain a comprehensive understanding of this field at the middle of the twentieth century it is necessary to summarize briefly some of the major accomplishments of the more significant workers. Some fifty individuals are therefore listed alphabetically to indicate some of the contributions of major workers in the field of group psychotherapy.

Joseph Abrahams has been concerned with the use of group methods in the rehabilitation of military prisoners and, with Lloyd McCorkle, has analyzed the use of guided group interaction [34]. He has also written on the use of group methods in the treatment of schizophrenics [1]. Nathan W. Ackerman has dealt with a wide variety of topics, including evaluations of psychoanalytic group procedures [9] and military uses of group methods [7]. I. M. Altshuler has emphasized the importance of music and rhythm in the group treatment of psychotics [14, 15].

George R. Bach has made a major contribution in a full-scale description of his intensive group procedure, which is noteworthy for its theoretical rationale, its complexity, and its length [19]. Bach's presentation gives evidence that the group method can parallel individual procedures in terms of depth of treatment. Dorothy Baruch and Hyman Miller, working together, have used group procedures including analyses of projective drawings [27], psychodrama, and nondirective discussions in the treatment of allergic patients [26, 263]. Lauretta Bender has experimented with group methods of treating institutionalized children in hospital wards [32] and, with A. G. Woltman [33], has discussed the use of puppets as a therapeutic medium. Joshua Bierer introduced a group psychotherapy to Great Britain and has developed the concept of therapeutic social clubs in mental hospitals [40, 43]. W. R. Bion, a member of the Tavistock Clinic in Great Britain, has experimented with groups [44, 46]. He has been more concerned with an analysis of processes that occur in groups than with evaluation of the effectiveness of such procedures [45]. Nathan Blackman has used group methods with aphasics [50] and has experimented with bibliotherapy with schizophrenics [48]. Edgar F. Borgatta has been the editor of *Sociometry* and *Group Psychotherapy*. He has investigated various aspects of the group process and has argued for the importance of scientific research in this field [52]. Robert W. Buck, an early follower of J. H. Pratt, used the class method in the treatment of essential hypertension [60].

M. H. Chappell, together with his collaborators, J. J. Stefano, J. S. Rogerson, and H. S. Pike, worked with matched groups of stomach ulcer patients and published the first experimental study of group psychotherapy in terms of a somatic condition [71]. This study was the first and in some ways is still the best in its particular area. Hubert Coffey, together with various collaborators, instituted a group therapy program in a church and has been employed in the construction of a complex system of describing group dynamics [76]. Robert R. Cohen is one of the first workers in this field to have used visual aids [78]. He has written chiefly about military applications of group therapeutic methods [77, 79].

Rudolf Dreikurs, a pupil of Alfred Adler, brought the method of family counseling to America and is the author of numerous articles in this field, stressing primarily the democratic implications of the therapeutic group [102, 104, 105]. He has been instrumental in the establishment of training centers for group therapists. As early as 1928 Dreikurs conducted groups with alcoholics. He was one of the first, together with Burrow, in employing group therapy in private practice. He also developed multiple therapy [103]. S. H. Foulkes is an outstanding exponent of the use of the psychoanalytic technique in group psychotherapy [123, 124]. He has written the most complete account of psychoanalytic group therapy. J. D. Frank has investigated a number of areas of interest in this field and has been concerned with research developments. With Florence Powdermaker, Frank has published a detailed study of the group process [290].

Joseph J. Geller is the statistician of the group therapy movement; he has made periodic surveys of its growth [133]. He has written one of the most satisfactory accounts of the introduction and use of group psychotherapy in a mental hospital [132]. Thomas Gordon, a client-centered counselor, has interpreted the group process in terms of Rogers' psychotherapeutic theory [140]. Leon Gorlow and his collaborators E. L. Hoch and Earl Telschow, also working in the client-centered frame of reference, have produced a scholarly research study of processes and evaluation of group therapy with college students [142]. S. B. Hadden has employed Pratt's class method [150, 151, 153], has been a student of the therapeutic process in groups [154], and is one of the historians of the movement [155].

Gertrude Harrow has conducted one of the most detailed studies of psychodrama in the treatment of schizophrenics [158]. Nicholas Hobbs, a client-centered group therapist, has in several publications discussed the theory and method of therapeutic group work [162, 163, 164, 165, 166]. Wilfred Hulse appears to be the international representative of this field [171, 172], has employed group therapy in military situations [169], and has been interested in various aspects of the group process [170]. Walter Joel and David Shapiro have conducted one of the most careful investigations of group mechanisms in therapy [181]. F. D. Jones and H. N. Peters have made some precise studies of processes and gains in group psychotherapy [184, 285].

One of the most prolific writers in this field and the author of the first general text in group psychotherapy is J. W. Klapman [199], who has developed a bibliotherapeutic method which stresses strongly the role of reason and logic in therapy [200, 201, 202, 203]. He has been a strong defender of didactic and directive procedures and is at one pole of the continuum at which Rogers is at the opposite end. He founded Resurgo, an organization of ex-mental hospital patients, using group activities for further development. Nathan S. Kline, a student of Paul Schilder, has investigated various aspects of group psychotherapy, including psychodrama [205, 206], and has been interested in ethical issues in this field. Investigations of the use of the Rorschach test for the evaluation of group psychotherapy have been made by Walter Klopfer [208]. Gisela Konopka has been a steady contributor to the literature, using the group method with children [211] and with delinquents [212]. Also, in the use of group therapy to combat prejudice she has made some original contributions [210]. Benjamin Kotkov has compiled a bibliography of group therapy [214], with Burchard and Michaels has attempted a conceptual structuring of the field [62], and has investigated group methods in obesity control [216]. Rudolf Lassner experimented with dramatic methods in correctional institutions, employing theatricals with delinquent children [218] and psychodrama with adult prisoners [219].

Stanley Lipkin, a client-centered psychotherapist, has used group methods in the treatment of military prisoners [231]. Abraham A. Low developed a unique procedure using community social clubs for exinmates of mental hospitals [239, 240]. Abraham Luchins used group methods in mental hospitals and has been concerned with evaluation of results [243, 244, 245]. The increasingly popular method of cotherapists has been studied by William H. Lundin and Bernard Aronov [246]. Willis Mc-

Cann, the originator, with his collaborator Albert Almada [251], of the round-table method, has made some highly original contributions to the theory and practice of group psychotherapy in mental hospitals; their method is an extension of the idea of milieu therapy. In addition, McCann has begun a long-range investigation of this procedure [250]. In the penal field, Lloyd McCorkle [254, 255, 257] is the outstanding exponent of the use of group methods. He employs a technique known as *guided group interaction*. He has written several accounts with others, including Joseph Abrahams [3, 4] and F. L. Bixby [47], of this method. In addition, McCorkle has surveyed the use of group methods in penal-correctional work [256].

Miguel Prados has centered his attention on the use of visual methods in group psychotherapy [292]. He has produced a series of motion pictures widely used in mental hygiene work [293]. Fritz Redl has employed group procedures in the treatment of disturbed children. His work approaches milieu therapy in concept. He has investigated a number of basic problems, including leadership and resistance [307, 309], and has been concerned with the diagnostic possibilities of the group [308]. Harold P. Rome has used the cinema for group therapy [319] and has employed group methods in military psychiatry [318, 320].

Paul Schilder has been important in group psychotherapy for several reasons [334, 335]. His penetrating observations and his enthusiasm for the potentials of groups helped establish the group method in this country, since his prestige in the field was great. He directly influenced such persons as Lauretta Bender, Frank Curran, Karl Bowman, Nathan Kline, S. H. Foulkes, and many others who later made contributions to this field. Donald A. Shaskan has demonstrated a wide diversity of interests in this area [343, 344]. With H. Lindt, Miriam Jolesch, Robert Plank, Helen Blum, Dorothy Conrad, and J. D. Grant he has investigated military uses of group therapy and the functioning and prediction of behavior in groups [345, 346, 347, 348]. Joel Shor was one of the first to modify Moreno's psychodrama in the form called *psychodramatic group therapy*, in which the auxiliary egos come out of the group itself [350]. This less complex procedure has also been used by Lassner [219] and by Boring and Deabler [53].

A most important person in group psychotherapy is S. R. Slavson, who about 1934 began to experiment with a permissive group method of dealing with disturbed youth in their latency period. This method, known as *activity group therapy*, has been described in detail in some of Slavson's many articles and books [354, 355, 356, 357, 358, 359, 360]. He has contributed much to the literature, with articles, reviews, textbook chapters, collections of articles, etc. He was the prime mover in establishing the American Group Therapy Association and in publishing *The Interna-*

tional Journal of Group Psychotherapy. He has influenced a number of persons, including Mortimer Schiffer, Betty Gabriel, and Saul Scheidlinger. J. D. Sutherland, a British psychiatrist, has used the group method in military situations and has been concerned with the question of training group therapists [381].

H. R. Teirich has written on a variety of issues in group psychotherapy; his major contribution may be his discussions of the status of this field in Europe [387, 388]. Zerka Toeman Moreno, under her maiden as well as her married name, has made a number of contributions to the literature of psychodrama and the therapeutic film [273, 392].

Louis Wender, an early worker in this field, has written on a variety of topics, including group dynamics [400], history of group therapy [405], and various applications of therapeutic groups [399, 401, 402, 404, 405, 406]. Carl A. Whitaker, with his collaborators John Warkentin and Nan Johnson, has discussed philosophic issues in group therapy and the use of supermultiple groups, in which one patient is treated by a number of therapists [409]. Alexander Wolf has been concerned with definitions and applications of psychoanalytic group psychotherapy [413, 414]. He has established a group workshop for investigation of the potentialities of groups operating under psychoanalytic principles. Katherine Wright and J. R. Jacobson [176, 416] have developed a unique procedure for use with deteriorated mental hospital patients.

CHAPTER 3

Group Psychotherapy and Theory

No scientifically based system of therapy can exist without theory. To meet new situations adequately and consistently, any practitioner of group therapy needs to have an understanding of the intervening dynamics between treatment and changes. To evaluate his results, he can not depend solely on observations but must establish a conceptual frame of reference from which he is able to make interpretations.

The group psychotherapist is continually forced to make decisions which may have important consequences. Wanting to make good decisions, he must rely on his past experiences, his readings, his interpretations and evaluations, and, finally, on his systematic theoretical position. How does he decide whom to select for a group and whom to reject; how does he know what to do in a group and what not to do; how can he respond to new situations? If he has some consistent articles of faith, he can respond immediately; otherwise he is lost. Theory serves him as a map in *terra incognita,* as a guide to action, as a compass on uncharted seas. His theory may be simple or complex; derived from the work of others or from his own work; implicit or explicit—but it must exist. He simply can not operate without theory.

Dangers of Theory

A theory, if we may paraphrase Gertrude Stein, is a theory is a theory. That is to say, it is not a law; it is only a guess, a speculation, a belief, an article of faith. It is when psychotherapists forget this and behave as though a theory were absolute truth that psychotherapy becomes programmatic and sterile. Those who accept theory as some persons accept religious dogma become impermeable to new ideas; they see reality through polarized lenses; they react emotionally and hostilely to whatever attacks their system of belief.

The danger of theory is that it may be regarded as law. Such an attitude may develop when communication is blocked between psychotherapists, when holders of one set of beliefs communicate only among themselves. This danger is augmented by the construction of new symbols of communication with esoteric meanings. The harm caused by the introduction of new words is incalculable.

It is important to understand various theories, to know how they came about and why contradictory theories are held. It is essential to learn to what extent theories are really different and to what extent they differ only with respect to terminology and metaphor, or with respect to area of concern. It does appear, fortunately for the advancement of psychotherapy, that the group situation permits closer inspection of operations than individual therapy and that group therapists are more willing to come to agreement than are individual therapists [107].

Theory: Individual and Group

Some psychotherapists believe that group and individual psychotherapy are based on the same laws. After all, they say, human nature is the same whether one is in a group situation of two or of ten persons: the same dynamics are at work, and changes come about in essentially the same way. Others take quite a different position and claim that individual therapy and group therapy are two different matters. An intermediate position might be that group therapy, because of its greater complexity of interactions, includes whatever is in individual therapy and has something else in addition.

Sigmund Freud appears to defend the first of these points of view in stating [127]:

The conflict between individual therapy and social or group psychology which at first might seem full of significance, loses a great deal of its sharpness when it is examined more closely . . . from the very first individual psychology is at the same time social psychology as well.

However, J. L. Moreno appears to attack this point of view when he says [269]:

Psychoanalysis has ceased to be the final word in everything psychological and social-psychiatric. . . . The evolution of science has gradually caught up with it. . . . In the last twenty years they [the group therapies] have led the way beyond psychoanalysis and the brilliant but speculative group psychologies of LeBon, McDougall and Freud. . . . The conceptual framework which was logical for the couch situation, libido, transference, resistance, abreaction, free association and so forth, had to undergo profound changes.

Leaving aside the issue of whether groups of two and groups of more than two, established for therapeutic purposes, have identical dynamics, it may be well to understand a variety of reactions concerning the issue.

Theories Held by Patients

Not only personality theorists but also patients have theories about psychotherapy. While this matter does not appear to have been made the subject of systematic research, every psychotherapist is well aware that his patients come to him with already formulated conceptions of what is to be done and why. While no definitive statement can be made at this point, it does appear that patients tend to hold to a cognitive-feeling-action theory that goes somewhat as follows: "I am now in distress and I do not function adequately. I feel that if I can learn what I am and how I have become what I am, this knowledge will lead to greater happiness and greater efficiency. I expect, in therapy, to learn more about myself, either through self-exploration or through directed explanations."

Theories Held by Therapists

It may be said that every psychotherapist holds on to some unique theory, which, no matter how much it may conform to some other person's theory, nevertheless manages to have individualistic elements. Those who hold somewhat similar theories, or, more cynically, who use the same idiom, form what may be called schools of thought, such as the Freudian, Adlerian, Jungian, Rankian, Rogerian, etc.

No worthwhile therapist holds undeviatingly to any particular set of beliefs. Freud is an outstanding example of a theorist who continually added to his system of thought. Alfred Adler maintained at least three quite different kinds of theories, the second of which is best known [106]. Rogers has made a statement to the effect that everything he believed at one time he discarded at another time [317]. From this it is evident that theory is a living, changing matter, varying among individuals and modifying itself in any individual from time to time on the basis of new experiences.

But many people are worried about the diversity of theories: why, they ask, are there so many different kinds of explanations of what happens in psychotherapy? There are many reasons for this state of affairs, which is not to be deplored, since a variety of viewpoints, especially if they are stated in ways that they can be tested experimentally, may lead more rapidly to final comprehension of human behavior. One answer is that various theories are concerned with different aspects of therapy. Another answer is that certain theories say essentially the same things in different ways. Another answer is that some theories do not appear to be capable of explaining certain events, and as a result, new explanations have to be found.

THE DEVELOPMENT OF A NEW THEORY

In order to make clear how a theory may arise, an example will be taken from the writer's experience. The fact that this theory may be unimportant and is accepted by no one is completely beside the point. What is important is that the reader, by sharing vicariously certain experiences, may learn how it is that new theories arise.

The writer at one time conducted a group consisting of a dozen members which operated under democratic, permissive rules. The usual method of therapy was psychodrama, but a variety of other techniques, suggested either by the therapist or by the members, were tried out at various times. Following a series of seven therapeutic sessions, the eighth session was reserved for discussions and evaluations of the members and of the previous sessions [83].

In this spirit of experimentation, almost every suggested method was tried out at least once. On the spur of the moment, the writer once suggested a procedure in which a member would talk about himself, then "retire" from the group psychologically but not physically, so that the rest of the group could discuss him as though he were not present. The "absent" member was to do nothing but listen. His back was turned to the group so that the others would not see his face and be inhibited in their discussion by seeing him face-to-face. Later on, this procedure, in somewhat more complex form, became the behind-the-back technique [86].

It appeared to be the unanimous opinion of the group that this method had something special in it and that it was worth further tryouts. Discussion brought forth three conclusions about the method: (*a*) it seemed that those who were subjected to this procedure believed that it had helped them; (*b*) it was reported by the other members that they could discuss the "absent" individual more frankly and freely than if he were psychologically present in the group or actually absent; (*c*) the subjects who were discussed "behind their backs" stated that they could listen to adverse criticism with a surprising lack of negative emotions.

Here were three reactions to a very unusual procedure. Why did they occur? What already formulated explanation was there to account for these reactions? Nothing known to the writer seemed adequate to explain the good results, the freedom the discussants felt, and the ease with which the subjects reacted.

This is what causes a theory to emerge: a need to explain events not adequately explained by other theories.

Why did people find this method good for them; why did others find they could talk more freely; why did subjects find they could accept what was said about them with equanimity? To answer these questions some postulates were formulated.

1. An individual has (*a*) an ideal conception of himself, (*b*) a perception of what he is like, (*c*) an understanding of how others react to him, and (*d*) a suspicion of how others really regard him.

2. A psychologically disturbed person is one who does not manage to combine these separate perceptions and conceptions into a coherent whole. A person is continually trying to find out in therapy what he is in terms of these four perceptions. He asks what should I be like; what am I like; how do others treat me; and how do others see me?

3. There is often a discrepancy, or the subject believes that there is, between *d* and the other three perceptions. A maladjusted individual may believe that others actually see him quite differently from the way he sees himself, the way he would like to be, and the way others act toward him. If he is able to have assurance about this fourth viewpoint, he will be able to feel much more comfortable.

4. Our society is based on the principle of tact. As the advertisements say, "Not even your best friend will tell you." There is a tendency in our society to talk and act one way before a person's face and another way behind his back. The gossip group is a case in point.

5. A subject who feels that others are thinking about him differently from the way they act begins to feel uncomfortable. If he has a valid understanding of how others feel about him, whether they feel favorably or unfavorably, he experiences a reduction in anxiety.

What has been said above is that this form of psychotherapy is, at least to some extent, a process of finding out what others think of one. How does this fit in with other forms of psychotherapy? In directive therapies, in which the analyst discusses with the individual his dynamics and life style, essentially the same process occurs. The therapist tells the patient how he sees him to be. In the nondirective therapies, the patient may discuss himself and the actions of others until he arrives at an understanding of what he is like from the point of view of the generalized "other." How then does the behind-the-back technique contribute to this understanding?

It is evident that it is a most direct method: the group actually discusses the individual in his presence. In short, they tell him directly what they think of him. But why this make-believe? Why cannot these results be attained by face-to-face discussions? Some further postulates become necessary.

1. People are socially conditioned not to discuss a person to his face, and even in the artificial situation of psychotherapy it is difficult for mem-

bers to feel free to utter critical remarks about another to his face. However, it is easy for people to criticize others behind their backs.

2. If a situation is constructed in which the discussants know that the individual is present but they cannot see him, the combination of the desire to help the fellow member by frank discussion and the releasing of socially conditioned inhibitions by not seeing him enables them to be exceedingly frank.

3. The same is true for the subjects. No matter how much a person may desire to hear the truth about himself, he reacts in an emotional manner when he hears and sees someone criticize him. This emotionalism interferes with his acceptance and understanding.

4. When a situation is created in which the subject does not see those who are discussing him, he does not become so emotional and is able to receive information about himself with calmness. He can hear what is said without becoming angry.

Consequently, it appears that this procedure makes use of two common psychological phenomena: release of inhibitions of discussion, as seen in gossip groups, when the subjection of discussion is absent; and freedom of emotional reaction to information when it is not presented in a face-to-face manner. It becomes evident that this peculiar procedure attains its results because of these dynamics. It is then possible to restate the theory more economically.

Social-personal maladjustments include discrepancies between what a person thinks he would like to be, what he is, how he finds others treat him, and what he believes others think of him. Psychotherapy is a process of bringing into adjustment these various conceptions. In group therapy these perceptions can be brought into line by oblique discussions. In the behind-the-back technique, the group discusses a person when he is absent psychologically although physically present. They are able to discuss him with unusual frankness because they do not see him; and he is able to accept unemotionally what they say because he does not see them.

It becomes evident that, if one took these arguments seriously, a school of psychotherapy could be based on this theory. It must be emphasized that the purpose of this section is to point out how, when some event occurs which cannot be explained otherwise, a new theory may arise.

AGREEMENTS ON THEORIES

It has been argued that almost every therapist holds a strictly personal theory and that members of various schools of thought in psychotherapy defend the points of view characteristic of their schools. But is the situation so diffuse? Does not some agreement exist in some areas? Despite real differences in viewpoints, there *is* considerable agreement as to what psychotherapy is and how it works. The next chapter will consider in detail mechanisms of group psychotherapy, and it will be seen that some apparent differences are merely semantic. At the present time it may be worth examining the theory just developed to note how it conforms to some other general concepts.

Alexander and French, writing from a psychoanalytic point of view, state [10], "In all forms of aetiological therapy the basic principle is the same: to reexpose the patient under more favorable circumstances which he could not handle in the past. The patient in order to be helped must undergo a corrective emotional experience suitable to repair the traumatic influence of previous experience."

Does this concept agree with the method and theory of behind-the-back? If not, then the general statement of Alexander and French about therapy does not hold for this procedure. Actually, their statement expresses the essence of behind-the-back, since this procedure is designed to allow the individual to expose himself to what were formerly traumatic events, but now under conditions that will not hurt. The patient discusses himself, delimiting the area of discussion; he indicates sensitive spots; he then listens to others talk about him, at the same time not seeing them; and finally, he enters the group as a full member and discusses himself. It seems evident that a sensitive individual listening to his fellow members discuss him with great frankness must undergo a corrective emotional experience.

Another version of what is the essence of psychotherapy is given by Cotton [91], who says that in psychotherapy a patient is put in a situation in which he cannot fail. This is exactly what occurs in this behind-the-back technique. First, he is given the floor and may talk as much as he likes and about whatever he likes; then he is asked to be passive and is placed so that no one can see him; next he is "called into the room" and he listens to the therapist, who summarizes the discussion that took place while he was "out of the room"; and finally, he participates in further discussion about himself.

As stated earlier, L. Cody Marsh [247] had this credo of group psychotherapy: "By the crowd have they been broken; by the crowd shall they be healed." It is evident that the social trauma suffered by individuals may be repaired by this new social experience.

Willis McCann states [250] that in psychotherapy a person must lose himself in order to find himself. This point needs a little attention, because it is not only the subject of the behind-the-back technique who is in therapy: all the members of the group are, and when they forget themselves and consider the subject, they are losing themselves in him.

On the basis of his investigations, Fiedler [119] came to the conclusion that psychotherapy is relationships. If good relationships are marked by unequivocal honesty, it would appear that the method of operating discussed, which because of its peculiar techniques stimulates unwonted frankness, does help to establish good interpersonal relationships. Exactly because this method tends to loosen individuals and allows them to speak out with frankness, the subjects enter into unusual relationships.

Ruesch and Bateson argue [326] that psychotherapy is a process of communication. At one point they state, "Successful communication with self and others implies correction by others as well as self-correction ... successful communication therefore becomes synonymous with adaption to life." The theory of behind-the-back is essentially an elaboration of the point of view of Ruesch and Bateson, namely that psychotherapy means effective communication. The argument is that maladjustment is based on perceptual discrepancies; and this method is designed to effect maximal communication.

Gordon states [140] that psychotherapy is a process of experimenting with new ways of relating to others. He says, "In the group he has a rare opportunity to discover and try out new ways of interacting that will free him from anxiety and bring him greater satisfaction." In behind-the-back this certainly seems to apply: both the subject and the discussants find an opportunity to engage in unusual social relationships.

From the above, it appears that a particular, unusual, and rather peculiar procedure, not generally used, nevertheless does appear to satisfy some criteria of a number of different theoretical conceptions of psychotherapy, which gives evidence that particular methods based on specific theories may nevertheless have a great deal in common with methods based on contrasting theories.

THERAPY IN OR BY THE GROUP?

Is group psychotherapy simultaneous individual therapy, or is it something else? Moreno, we have shown, does not believe that the principles of psychoanalysis apply to groups; he believes that explanations which might apply to individual therapy situations do not satisfactorily account for results in group situations. Freud, on the other hand, believed that individual and group psychology were identical or nearly so. With respect to group therapy, the question remains whether everyone in the group benefits independently of the other members or whether a group experience takes place.

Lowrey states [242], "Therapy is in the group but not by the group. Lines of therapeutic relationships are from each individual to the therapist." This is a startling statement and an unequivocal claim that group therapy is mass therapy of individuals, each of whom gains and makes advances independently of others, in terms of his relationship to the therapist. But it becomes evident on examination that Lowrey's statement holds true only for certain kinds of therapeutic groups. For example, in McCann's round-table therapy, the therapist does not enter into the interactions to any great extent; the same is true for Bion's leaderless procedures. And even in circular discussional groups, of the kind with which Lowery is presumably best acquainted, it is difficult to see how his statement can be justified if a nondirective approach is accepted. In the highly directive methods, where interaction is maintained between the therapist and the members and intermember relationships are discouraged, as in the repressive-inspirational technique, then such a statement may have justification.

Moreno's early concept of group therapy involved the belief that one person was the therapeutic agent of another. In his earliest formulation, the therapist did not even have to know the subjects; he could make up therapeutic groups on the basis of diagnostic evidence, and the subjects would, in effect, treat one another.

The question of therapy in or by the group is not simple: some methods apparently draw on particular dynamics, and other methods on quite different ones. The greater the feeling of togetherness, the fewer the restrictions on communication, the more that members become a group— the more the group becomes the therapeutic agent.

If so, where does the therapist stand? He is a member of the group; while he may generally be of greater value, in terms of what happens, than any other single member, he is not the sole element to be considered. He serves as a symbol for the group, gives his authority to it, and makes possible more rapid operations because of his special knowledge; but to state that lines of relationship develop solely between the therapist and each patient, disregarding the relationships between patients, is incorrect.

SOME THEORIES

There are four major theories of psychotherapy which underlie many therapeutic groups. Stated in alphabetic order in terms of the men with whom they are most often identified, they are the theory of *individual psychology* as formulated by Alfred Adler, the *psychoanalytic theory* of Sigmund Freud, the *spontaneity-sociometric* theory developed by Moreno, and the *client-centered* theory held by Carl Rogers.

In the subsequent discussion of these theories, which the reader should supplement with more adequate descriptions [106, 128, 270, 316], it should be of interest to note to what extent the theories are really in conflict. Are some theories concerned with material not taken up by other theories? Are differences more in language or in slants than in real issues? Is it possible for a therapist to hold all four of these theories simultaneously?

Below, when required, the theories will be considered in terms of group psychotherapy. How each of them is applied to concrete clinical situations will be illustrated in the second part of this volume.

Individual Psychology

The psychotherapeutic system of Alfred Adler went through at least three identifiable phases, of which the last, and perhaps the least understood, is the most important. The discussion below is based primarily on the writings of Rudolf Dreikurs [102, 106], Adler's pupil and chief American exponent of Adler's theory.

Individual psychology is based on the concept of the individual as a holistic, goal-seeking organism. To understand a person one must know his goals. If we have a comprehension of what he is after and if we understand his characteristic ways of operating—his life style—then we know him. Understanding is important in this system of therapy; the individual who has been pursuing unhealthy or unrealistic goals or trying to reach goals in an inefficient manner may, with new knowledge or insight, change his aims or tactics and thus arrive at a more satisfactory way of life. But such understanding is not easy for either the therapist or the client, since there are so many goals and so many diverse and cryptic ways of attaining them.

Though goals differ for every person and though every person has a hierarchy of complex goals, it is possible to separate goals into four overall groups. Dreikurs, in discussing children's goals, labels these attention, power, revenge, and defeat [102, 106].

Attention. The primary goal for every individual is belonging. Man is a social creature, and he needs the attention of others; first, on a biologic survival basis, but later on a social-psychological basis. Attention does not mean *only* recognition. The desire for attention includes the longing to be recognized, to be given honors, to be made a fuss over, to be accepted, to belong. The individual has a supreme desire to find out who he is and where he belongs. He wants to become a part of his social world.

The Adlerian believes that a primary drive is social belonging. The goal of attention exemplifies this drive.

Power. Not only does an individual want to be given attention in a favorable manner, but he also wants power, that is to say control over himself and others. Such diverse examples as the child who does not want to be carried but wants to walk on his own and the dictator who seeks world dominance are evidence of the power drive. The desire to get more education so that one will be more competent, the desire to save money, to become physically stronger, etc., are all examples of the drive for power.

Revenge. This third drive identified by Dreikurs is of special interest in social maladjustments because of its demands on the psychological economy. Revenge is the consequence of frustration of the two primary goals listed above. Not being able to get one's own way, defeated by social obstacles, the individual abandons to some extent his original drives toward the goals of *attention* and *power* and now wants to get vengeance. This drive is seen in its simpler forms in noncooperation and negativism and is found in more elaborate forms in delinquency and hypochondria.

Defeat. The most difficult goal to understand is that of defeat. It means simply that the individual has given up his struggles for power and attention and even for revenge; not finding an answer for his demands he is now occupied with defeating himself. The inferiority complex is an example of defeat. The defeated individual tries to prove that he can not succeed, he accepts self-concepts that may be unrealistic, designed to prove that he is unworthy. Defeat may show itself by excessive shyness and, in the final stage, by a complete withdrawal from social life through a psychosis.

These four goals exist in all people to varying extents. The extreme extension of any one of these goals leads to psychic difficulties. How the goals are sought is exemplified by the *life style*, which represents the complex series of characteristic behavior activities that makes up personality. The life style is established early in life and develops as a reaction to the individual's family constellation, which represents not the birth order of the individual or his structural relationship to his siblings and his parents, as is commonly thought, but rather the dynamic picture in the individual's early social relationships. One child may learn that he gains attention by being good, and he may assume the life style of the good boy; another child finds that he gains attention by being demanding, and this becomes his way of life, or his major thema of behavior.

As can be seen by this concentrated statement, the Adlerian viewpoint is social. Such matters as physical anomalies or instinctual drives are viewed as elements within the individual's economy that may affect his aims or the way in which they are obtained, but the primary consideration is given to goal striving. The Adlerian method, as its name—individual psychology—indicates, is concerned with the individuum, or the unit organism. The whole conception of separation of the person into parts is unpalatable to Adlerians, and consequently the idea of analyzing psychology into elements is seen as worthless.

In terms of clinical practice, Dreikurs makes a sharp differentiation between two modes of treatment. Guidance, or counseling, refers to direct advice and interpretation. It is a teaching process, and the individual is seen as one who needs to be taught new and better ways of operating. He is told, in effect, that his present method is not efficient, or is psychologically unsound, and that a new method would be better. This treatment works from the outside in, as it were. Instead of trying to find out what may be basically wrong with people, finding out their covert aims, analyzing their deeper motives, the counselor merely learns how the subject operates and informs him how to operate differently. He does this by a combination of persuasion and instruction. As a result of behavior changes which come about through direction, the individual experiences success; he finds that these better ways give him greater satisfaction; and internal consequences occur. This is a thoroughly common-sense point of view, which meets with approbation with clients who tend to hold to intellectual theories of psychotherapy. This theory will be seen in operation in the description of family counseling.

Adlerian group therapy, on the other hand, involves free discussions among members. The therapist strives to understand goals and life style, and, once having this understanding, he attempts to point out to the individual how he is operating and why. By acting as a mirror and pointing out to individuals the way they are acting, the therapist helps them see themselves as they are and learn to change their aims or to reach them in more effective ways.

According to the Adler-Dreikurs conception of society as a basic factor in maladjustments, there is a fundamental social error which confuses differences between people with inferiority and superiority. People continually evaluate themselves in terms of status and try to become bigger, stronger, and smarter than others. As a result they often set unrealistic goals, which inevitably lead to feelings of inadequacy, which in turn lead to intensification of unrealistic goals and consequent maladjustment. On the other hand, the logical consequent of a philosophy which states that differences do not necessarily mean superiority or inferiority is democracy, in which all individuals accept themselves for what they are and attempt to develop themselves without regard to status differences.

Psychoanalysis

Although psychoanalysis is the oldest of the schools of dynamic psychology and the one about which most has been written, it is nevertheless extremely difficult to summarize, for a number of reasons. One reason is that the vast amount of literature, often written in difficult style, is so heterogeneous and diffuse that it becomes difficult to find simple unifying concepts. A second reason is that within the framework of the psychoanalytic school a number of other schools have developed, which, depending on one's point of view, may or may not be said to belong to the main stream of psychoanalysis.

In the discussion below, the writer will attempt to stick close to the later writings of Sigmund Freud, presenting material which, more or less, is still acceptable to current thinkers in this field.

Psychoanalysis is the uncovering of unconscious emotions and conflicts. This uncovering leads eventually to insights, that is to an understanding on the part of the patient of the role that formerly repressed ideas and feelings are playing in his pathological state of mind or behavior. The transformation of unconscious processes into conscious ones takes place through the recall of forgotten memories by the process of free association and other techniques which overcome resistance.

Freud regarded all mental forces as deriving primarily from basic instincts which were categorized under two headings: *eros,* or the life-preserving instinct, and *thanatos,* or the death instinct. These instincts were felt to possess great vitality and persistence and were considered to be directed toward affective charges or demands. It is of interest that many modern students of psychoanalysis have abandoned the concept of the importance of instincts.

Life demands are regulated at first by the pleasure-pain principle, but gradually their expression is controlled by the reality principle, which develops out of social interaction and in adaptation to the real external world.

The whole mind is topologically conceived as made up of the id, the ego, and the superego. The id is the reservoir of instinctual demand. The ego develops out of the id; it has awareness and is the integral part of the personality, acting as a mediator between instinctual urges and the external environment, as well as between the id and the superego. The superego, or conscience, develops through the child's identification with standards set by his parental surrogates; if it is too strict, it may dominate the ego.

However, the way psychoanalysts actually conduct their therapeutic groups probably differs very little from the way of the Adlerians, the Rogerians, or the eclectics, who make use of circular discussional techniques. The difference between these various groups depends on the nature of interpretations—or, in the case of the Rogerian groups, the lack of interpretations—given to the members. Probably the best explanation of the psychoanalytic procedure in group psychotherapy is provided by Foulkes [124].

Freud, like Adler, does not appear to have discussed group psychotherapy per se, but he was interested in the psychology of the group and attempted analysis of group psychology. Durkin has catalogued five postulates that Freud developed about groups. They are:

1. A predominance of unconscious emotional processes
2. A tendency to turn impulses into action
3. An emotional contagion between members
4. Libidinal ties
5. A reduction of thinking

On the basis of her experiences with therapeutic groups, Durkin was able to find evidence only for the third of these five postulates [109].

Spontaneity-Sociometry Theory

The most difficult of the four schools of thought to discuss is that of Moreno, because of both its inchoate character and Moreno's rather difficult style of writing.

To understand Moreno, four separate aspects should be considered: (*a*) his philosophic postulates, (*b*) his sociometric method, (*c*) his concept of the ideal person, and (*d*) his preferred therapeutic instrument—psychodrama. While these four parts often do not appear to have much relationship to one another, nevertheless they form part of a connected system.

Philosophy. Moreno may be best understood as a religious mystic. His first several books were on religious themes. We learn from some of his autobiographical segments that in his youth he attempted to establish a new religion, but not finding any adherents, he decided to prove the worth of his ideas through a practical demonstration of their validity [270]. Consequently, even though the connection between psychodrama, sociometry, and his other procedures may not appear to have axiological connotations, they do derive from his basic philosophical principles.

Moreno's fundamental postulate goes somewhat as follows. Man is part of God and has divine attributes. Like God, he is a creator; a genius. Man's goal is to attain his potentialities. But the devil is the machine: civilization, with all its measures for denying man's ineffable uniqueness. The rituals of society, the limitations of convention, the restrictions of social usages are seen as denying man his God-like uniqueness. The task of psychotherapy is to permit men to regain their spontaneity. Psychotherapy is the instrument for regaining freedom, originality, and creativity.

Moreno associates himself with Jesus, Buddha, and Socrates, his major inspirations. As do the Adlerians, but for different reasons, Moreno rejects the importance of the instincts. Consequently, his orientation is primarily social, not physiological.

Sociometry. Moreno's concept of life is somewhat similar to that of Trigant Burrow, on which his phyloanalysis is based. Man is not a unit entity alone; he is a part of a group. To understand an individual, one has to know how he belongs to the group, or social atom, of which he is a part. Individuals send out positive and negative forces, known as *tele*, between themselves. Tele is a force that binds individuals into groups. A group works well if tele forces are positive. To obtain a picture of the status of a group, it is necessary to measure tele. This is done simply by finding out, for any group, how each member feels about every other member and then charting out the relationships in a sociometric diagram. If people who have positive tele are placed in close relationships, they will work together better, supplement one another, and attain a higher state of effective functioning.

Psychodrama. Our major attention must be drawn to psychodrama, Moreno's chosen instrument for psychotherapy. How does it relate to his philosophy, his sociometry, and his ideal man? On the basis of the idea that man has been the victim of the "machine," Moreno gives him an opportunity, in a protective situation, to test reality and to create on his feet, in the midst of others, a new personality. Sociometry does not appear to be related to psychodrama as a psychotherapeutic method, but it is used to measure changes in the group's affective patterns. The ideal man would, of course, as a result of shedding his inhibitions and acting out his impulses, tend to approach the creative, spontaneous individual envisaged by Moreno. From another point of view, in the psychodrama a patient gets the experience of reliving old conflicts, trying out new patterns, and, since he can never fail, obtaining a sense of security.

Examples. No one can really get the flavor of Moreno's thoughts without sampling his language. The following excerpts come from Moreno's major work, "Who Shall Survive?" [270] and may clarify previous discussion.

The fact that Christianity, Buddhism, Judaism and other religions of the past had limited success did not prove that the concept of religion itself had failed. My contention was that religion was to be tried again, a religion of a *new* sort, its inspirations modified and its techniques improved by the insights which science has given us—and by no means excluding some of the insights which Marxism and psychoanalysis have brought forth. My proposition was threefold: first, the hypothesis of spontaneity-creativity as a propelling force in human progress, beyond and independent from libido and socio-economic motives—which does not deny the fact that they are frequently interwoven, but which does deny the contention that they are merely a function and a derivative; second, the hypothesis of having faith in our fellowman's intentions—outside of obedience resulting from physical and legalistic coercion—the hypothesis of love and mutual sharing as a powerful indispensable working principle in group life; and third, the hypothesis of a superdynamic community based upon these principles which can be brought to realization through newer techniques. [270, p. xv]

Human society has an atomic structure which is analogous to the atomic structure of matter. . . . There are two significant microscopic formulations of the atom, the social atom and the cultural atom. Their existence has been brought to empirical test by means of social microscopy. A pattern of attractions, repulsions and indifferences can be discerned on the threshold between individual and group. [270, p. 69]

The theoretical principle of psychodrama is that the director acts directly upon the level of the subject's spontaneity—obviously, it makes little difference to the operation whether one calls the subject's spontaneity his "unconscious"— that the subject enters actually the areas of objects and persons, however confused and fragmented, to which his spontaneous energy is related. [270, p. 86]

Client-centered Theory

Although Carl Rogers generously credits a number of other people, notably Rank and Taft, for some of the ideas that he has disseminated, it is evident that while he has incorporated a variety of concepts from these as well as other persons, their ideas form a background to a rather clearly differentiated procedure and philosophy of psychotherapy. To understand this fact we must consider his theory, philosophy, and method separately. Rogers' theory is still in process of formulation, although at the present time it has begun to assume shape; his methods have varied slightly; but it is his philosophy which has remained constant and which has directed theory and action.

Like Adler, Moreno, and Freud, Rogers assumes a philosophical point of view, which to date has not been made explicit but which is certainly the most significant part of his whole production. Only by understanding this can his theory and method be comprehended.

Philosophy. Rogers believes that in order for a therapist to help others, he has to give of himself. The therapist must have genuine interest in the patient, be willing to listen to him carefully to understand him, and must provide an atmosphere of real acceptance. Rogers believes that every individual has within himself the potentiality of growth, latent if not actualized, which he can make use of under psychologically proper circumstances. In this philosophy, there is a great deal of confidence in the unique capacity of the patient to find his own solutions. The therapist must respect the individual and must allow him his own way in finding his own solutions.

Theory. Though Rogers' theory is in the process of formulation and is developing, uniquely for psychotherapeutic theories, in conjunction with carefully formulated research studies, it has assumed, for the present, a phenomenological character. Every individual is aware of his own perception, and to him what his senses present is reality. Perceptions may be wrong, in the sense that they may not be veridical, that is to say, they may not reflect reality, but for the individual, whether a perception is veridical is not so important; this is the way he sees things, and therefore this is the way they are for him. Behavior is a consequent of perception. Unsuccessful behavior is related to poor perception, i.e., a person may not see himself, others, and events in the way that they really are. It is the purpose of therapy to permit the individual to explore himself and his perceptions in order to come to an understanding of reality consistent with truth. The fully functioning person is one who is open to his own feelings and to the people and events in the world outside and who can deal with them adequately.

Method. Rogers' espousal of the nondirective method, which in practice avoids interpretations, advice, explanations, suggestions, or questions, follows directly from his major premise that every person has inner capacities to solve his own problems. The therapist attempts to provide for the patient an emotionally neutral field of interaction in which he can express whatever thoughts he has without criticism and in which he will feel safe to explore his deepest thoughts. The therapist contributes to the process of the individual's therapy by indicating acceptance, although not approval, of statements and by attempting to show the patient that he understands what the patient is trying to communicate. In a very real sense, the direction of the therapy is set by the patient, and the therapist follows in his lead. Since the therapist sets limits on himself and not on the patient, this method may be said to differ from all other methods here considered.

COMPARISONS

It may be evident from the above that, even though the four theories and the procedures associated with them differ, in few cases is there direct contradiction. The differences seem to lie in emphasis, or in selecting particular aspects of a total theory of psychotherapy. An observer in a therapeutic group might well find difficulty in deciding under which of the various theories to classify it. In actuality, at least in terms of procedures, it may be said that persons with specific theoretical orientations may cut across lines, using methods developed by those of different theoretical orientation.

CHAPTER 4   *Mechanisms of Group Psychotherapy*

In the previous chapter, several schools of thought were summarized. Each of these schools is the resultant of the brilliant insights of one person, who later conceptualized his major hypotheses into a connected system until a logical structure was obtained. These theories were modified by clinical evidence and by critical attacks. New evidence and blows from critics help a theory develop to maturation.

In communicating ideas, personality theorists have a tendency to use special symbols to make more precise denotations of new concepts. These symbols, i.e., words and phrases such as *Oedipus complex, life style, acceptance, transference, tele,* etc., have the purpose of conveying complex information in an economical manner, but they manage to prevent communication, because symbols, which often are not defined precisely, may be variously understood and, consequently, used and interpreted in different ways. In short, terms created to improve communication may actually hinder it.

To give an example, let us take the term *transference,* commonly found in the literature. To some, this word means merely a positive emotional relationship that develops between two people in psychotherapy. To others, transference means a neurotic dependency engendered by psychotherapy. To others, transference means transferring unconscious attitudes about one person to another. And to still others, this term refers to the channeling of libidinal forces toward the therapist. From the point of view found in "Through the Looking-Glass," a word means what the speaker chooses it to mean. And when new and unusual terms are constructed and given vague and equivocal definitions, especially when the definitions are themselves defined in terms of unusual and nonoperational language, confusion results. It is the story of Babel all over again.

It may appear that this elementary discussion of semantics is inappropiate to this volume, but we shall run into the need for some standard system in discussing a number of methods of group psychotherapy, and

38

it will be useful to have an understanding of which major terms will be used and how they will be interpreted.

An Approach to Unequivocality

Let us examine a specific example of the above problem. During group psychotherapy certain processes occur which lead to favorable results. What are these dynamic processes: what are the *names* of the mechanisms of group psychotherapy? A service has been done by Slavson [358], Hadden [154], and Cotton [92], each of whom identified five major mechanisms of group psychotherapy. Table 2 lists them.

Table 2

Cotton	Hadden	Slavson
Reassurance	Abreaction	Relationships
Reeducation	Loss of isolation	Insight
Desensitization	Ego support	Reality testing
Transference	Transference	Sublimation
Catharsis	Catharsis	Catharsis

The reader will do well to study this table and ponder its implications. Let us ask some naïve questions. If Cotton believes that reassurance is a major mechanism of group psychotherapy, how is it that neither Slavson nor Hadden mentioned it? Hadden states that one of the five major mechanisms is abreaction. Why then did Slavson and Cotton neglect it entirely? Slavson states that relationships is a major mechanism, but why do Hadden and Cotton not list it? Perhaps the answer lies in the equivocality of language. Perhaps one term as used by Cotton means the same as a different term used by Hadden or Slavson. Could it be that reassurance means ego support or relationships? Is reeducation the same as abreaction or insight?

Or perhaps there is really only one mechanism in group psychotherapy: catharsis, which all three agree on? Or maybe there are 12 different ones, each of these three authorities seeing only some of them?

An inductive solution to this problem of semantics has been proposed by Corsini and Rosenberg [90], who searched 300 articles in the literature of group psychotherapy and found cited no fewer than 166 mechanisms. Are there then really this many separate dynamic processes in group psychotherapy? Basing their work on the premise that there are really fewer distinct processes than 166 and that some identical mechanisms are described in various manners, the investigators undertook clinical factor analysis, described in detail in their article, and emerged with nine major classes of mechanisms, which could be placed into three broad areas. They are *acceptance, altruism,* and *transference* (EMOTIONAL);

spectator therapy, universalization, and *intellectualization* (COGNITIVE); and *reality testing, ventilation,* and *interaction* (ACTIONAL). In addition, a number of other specific mechanisms not classifiable into these nine major classes were found.

Emotional Factors

Acceptance. Lipkin states [231], "The common factor in various techniques is the therapist's acceptance, tolerance and confidence in the patient." The essential idea of acceptance appears to be implicit also in the following terms employed by a variety of therapists in efforts to explain the major processes involved in group psychotherapy: *friendly environment, esprit de corps, communal feeling, togetherness, supportive relations, identification with others, loss of isolation,* etc.

Acceptance seems to be a feeling that one belongs in the group, that one is an equal and valued member of the group, and that others in the group will show and maintain friendly relations. It is certainly engendered in the group by the therapist's own attitude toward the members.

Altruism. Greenblatt says [144], ". . . group therapy facilitates relaxed, less anxious, more responsible sort of living which contributes to altruism of relationships." Altruism has much in common with acceptance, but it goes farther. Acceptance implies passivity: it is tolerance and liking; but altruism implies helping the other person, a positive desire to exert oneself for the benefit of the other. Altruism helps both the one who "loses himself in others," as McCann states it [250], and the one who is the recipient of the altruism. This central concept of altruism is implied in some of the terms used by group therapists, such as *advice by patients* and *encouragement* and *interpretation by patients.* Some therapists have stated that *the patient is a therapist to other patients* and that *patients sacrifice personal interest to the group,* which are additional examples of altruism. In doing this, as stated by one therapist, *one is giving love.*

Why altruism is an important aspect of group psychotherapy is evident in that it is an expression of love. One is willing to sacrifice one's own selfish interests for the benefit of another. To listen sympathetically to another, to attempt to understand him, to want to help him to make advances, to encourage and to advise him are all expressions of altruism, and, as Portia said about mercy, it is twice blessed. This sense of *being important in the lives of others* seems to be of value in making therapeutic gains. And, as in the case of acceptance, it is certain that, as Gordon states [140], members of groups take the therapist as a model; if he demonstrates altruism, others will imitate him.

Transference. Sternbach says [377], "The cement that makes a group . . . is the identification with each other through the common attachment to the leader." Klapman states [199], ". . . one of the principal effects of group psychotherapy is to quicken or expedite the application of transference to the therapist in a commensurate manner also between the various members of the group." Pederson-Krag claims [283], "Much of the value of group psychotherapy is in the unconscious factors that result in various relationships to the group leader...." A patient, quoted by Hadden, stated [151], "I felt so isolated before I attended; now I feel I have people fighting the same thing that I am fighting."

Transference may be considered a strong bond of relationships between members of the group. It has been called a "continued flow of emotional support." It means *liking, mutual attraction, sympathy,* or just plain love.

We may now try to order and connect these three EMOTIONAL factors involved in group psychotherapy. Acceptance, altruism, and transference seem to be steps in the same dynamic process of *love.* First one takes an attitude of tolerance, then one wants to do something for the other person, and finally one comes genuinely to like the other. How these steps may actually appear in any one individual, whether in this order or in any other, or whether they appear simultaneously is not at issue. What does appear to be true is that all of them are essentially expressions of affection for one's fellow man. Therapists tend to avoid this four-letter word, but we are inescapably drawn to the conclusion that the first of three major complexes of therapeutic mechanisms is love.

From this we may conclude that the therapist must maintain a general attitude toward his patients of genuine affection, based on a feeling of good will to all men, an unconditional regard and respect for others. In demonstrating this by his own acceptance, altruism, and transference, he provides for his patients at the same time a feeling of worthwhileness and an example for others. Once again, to use the four-letter word, we must conclude that the therapist must love his patients for psychotherapy to occur.

Intellectual Factors

Spectator Therapy. McCann states [250], "Every patient, without exception, has commented that hearing others tell about their problems ... has made his problems seem less important by comparison. This reevaluation of his problems seems to open the way for him to gain a better understanding of himself and a clearer insight into his symptoms."

Moreno, who introduced the term spectator therapy [265], referred to passive participation. In essence this is what Aristotle meant when he referred to the cathartic effect of the drama. Psychotherapists when they talk about *watching the examples of others* and *listening to the testimony of others* are stating in essence that one may be able to make therapeutic gains by learning, vicariously, from the experiences of others.

Spectator therapy is a complex phenomenon. Group therapy is far from being independent individual therapy occurring simultaneously; in any truly interactive group, the members progress roughly at the same rate. If we think of discussions in terms of intensity, there seems no doubt that any member can accelerate or decelerate the progress of others by his own movements. The more venturesome and courageous members advance the level or depth of therapy, while the more timid hold it back. Watching some members take chances in self-revelation impels others to do likewise; seeing some obtain benefits gives the other members confidence.

Spectator therapy may also be considered from the point of view of the object of attention. There seems little doubt that there is a great emotional impact on the main actor when he discusses himself in front of the group. Moreover, it may be that the more symmetrical the group is, i.e., the more the members of the group are like the active member, the greater is the impact.

The therapist probably contributes to this mechanism by being a real spectator, that is by giving members full and undivided attention and by regarding them highly in terms of their productions. When people obtain unqualified attention, there is a tendency to want to continue getting this attention.

Universalization. Schilder stated [335], "In a group the patients realize with astonishment that the thoughts that have seemed to isolate them are common to all of them." Teirich quotes a patient [387], "Group therapy helps me to realize that other people have the same problems and difficulties, and this knowledge reduces my feelings of loneliness." Another patient as quoted by Hadden stated [151], "Realizing so many other normal-looking patients were similarly affected was the means of restoring my courage."

For a patient to learn that his behavior has been *duplicated by many of his mates, that others have similar problems* is to come to the realization that he is not unique. When he learns that others are fighting the problems that "I am fighting" and that others have the same kind of difficulty, a feeling of *resonance* with others is engendered. In other words, one becomes a member of the human race. There seems to be no question that what we call neurosis is essentially a breakdown of communications, in which one comes to feel that he is different from others, that he is uniquely special. A person begins to feel that he is "an ilande unto himself," and he isolates himself when he begins to develop complexes of maladjustment. To rejoin the human race is the essence of universalization, which appears to be one of the major mechanisms of group psychotherapy.

It appears to come as a shock to many, and this is often expressed by patients, to learn that they are not different from others, that others have similar problems. A patient learns that he has exiled himself from the rest of the world and that he is a victim of what Allport calls *pluralistic error* [13]. Consequently, the mere learning that others have similar problems, that one is not unique, and that what one had felt to be his own special and private feelings are shared by others comes as an intellectual shock.

How may the therapist contribute to universalization? One way is to permit, as do the client-centered therapists, a maximum amount of free communication in a nonthreatening social situation. Another way is to point out resemblances between the problems of people, or to make direct comparisons between feelings of two or more people.

Intellectualization. Snowden states [363], "Once the patient realizes that symptoms need not cause anxiety and that the originating cause is in the past, the way is open for education." Blackman, in describing group psychotherapy, stated [49], "A setting is provided where the patient finds it possible to re-evaluate his concepts."

Many patients and therapists center their understanding of psychotherapy on the cognitive aspect of insight. Patients often remark, "I never knew...," "I never would have believed...," "I never thought until now...," expressing new understandings about themselves and others. Such statements may be considered evidence that in the group situation the members have come to attain insights.

It is evident that there is an intellectual aspect to group psychotherapy, that one does learn new things. This occurs in two general ways: autonomously—by coming to one's own conclusions—and by being given information by others. By learning of the thoughts that one has in common with others and by understanding the defenses of others, one comes to have a general awareness of interpersonal relations.

There is, however, one puzzling aspect about intellectualization. The patient often appears to have learned what he knew all along. Such statements as "I always knew it, but I never really understood...," or "I have been told this many times, but somehow I never could believe..." illustrate the paradox of learning in psychotherapy. It is acceptance of what one already knows. A patient may say, "Others have told me this...I know they are right...but somehow I can't really see it." Intellectualization is not learning in the sense of getting brand new information; it rather represents a capacity to understand what one has known all along.

These three processes—*spectator therapy, universalization,* and *intellectualization* grouped under the area of COGNITION—are steps along a continuum. First, one listens to others; then he comes to realize that others are like himself; then he comes to understand himself. The therapist contributes to the movements of these processes primarily by facilitating maximum communication.

If the first of the major factors in group psychotherapy is *love*, the second is *understanding*. Aphoristically, the first is "Love thy neighbor," and the second is, "Know thyself."

Action Factors

Psychotherapy depends on love and understanding, or feeling and knowledge, or EMOTIONAL and INTELLECTUAL factors, but these elements are not enough. Psychotherapy depends also on "good works," to use religious language, or ACTION.

Reality Testing. Coffey states, ". . . reality testing lies at the heart of group psychotherapy" [75]. This statement is remarkable coming from one who weighs his words carefully, but on consideration Coffey's statement is well justified.

Therapy is artificial, in the sense that it does not accurately reflect the world outside. The person who enters a therapeutic group may, as it were, lick his wounds and thereby recover from the trauma of reality. He is able to repair damage in a social setting where he will find love and understanding. But to experience good feelings and to come to have superior understanding may not be sufficient to cause changes. One needs real experiences in successful relationships. Can one obtain this real experience in the unrealistic and artificial environment of a therapeutic group?

Therapeutic groups provide a field for social relationships in which a person can test his defenses, where he can relive old family conflicts, live out ego frustrations, and find outlets for aggression. He can find a method whereby he can relate himself to others. By structuring and arranging relations in an atmosphere of protection, it is possible for an individual to test himself. He may experiment with new ways of relating and acting with the members of the group. In other words, he practices being his new and desired self in a social field that is nonthreatening and accepting.

An example may be given from experience with boys in a training school. A boy complained that he was afraid of everyone and was constantly bullied. Everybody picked on him. He stated a desire to be able to "beat up" others. He was given an opportunity to be the bully of the group, and for a half-hour he terrorized the other members, scolding them, hitting them, kicking them, and otherwise venting his direct hostility, while the rest of the group, therapist included, cowered at his assaults and took verbal and physical punishment without attempting to strike back. After the session was over, this formerly meek person engaged in a series of battles, some of which he won, in the institution proper, and he emerged a normally self-confident individual.

In the therapeutic group the patient can work through problems, since he is put in a situation where he cannot fail. The group becomes a testing forum, a practice field for social relations.

Often-defeated individuals are provided with an opportunity in therapeutic groups to express themselves without danger, to take chances that will not fail, and to expose themselves without harm. The patient in the group may express hostility to other members, he may declare his most private thoughts, and no matter how he might be rejected or punished in the world outside, he finds that he is still loved and valued. Given complete permissivism, not finding himself limited or blocked, able to say or do whatever he wants, and finding always a sympathetic group who attempt to understand him, he begins to gain a new feeling of freedom, and he loses fears and hatred.

The therapist provides the possibility of making therapeutic gains in permitting individuals to act out feelings through maintaining an attitude of respect and confidence. The therapist may do this either by permitting the individual to act out his feelings directly if he desires to, or by facilitating this acting out through the structure of the therapy, as in a method such as psychodrama, which requires such overt behavior.

Ventilation. Wolf et al. state [414], "... even these severely immobilized analysands can frequently be activated by the explosive atmosphere of the group." Expressions such as *emotional release, expression of repressed drives, release of unconscious material,* etc., convey the idea that one of the essential processes in successful therapy is catharsis, or ventilation.

A maladjusted person is one who is bottled up, who cannot communicate freely with others, who is repressing his aggressions and hostilities. Watching himself with utmost care, he is afraid to reveal himself as he is, and he is unable to experience the world as it is. He is not fully functioning, he mistrusts people, he fears them, seeing everyone and everything as potentially hostile. A good deal of his personal economy is spent in watching himself.

The therapeutic group with its permissivism, in which one can do what one wishes within broad limits, gives the individual the opportunity to expose inner feelings, self-condemnatory or hostile in nature, with impunity. Instead of meeting shock, counteraggression, or expulsion from the group, he finds that he continues to be regarded with love. The maladjusted individual who acts out his aggressions in the real world goes either to prison or to a mental hospital. In a social group he suffers ostracism. In the therapeutic group, his ventilations are accepted, discussed, and understood. Instead of being rejected as a result of his ventilation, he may find that others will be impelled to imitate him. He learns that rapid emotional releases are tolerated, and as a result, he becomes more rational and finds that the act of ventilation has the effect of reducing the pressure. He has blown his top and he feels better.

Ventilation is a signal to the therapist that confidence in the group has been reached. When one person dares to express himself, this often sets off a chain reaction. While ventilation by itself solves no problems, it does permit the individual to become free of major tensions and able to attend to other aspects of self and the world.

The therapist contributes to ventilation by the assumption of an attitude of honest inquiry, by showing interest in the productions of the members, and by avoiding indications of disapproval. As always, a desire to understand and to accept permits fuller expressions from the members.

Interaction. Curran and Schilder write [95], "Group discussion with children provides relief from fears and anxieties by sharing of mutual experience and conviction of social approval."

When various statements by group therapists were analyzed and classified by the method of semantic factor analysis, a number of terms which did not seem to have any specific name, but which appeared to belong to the same class, emerged. The terms *relationships, contagion, relationship pattern, sociometric relationships,* and *interstimulation* occurred, and it was evident that group therapists had found that interactions, otherwise unspecified, between members had therapeutic benefit. It appeared that if a group of individuals met for therapy, regardless of the nature of the specific interaction, beneficial results would be obtained. On this basis it also appeared that the specific nature of the interaction is not so important as the fact that there *is* interaction. One might go further and say that if a group meets in which every member intends to enter into a communication network and if the discussions are such as to permit maximal relationships, regardless of method used, benefits will accrue.

The three ACTIONAL factors—*reality testing, ventilation,* and *interaction* —can now be seen to represent overt processes, visible to all members, which supplement and complement the EMOTIONAL and COGNITIVE factors. However, it should be made clear that no analysis can do justice to the complex here-and-now situation in group therapy and that while the nine mechanisms discussed probably are in operation in any therapeutic group, they may occur with various intensities at various times.

The therapist who is aware of these processes and their implications may examine his own behavior in the group and may experiment with modifications of his own processes to see whether changes in his method of dealing with the group will result in changes in these mechanisms. But no matter how complex the relationships of these processes and mechanisms are, it must not be considered that these are the only mechanisms or dynamics of therapy. Even though this list is more complex and complete than any other system described thus far, there may still be other dynamics of major importance for any single individual.

Other Factors

In classifying the 166 mechanisms cited in the literature, a majority fitted into the scheme developed above, but a number of others could not be so neatly pigeonholed. In listing some of these other mechanisms below, it should not be felt because they do not appear to fit this neat scheme that they are less important.

Suggestion. Freud believed that groups are in a hypnotic, or suggestion, relationship. The suggestibility of a group has been cited as a major process in group psychotherapy. There is probably no question that members affect each other in unconscious ways and that therapeutic advances by one member impel other members to follow along.

Authority. Closely related to suggestion is authority. Many weak individuals who appear to have strong needs to become dependent form dependency ties to the therapist, to specific members, or to the group as a whole and appear to make changes on the basis of the authority of others. *The patient's confidence in the therapist* has been cited as a major mechanism.

Rivalry. It has been stated that *rivalry for improvement* occurs in groups. Many people in a group begin to pit themselves against others and in a competitive way want to make improvements faster than others. The group becomes a kind of a family where sibling rivalry occurs, not only for the attention of the therapist and the other members, but also in terms of advances. One may be *inspired by others to greater effort,* as one writer puts it. Rivalry is frequently at an unconscious level.

Relaxation. It has been jokingly said that the major value in classical psychoanalysis lies in the relaxation that one gets from lying down on a couch. It may be that the very atmosphere of a group where one feels free to be himself in a social situation, where he does not have to be on guard, where he feels completely accepted and therefore relaxed has therapeutic benefit.

Tension. Exactly the opposite idea has been suggested, that in a group tension occurs and that it is the tension that leads to improvements. *Heightening of action, shock,* and *intensification of situations* have been cited as leading to gains. The argument is that neurotic individuals are in a constant state of subtension, and that developing the tension and letting areas of sensitivity build up and then become unbearable may lead to benefits.

Sharing. Somewhat related to the concepts of altruism and universalization is the idea of the benefits of sharing. There is a *loss of isolation through sharing.* If A tells B his problems, and if B then shares his problems with A, this exchange is felt to be of benefit.

Reassurance. Related to authority is the concept of reassurance. It is also related to altruism. In reassurance, a member is given expressions of confidence that he can solve his problems, that he can sustain his discomfort, etc. An insecure person may feel that if others believe in him, he can then believe in himself. However, it is probable that the major value of reassurance to the insecure person is that it is an expression of the interest that other members have in him.

SUMMARY

Group psychotherapy consists of interactions among members. Interactions lead to covert emotional and intellectual processes. These processes have been discussed by a large number of group therapists. The assumption held in this chapter is that a synthesis of the opinions of a great many persons will give a more complete picture of the effecting dynamics of personality and behavioral improvement than any arbitrary deductive system.

It has been seen that when 166 specifically named mechanisms were gathered into clusters, nine major factors appeared. Three of them were in the area of the EMOTIONS—*acceptance, altruism,* and *transference;* three were in the area of COGNITION—*spectator therapy, universalization,* and *intellectualization;* and three were in the area of ACTION—*reality testing, ventilation,* and *interaction.*

More generally, in effective group psychotherapy there must be *love, understanding* and *action.* There must be love of fellow men, knowledge of oneself, and good works. It is evident, as stated earlier that religion and psychotherapy have the same general aims—establishment on earth of a community based on ethical principles. Furthermore it is clear that the religious and therapeutic means whereby the good life is to be attained are essentially the same.

Members of groups, in order to make advances with respect to their own personal lives, must be led or permitted to find new ways of relating to others in accordance with the principles of ethical behavior. Illustrating how this can be done is in effect the purpose of the rest of the book.

CHAPTER 5 *Individual and Group Therapy*

Although many therapists divide psychotherapy into individual and group, this distinction is logically unsatisfactory. A better scheme is to separate therapy into *autonomous, individual, small group,* and *large group.* But if it is considered necessary to make a dichotomy, it seems that a better division can be based on *autonomy* and *interaction.* Consequently, individual and group therapy become examples of the same kind of process. In one case the group consists of two persons, in the other case the group consists of three or more persons.

This point of view has been presented by others. Ackerman, states [6], "... in individual therapy, such as psychoanalysis ... these two persons, the patient and the therapist, are a group. ..." Spotnitz says [372], "It has been observed frequently that individual therapy can be beneficial not only for the patient but for the therapists. In this sense then, individual therapy too is group therapy."

Whether individual therapy has been misnamed, since it is in reality a form of group therapy, is not important. Following convention, any therapeutic form that involves only two persons in interaction will be called individual therapy, and any form involving three or more who meet under formal conditions for the purpose of therapy will be regarded as group therapy.

Dynamics

The question may be asked whether dynamic processes in individual and group therapy are the same. If they are, it would be evidence that the two modes are different only arbitrarily. One evidence for similarity or identity comes from the fact that the major schools of individual psychotherapy are able to adapt themselves to the group procedure. Sternbach says [377], "Essentially, the dynamics of therapy of an individual are the same whether it is undertaken in an individual relation or in a group." Miller and Baruch, in agreement, state [263], "The process of psychotherapy by the group method is essentially the same as that for group therapy."

49

But in this field we rarely find complete agreement on any issue. It may be surprising to note that J. L. Moreno and S. R. Slavson, who generally do not agree on much in this area of concern, do have a common opinion that individual and group forms of therapy are not identical with respect to dynamics. Moreno has commented [267] that some workers have "inappropriately tried to apply concepts from psychoanalysis to groups," and Slavson, a psychoanalytically oriented group worker, has stated [355], "The dynamics of group therapy although analogous are vastly different from those in individual therapy."

INDIVIDUAL VS. GROUP THERAPY

A reasonable point of view with respect to the two modes of psychotherapy, individual and group, is that a particular method may be better for some therapists and for some members. It may also be that certain kinds of problems may be met better by one procedure than another. It is probable that most group therapists, who usually also undertake individual therapy, take this attitude. Nevertheless, it is possible to take the attitude that either group or individual therapy is generally better than the other form. To give an indication of some attitudes, a number of statements culled from the literature will be cited.

Superiority of Individual Methods

"Nothing can replace individual methods" [380].

"Group psychotherapy is superficial and can not deal directly with deeply repressed unconscious conflicts" [332].

"Group therapy can not replace or substitute for the deep insights gained in individual analytic therapy and is not particularly useful for those cases in which such prolonged and searching therapy is indicated" [92].

"Group therapy can not substitute for individual therapy for severe deeply rooted fears and anxieties" [321].

"In some cases the therapeutic benefits of open and free discussions in the group were not sufficient to ensure the patients' ability to make a good adjustment. In these cases, individual therapy supplemented that of the group" [343].

"Its shortcomings seem to be that it is apt to be more of an intellectual participation rather than emotional" [5].

Superiority of Group Methods

"Perhaps the most important development in psychological treatment has been the application of group therapy" [5].

"Group treatment has proven to have advantages over individual treatment" [33].

"My own experience has been that group therapy will produce more intimate self-revelations in a short period of time than will occur in individual therapy" [151].

"Group therapy bids fair to at least equal if not surpass any other single contribution to our therapeutic armamentarium" [68].

"The patient sees group therapy as an educational process and is not as resistant to it as to individual therapy" [222].

"In our experience...dramatization of the psychodynamics has had greater therapeutic effect from the amount of time that has been spent on them than any other method with which we are familiar" [365].

"It was found that the usual resistances met in psychoanalytic therapy are more readily broken through with the aid of group therapy" [234].

"When we have introduced our own resistive patients from individual to group analysis, they have not infrequently emerged in a manner never before evident in their prior work with us..." [413].

"Most striking is the fact that the best therapeutic results in the treatment of certain social psychopaths and of delinquents with severe primary disorders have heretofore been achieved almost exclusively through group therapy..." [377].

"Although the method was adopted primarily as a matter of expedience during the last war, the feeling is now that group therapy has value far beyond that of mere convenience" [142].

"...it is obvious that here is a technique which is as effective as individual therapy" [241].

Whenever there is a difference of opinion in science, the proper procedure is to attempt to test operationally. No one has yet tried any adequate objective evaluation of whether or not individual therapy is superior to group therapy; or whether either mode is superior economically, or for certain types of patients, or for certain kinds of problems. The question of relative superiority of these modes must be kept open until much more information is available. However, one can take some comfort from Baehr's investigation [21], which showed that a combination of individual therapy and group therapy was superior in effectiveness to either method alone.

ADVANTAGES OF GROUP THERAPY

A number of writers have attempted to analyze the advantages of the group method. In reading the lists below, one may attempt to weigh the validity of the various statements and compare the claimed advantages with those claimed for the individual method.

One of the earliest statements about the advantages of the group method was by Marsh [249]. He made six major points about group therapy:

1. There is a therapeutic compulsion to improve.
2. Strong transferences can be easily broken.
3. It has educational advantages.
4. Resistances are easily broken.
5. Enthusiasm is engendered.
6. It is an impersonal situation.

Kadis and Lazarfeld, who operate in an Adlerian frame of reference and whose discussion concerned the use of group methods with children, make the following comments [188]:

1. Children feel unconditionally accepted.
2. It lets them understand that adults have similar problems.
3. They realize that failures are a part of development.
4. Parents realize that failures are not exceptional.
5. Parents gain an objective outlook.

Joshua Bierer, also an Adlerian, discussing the advantages of the group method in a mental hospital, gives the following arguments for its use [42]:

1. It enables the psychiatrist to study patients in a group setting.
2. It enables the psychiatrist to make contact with a maximum number of patients.
3. It helps patients to relieve pent-up feelings.
4. Patients who need more intensive therapy can be selected through the group method.
5. By exchanging views, patients are saved from intellectual rot and deterioration.
6. The group method is helpful in maintaining the discipline of the hospital.

Schwartz discusses the economic advantage of the group method, which has been used, perhaps wrongly, as a major argument for group therapy [339].

1. Treatment is shortened for neurotics.
2. It requires fewer trained therapists.

Lauretta Bender, who has had extensive experience with group methods for severely maladjusted children, presents the following advantages of the group method [32]:

1. It frees expressions of neurotic complexes.
2. It gives relief of feelings of guilt, anxiety, inferiority, and insecurity.
3. It permits demonstrations of affection by adults.

4. The child can express affection and aggression.

5. It gives the child an opportunity to be at ease in a group.

6. It permits the crystallization of ideologies.

Somers and Pouppirt [368] summarize the advantages of group psychotherapy as follows:

1. It gives therapy for those who would not otherwise get any.

2. Employed patients can be seen without interference with work.

3. It permits reeducation of relatives and friends.

4. Patients get experience in group adjustment.

5. The therapist can see the patient in a social situation.

6. Professional people can best be treated in this way.

7. The group spirit helps offset setbacks.

8. Patients are aided in beginning outside activities.

Wender [404] finds that in group therapy, the following advantages are involved:

1. The patient is able to express himself without fear of punishment.

2. He does not have to identify with or depend on a leader.

3. Resistances and transferences are more easily managed.

Jones states [186] that the following conditions occur in group therapy:

1. Objective attitudes to neurotic symptoms can be maintained.

2. Informality leads to receptive attitudes.

3. Patients learn not to fear symptoms.

4. Enormous economies of the doctor's time are effected.

Many other statements are found in the literature concerning the advantages of the group method.

DISADVANTAGES OF GROUP THERAPY

Just as some defenders of the group method have been able to list its advantages, critics have listed its disadvantages. As before, the reader should test them for validity and compare these disadvantages with those of the individual method.

According to Ebaugh [111], some of the weaknesses of the group method are:

1. It fosters an acute sibling rivalry.

2. A group tears defenses down too rapidly.

3. It is difficult to reach some departments of conflict.

4. It is difficult to use with people who know each other.

5. It is too slow.

Meier [260], a Swiss psychiatrist, who says the very word *group* makes a good Swiss citizen shudder, and who states that he speaks from preconceptions and not from experience, presents the following rather unusual arguments against group therapy:

1. It raises the danger of collectivism.
2. It decreases personal responsibility.
3. It aids a person to escape from conflicts.
4. It implies neglect of the patient's responsibility.
5. There is danger of accumulating the unconscious of various patients.
6. A substitute reality is provided by the group.

DIFFERENTIAL APPLICATIONS

It has been suggested that there is no real conflict between group and individual forms of psychotherapy, and that it is possible that either method is superior in particular situations. A therapist has to take many considerations into account when the question arises whether a particular patient should enter group therapy. A search of the literature indicates, however, that no agreement, at least not to any apparent extent, exists between psychotherapists about who should and who should not be in group therapy.

Some therapists state that a particular kind of patient is not suitable, and in the same issue of the journal in which the statement appeared, one may find an enthusiastic account of successful therapy with that very kind of patient. The answer to this is simple. Therapists differ in their own personalities, and one may be able to work well with the very kind of patient that another failed with. Then, too, therapists may have different standards of diagnosing and different levels of evaluation of success. Also the methods of two therapists may differ, so that while each calls his method group psychotherapy, they are actually using two different kinds of procedure.

Some understanding of differences and agreements about the issue of who should be given group psychotherapy comes from a questionnaire prepared by Corsini and Lundin [89], which was sent to 100 institutions and agencies in the Middle West that were believed to be engaged in group therapy. Replies were obtained from 42 institutions. One of the questions in this questionnaire was: "What kind of people benefit mostly from group therapy and which kinds ought to be excluded?" Table 3 illustrates the summary of opinions.

To understand the significance of this table, it must be recalled that the 42 respondents were asked, without being given any frame of reference, to indicate what types of patients were or were not suitable for therapy. While there was agreement by 5 people that psychoneurotics are suitable, 37 of the respondents did not mention psychoneurotics as suitable. Also, while all those who did mention psychopaths felt that they were unsuitable for group therapy, 38 of the 42 respondents did not mention psychopaths at all. Yet there is a literature concerning the superiority of the group method over the individual methods with alcoholics, drug addicts, delinquents, and criminals. A great deal of successful work has been reported with psychotics, and yet there is almost complete agreement on the part of these respondents that the actively delusional, the psychotics, and hyperactives (manics) are not suitable for therapy.

The literature in the field is replete with cautions about certain diagnostic groups, but the advice is often in contradiction to that of other authorities. We suggest that no one's opinion is to be trusted but one's own, for every therapist is his own measure, and certain kinds of cases

Table 3. Patients Considered Suitable and Unsuitable for Group Psychotherapy by 42 Respondents

Classification	Suitable	Unsuitable
Psychoneurotic	5	0
Nonpsychotic	3	0
Passive	3	0
Psychsomatic	2	1
Having average IQ or higher	1	0
Chronically ill	1	0
Schizoid	1	0
Depressed	1	0
Verbally aggressive	1	0
Senile	0	1
Hyperactive	0	1
Actively delusional	0	2
Having character disorders	0	2
Organically ill	0	3
Psychotic	1	4
Acutely disturbed	1	5
Psychopathic	0	4

not treatable by one therapist using one particular method in one particular frame of reference may be quite satisfactorily treated by another. At the present time, especially in view of the gross unreliability of diagnoses, it is extremely unwise to make any sort of statement about the treatability of any person in terms of some label that someone has placed on him.

Some patients are difficult to deal with whether one tries group or individual therapy. Two persons with identical diagnoses may nevertheless react quite differently to either group or individual therapy.

In concluding this section, it is clear that group and individual therapy are not in competition. There is need for both. Nevertheless, it is perfectly proper to attempt to examine them in terms of respective strengths and weaknesses. There are contradictory opinions about relative values. It is the writer's opinion that those who favor group therapy are in a stronger position, since those who argue against it have had, for the most part, no direct experience in its use, while those who extol its advantages have, for the most part, also practiced individual therapy. Another point to be kept in mind, whether reports are favorable or not, is the common confusion between group psychotherapy and a single method of group psychotherapy. Often when a person says, "Group psychotherapy is not suitable for patients of category Alpha," what he really means is, "I have tried method Beta with a number of patients Alpha and I did not appear to get favorable results."

In view of the disparity of conclusions, direct contradictions, and variations in diagnostic categories, it must be concluded that at the present time very little is known about the relative advantages and disadvantages of group and individual therapy, of specific optimal applications, or of comparative effectiveness. The question is open.

CHAPTER 6 *Methods of Group Psychotherapy*

Individual psychotherapy, as developed, has two major formats, or position-space procedures. Either the patient sits up and talks with the therapist, or he lies down and, with the therapist out of his sight, he free-associates. In contrast, group psychotherapy has developed more than 25 distinct methods [88]. Some of these methods will be discussed in this chapter. Four major procedures will be analyzed in the second half of this book.

More than a dozen schemes have been devised to classify the group therapies. In the interests of simplicity and completeness, still another system will be used in this book. Eight classifications will be achieved through a triple dichotomy. A method will be called *directive* or *nondirective, verbal* or *actional,* and *superficial* or *deep.* A method may have the possibility of variation in direction, style, or depth. Dichotomizing calls for arbitrary decisions to determine on which side of the dividing line a method falls.

In terms of this system, there are, then, eight possible classes, or kinds, of group psychotherapy. They are:
1. Directive-verbal-superficial
2. Directive-verbal-deep
3. Directive-actional-superficial
4. Directive-actional-deep
5. Nondirective-verbal-superficial
6. Nondirective-verbal-deep
7. Nondirective-actional-superficial
8. Nondirective-actional-deep

Directive and Nondirective Methods

The first dimension refers to the role the therapist plays in the group. A directive therapist's role may call for autocratic control: he may set the agenda, which means he determines what will occur in the group;

57

he may do all the talking; and he may make every decision. Or he may permit the group some latitude but will reserve for himself certain functions, such as having the final word about interpretations. A non-directive therapist may also play a variety of roles. He may take certain responsibilities but refuse others. He may assume or accept certain powers but will not accept others. Or he may refused to accept any responsibilities. In general, in deciding whether a method is directive or non-directive, the amount of decision making exercised by the therapist is crucial, especially decision making with respect to interpretations. If the group is permitted latitude of decisions, that group may be called non-directive.

Generally, the directive therapist sets limits on the members of the group; the nondirective therapist sets limits on himself.

Verbal and Nonverbal Methods

Some methods are completely verbal. Everything that is connected with the therapy consists of words. But there are methods of group psychotherapy in which, in addition to language, or even in place of it, communication is effected through behavior or through nonverbal stimuli.

As used here, actional or nonverbal methods are those in which some behavioral elements or nonverbal processes are involved as an integral part.

Superficial and Depth Methods

Some methods are self-limiting with respect to depth, being so structured and conducted that limited objectives are sought. Other methods, on the other hand, have potentiality for depth. The potential depth of the method depends in part on the size of the group. In general, the larger the group, the more superficial the method. Another rule for determining the depth of the method depends on the possibility for intercommunication; the more limits that are placed on communications between members, the more superficial the method. Still another criterion depends on the possibilities for self-revelation. The more one can discuss oneself, the more potentially deep the method.

REASONS FOR DIVERSITY OF METHODS

Writing in 1948, Bettis made the following remark [37]: "At the present time there are as many methods of group psychotherapy as there are group psychotherapists, for each group therapist has attempted to devise methods which will fit the needs of his particular group." The first half of this statement is probably an exaggeration, since it is necessary to distinguish between different methods and different styles of conducting similar methods; but there is a great deal of truth in the second half of the quotation, since no matter how the therapist may conceive of how he should operate, the interaction of the group will affect its actual procedures.

To understand how different methods came to be and why different therapists use such a variety of techniques, at least five considerations are necessary. One should understand (*a*) the therapist's exposure to group therapy, (*b*) the therapist's theoretic orientation, (*c*) the therapist's personality, (*d*) the nature and size of the group, and (*e*) the setting in which the therapy takes place. Any one of these five factors may affect the kind of group therapy carried out.

Training. A therapist who decides to use group therapy will tend to employ a method with which he is familiar, from experience as a patient, from previous experience as a therapist, from observation of groups, or from films, lectures, books, or articles. If Dr. Jones is working in Zeta Hospital and there is introduced by Dr. Smith to group therapy, and if Dr. Smith uses method Alpha, then it is to be expected that if Dr. Jones is himself to try group therapy he will use method Alpha rather than Beta or Gamma.

Dr. Jones may use a method inappropriate for a certain group, and if so, he may find that he will modify the method to suit the needs of that group. A therapist who knows of only one method which happens to be inappropriate for himself and his group may well feel discouraged and come to the conclusion that he does not have the aptitude for group therapy, when in truth he may not have an aptitude for that particular technique. The writer has known persons who were completely at sea using one procedure but who felt very comfortable in another. One of the major reasons for writing this book was to indicate the complexity of the field and to counteract the tendency of enthusiasts of one particular procedure, who give the impression that there is only one way to carry out group psychotherapy.

Theory. Therapeutic behavior is a function of theory. Every therapist has developed or accepted some particular theory of human behavior and of change of personality. To be successful in his group therapeutic endeavors, the procedure he uses should be consistent with his theoretic formulations. For example, if a person who held to Rogers' theory of psychotherapy, which has nondirective procedures implicit in it, were to attempt to use a method that was highly directive, then he would certainly be unhappy with it.

Personality. The therapist's own personality is another crucial factor to consider with respect to method. A therapist who is essentially shy and modest may find quite unacceptable a procedure which calls for him to be aggressive and bold; while a domineering therapist may find a procedure which holds him back just as unsupportable. Therefore, no matter what procedure may be used, there is no question that it will be affected, if not completely changed, by the therapist's own needs. What is good for one therapist may not be good for another.

The Group. We have discussed the training of the therapist, his theory, and his personality, but now we must consider the group. The method employed will be a function of the size and kind of the group. A method suitable for a half dozen college students may be quite inappropriate for 50 delinquents; and a method that will work with children may not work with adults. A method suitable for people with one kind of problem may not be appropriate to people with a different kind of problem. The therapist who comes to use some method on the basis of his own needs may find that the method does not fit the size of his group or the nature of its members.

The Setting. While the setting of the group is probably not often considered in connection with which method to use, it may have crucial importance. The privacy of the location, the size of the room, outside noises, etc., may be important in determining the best method. Also, such questions as whether visitors will come into the group without the group's invitation, whether the setting is such that the group members are mobile, etc., are pertinent.

Examples

Some examples will be cited to indicate the role of these various factors.

Dr. Brown learned how to carry out group psychotherapy in a mental hospital from Dr. White, who had student nurses in his group. Dr. White began his particular method by a detailed consideration of the nervous system. Dr. Brown was transferred to a mental hospital and was asked to do group therapy with patients. He began to employ the method of Dr. White but found that he could not get or hold the attention of patients in this manner.

Dr. Sanderson, who held to a client-centered theory of personality growth, was asked by Dr. Smith to conduct a group according to a method developed by Dr. Smith which consisted of carefully outlined lectures. Dr. Sanderson gave the lectures but felt most unhappy about them, minimized their value, and began to modify the procedure to permit the group greater latitude of expression. Dr. Smith complained, stating that errors in thinking would occur, since the proper procedure was to give the lectures without permitting any additions.

Dr. Green was introduced to group psychotherapy of the permissive circular discussional type, in which every member's opinion is respected, but when he began to use this particular method, he found that he could not tolerate the sloppy thinking of the members. He began to give longer and longer explanations of the dynamics of human behavior, and soon the group became the audience for his lectures.

Dr. Thomas wanted to use a dramatic method of group psychotherapy, but he found his group totally unresponsive. Cajoling them, flattering them, encouraging them, and bullying them did no good. They were resistive to the procedure as he saw it and as he tried it out.

Dr. Conrad found his group unresponsive. He tried to allow them freedom but obtained little participation. Finally he was told that the room, which had a glass door, through which the members could see others going about and those outside could see in, was unsuited for the method. He had the glass door made opaque; immediately a greater feeling of security was obtained, and discussions improved.

DIRECTIVE METHODS

The directive therapist believes that he is the most suitable person in the group to make decisions. He may argue as follows. Many members in a group are weak, uncertain, dependent; they desire and need a strong, confident, well-informed leader. They will feel more secure and more comfortable in a group where the therapist is ready to assume responsibilities. The therapist, after all, is a specialist in human relations, he has a greater knowledge of personality and of therapy than the other members, and he must give of himself and of his abilities. An experienced, impartial, and devoted group therapist is able to lead a group economically and efficiently; a group without leadership disintegrates into a social group. A directive therapist has the welfare of every member in mind, and, with his greater understanding and objectivity, he can allocate the time and direct the attention of the group so that every member will benefit. Some members of the group will want to dominate it; they will either get all the attention for themselves or cause the group to become disatisfied. A group that is not directed in an intelligent manner becomes disrupted.

While directive therapists may vary in many respects, they generally tend to be aggressive; they hold to rationalistic theories of personality, having high regard for the will and the intellect. They are likely to have forceful personalities and may be effective with short-term and difficult groups.

Persons working in a directive manner may use verbal and nonverbal methods, and the depth of the therapy may vary considerably.

Directive-verbal-deep Methods

Multiple Therapy. If group therapy is considered to have economic value, principally because one therapist meets with more than one patient, then multiple therapy is only one-half as efficient as individual therapy, since in this form two therapies meet with one patient.

Introduced by Rudolf Dreikurs [103], the interactional possibilities are from the patient to either or to both of the therapists, and for each therapist to the patient or the other therapist or to the other therapist and the patient. The therapists may assume coequal roles, or one may take the leading role and the other a subordinate role. The major argument for this triangular procedure, as given by Dreikurs, is that it is more economical than ordinary individual therapy in that much more rapid improvements are made.

As used according to the Adlerian theory of psychotherapy which conceives the problem of therapy as education, the therapists are concerned with understanding how the individual came to use certain life techniques, what his unconscious motives are, and how he may establish more satisfactory ways of obtaining proper goals. During the process, one or both of the therapists may question the patient in order to come to a diagnosis of the reasons for the present assumption of values and life style. The therapists may begin to interact between themselves, while the patient listens to the discussion about him, and they may come to tentative agreements or may even disagree. The patient may intervene to give more information or to suggest other explanations. In short, the three people in the room are united in a common effort to understand the patient's motivations and to find new procedures superior to old ones.

This method is primarily directive, in that the therapists ask questions, come to conclusions, and make suggestions: it is also democratic, in that the three are engaged in a common problem of working out the difficulties of one of the three and of doing so on an equality basis.

Analytic Therapy. Probably the single most popular method of group psychotherapy is the *circular discussional,* which operates as follows. The therapist sets the stage by indicating that any member of the group may take the floor. When one of the members talks, the rest of the group listens. When he finishes, the therapist or any of the members may comment or ask questions, or another member may begin to talk about himself. At his discretion, the therapist may ask other members to comment, ask them questions, and in other ways attempt to get the group as a whole to participate. His major objective is to come to conclusions about the particular dynamics of a single individual, or about the group as a whole, or about people in general. What distinguishes various schools of thought, such as the Freudians, Adlerians, or eclectics, is not the procedure proper, but rather the nature of the explanation.

In the procedure used by Bach [19], almost any variation, including role playing, may be used, depending on the judgment of the therapist or the desire of a member. However, the final common objective of analytic methods is to analyze; the analysis may come from the participants but more usually comes from the therapist, who is regarded as the final judge in most cases.

The therapist may assume varying degrees of authority, ranging from complete control to passive participation, and he may vary his amount of control from session to session, permitting the group more freedom the longer it continues. This depends on his judgment of what will best achieve the purposes of therapy. He may, for example, find it advantageous to pull together the discussion, lecturing on some topic and indicating how each of the members may be working on the basis of some principle. He may offer dream interpretations. He may initiate discussions on some topic and may then act as a facilitator, using techniques of encouragement and reflection. In short, in analytic therapy, the procedures used by any therapist may vary considerably within one session or from session to session, but the final aim is to come to understand every individual by means of group discussions.

Cotherapist Methods. A number of therapists have found it advantageous to have coleadership of groups. Among those who have employed this procedure are Lundin and Aronov [246], Baruch and Miller [27], and Loeffler and Weinstein [237]. The advantages of cotherapists in group psychotherapy are cited by the latter pair as follows:

1. The patient can choose a less threatening therapist.
2. The method facilitates a more rapid expression of negative statements.
3. Given two styles of verbalization, one may be easier for the patient to understand.
4. This method is a concrete example of good interpersonal relationships (between the therapists).
5. More effective interpretations and plannings are possible.
6. The efforts of the two therapists concatenate, each man helping the other.

The therapists may have equal rank. In some cases, as reported by Powdermaker and Frank [290], one serves as an observer, who may report to the group as a whole or only to the main therapist on his observations and conclusions. Solomon, Loeffler, and Frank [366] have discussed this method and cite its advantages as follows:

1. It is an effective training procedure.
2. The therapist can objectively evaluate the behavior that he observes.
3. It serves to duplicate more closely the reality of patients' own conflicts.
4. It offers patients a broader dynamic area to which they can react.

5. It makes possible the handling of larger groups without diminishing therapeutic effectiveness.

Behind-the-back Technique. This procedure, discussed earlier, is directive, in that the form is established by the therapist. A patient who has volunteered to be the subject discusses himself, then he "goes out of the room" simply by turning his back to the group or hiding behind some object, while the rest of the group discuss and analyze him. Then the member "comes back into the group," and the therapist, maintaining the fiction that the patient was actually out of the room, gives a summary of what was said. Then after the patient comments on the summary, the group as a whole discusses him.

Eleanore Redwin [310] has used this procedure in a married couples' group, sending "out of the room" both members of the couple while the rest of the members discussed the "absent" pair.

Projective Methods. Baruch and Miller [27] have employed a procedure of the circular discussional type in which the various members were asked to produce spontaneous drawings, which were then analyzed by the group as a whole. The theory behind this method is that patients will express their underlying problems symbolically by such drawings, and that through discussions, the meanings of the productions will become evident.

Directive-verbal-superficial Methods

Will Training. A unique method of group psychotherapy associated with the name of the late A. A. Low [239, 240] is known as will training. It is important because of the nature of the persons to whom it is directed, because it is used by more than 40 groups in a dozen states, and because of its unusual theory and method. It presents a curious combination of contradictory elements of authoritarianism and democracy.

Low's basic proposition was that an effective psychiatry for the masses had to be simple and cheap. Without criticizing other methods, he found that none of them had these qualities. His will training meets these two requirements.

The theory of will training is simple. Mental disorders show themselves by improper behavior, of which peculiar language is a prime and most important example. A mentally ill person demonstrates his condition by inappropriate language. To help a patient, it might be enough if one worked with language, instead of trying to get to his basic personality structure, rooted in the past. If one could get a patient to talk more sensibly, then perhaps he might think more sensibly. As can be seen, the theory of this procedure depends on semantics.

In practice, the therapist and the members of the group concern themselves with language productions of members. It becomes crucial to be aware of verbal errors, to "spot" statements that indicate "self-sabotage" or "confusion." A patient may say, "I simply can not stand my pain!" The therapist might respond, "You *are* standing your pain. Besides, all pain can be borne. You are not stating facts correctly." Or a patient may say, "I am completely unable to go into stores." The therapist may reply, "Perhaps you do not go into stores. Certainly you think you can not go. But the plain truth of the matter is you can go into stores." Even a delusion is handled in this forthright manner. The therapist might say, "You say that you see something. I can not see it. No one else in the group sees it. You are merely reporting that you have a private experience, which we can not share."

Will-therapy groups are composed primarily of ex-mental hospital patients, psychotics in remission. Groups meet at members' homes for sessions rigidly prescribed by a manual of operations [240], written by Low, which serves as the bible for the group. During the sessions, members may read from the text, will listen to phonographic recordings by Low, will listen to testimonials and experiences by members, and will be controlled by the senior member. The senior member, himself an expatient, serves as therapist.

According to Low, a therapist, to be effective with ex-psychotics, must have two qualities. He must be viewed as a sympathetic person, and he must be viewed as having understanding. The fact that senior members themselves have been mentally ill serves to create a feeling on the part of the other members that senior members *are* sympathetic; and since senior members have been trained by Low, they are viewed as having a comprehensive knowledge of the particular theory and method.

The method, as can be seen, is authoritarian, since a patient is not permitted to speak in his own idiom if this idiom is considered to be improper. Members of the group are alerted to the possibilities of semantic self-sabotage and are quick to spot verbal deviations. On the other hand, the groups are an example of self-direction and control. Because the groups are run by patients, it may be said that will-training groups are an example of democracy.

Group Counseling. Alfred Adler was the first of Freud's followers to desert him, rebelling against the master's insistence on the importance of sex. For Adler, the drive to power and the social need to belong to the group were more potent factors in personality development. In 1922 Adler began what was in some respects a most revolutionary procedure. Up to this time, spectators had been permitted to observe surgical operations, but no one had been permitted to overhear psychiatric consultations. It was exactly this that Adler permitted, interviewing children and their parents, exactly as he had in his private office, in front of others. The "others" were physicians, social workers, psychologists, and teachers, and they were present to learn more about Adler's theories and his methods of practice. The realization soon came that there were two unexpected advantages to the procedure. The presence of the group, instead of inhibiting the counselee, appeared, paradoxically, to stimulate him. Children who might have been shy, mute, negative, or hostile in the private office were actually more communicative in front of a group. The second advantage was that the auditors not only learned more about Adler's methods and theories, but also in many cases felt that they had made personal gains [342].

Adler, however, never paid much attention to the group, and he does not appear to have written anything specifically about group psychotherapy. It was his followers, Bierer in England; Dreikurs, Redwin, and Kadis in America, who developed Adlerian group therapy to a high point.

The particular version which Dreikurs elaborated will be discussed in greater detail in the second part of this book. While maintaining the essential features of Adler's early procedures, it has become the most complex of the methods of group psychotherapy.

Lecture Methods. A number of procedures have the following in common: the therapist acts the part of the lecturer, presenting verbal, visual, or a combination of verbal and visual material to the members of the group, who are supposed to accept the visual or auditory stimuli without response, or who may be allowed to ask questions. Lecture methods are generally used with large groups, with unresponsive members, such as psychotics, and are most frequently used by inexperienced therapists.

THE CLASS METHOD. The method used by Pratt in 1905 and later developed at the Boston Dispensary in 1930 consisted for the most part of lectures by the therapist. Later, testimonials by members, often by means of notes which were read by the therapist, were included. Members were seated in terms of the number of sessions they had attended, and senior members were permitted to sit up on the platform facing the rest of the group [305].

THE REPRESSIVE-INSPIRATIONAL TECHNIQUE. Similar to the class method were a variety of procedures used by Marsh, Lazell, Emerson, Smilie, Altshuler, and others, in which the therapist presented a variety of auditory stimuli, often including music, to gain the attention of subjects and to enable them to experience some kind of social stimulation. Subjects might be asked to whistle, hum, clap hands, or sing in unison. News might be read to the members. Members might be asked to give short talks or engage in debates, but usually the essence of the meeting was the discussion, intended to keep the morale of the group up, to encourage the members, and to help them avoid feelings of loneliness. This method has been used for the most part with large groups of psychotics in mental hospitals, and it continues to be one of the most popular of procedures. As used originally, it was not intended for psychotherapy but rather for prophylaxis, to keep patients from deteriorating under institutional conditions.

REPETITION LECTURES. The following procedure, to the writer's knowledge, has never been published; this account is based on personal experience. About 1934, David C. Schmidt, a psychiatrist at San Quentin Prison in California, began to give therapeutic lectures to prisoners, which he continued for more than 20 years. Finally, the lectures became one lecture, which Dr. Schmidt repeated thousands of times, and some inmates heard the very same lecture hundreds of times! The theory behind the procedure was that the lecture, which contained the essence of the speaker's philosophy of life, by constant repetition might eventually sink into the minds of the auditors. It may easily be imagined how some of the subjects reacted to this constant and almost unvarying lecture.

VISUAL AIDS. A number of therapists have used visual aids, primarily moving pictures and slides, to supplement or supplant the lecturer. Bettis [37], Prados [292], and Stein [376] are among those who have made use of such aids. Bettis gives the following list of advantages for his own procedure, which employs posters.

1. They stimulate attention and interest.

2. They put discussions on a level that even an illiterate can understand.

3. They illustrate mechanisms without pedantry.

4. They relate vividly early experiences and behavior patterns to present behavior.

5. They give intellectual comfort to anxiety-ridden subjects and assist in dealing with painful material brought to consciousness.

A currently popular use of lectures, either with or without visual aids, is to prepare a larger group for more intensive individual or group therapy. Altshuler [15], Prados [293], and Luchins [245] have used this particular approach.

While therapeutic lectures certainly do have a place, there are some cautions that must be kept in mind. It is very easy for a therapist, who generally comes from an upper social class and who has had greater educational and cultural opportunities, to talk over the heads of the group. Since such groups are often held captive, either in mental hospitals, schools, or prisons, the corrective experience of having a group oppose the lecturer does not often occur, and it is possible for a therapist to continue to employ a procedure which may not have much value. Historically, it may be noted that the lecture method has almost disappeared from the literature. Kelley's article on "Semantic Therapy" [193] is one of the few recent discussions of this method.

Case Histories. Wender [400] uses a method which depends on the presentation of a disguised case history and later discussions. A real case, which may be of one of the members of the group or of someone else, is presented to the group by the therapist. The identity of the individual is not made known, and if he were to be identifiable, some of the salient elements may be distorted in order to prevent exposure. The therapist initiates and encourages discussion. Since the therapist generally has had more complete sources of information about the subject of discussion, he is in the position of serving as the authority about the dynamics of the person under discussion.

Anonymous Participation. This method illustrates the truism that there is nothing new under the sun. For centuries, in the Catholic church during a period of silent meditation known as a "retreat," directors have answered questions on faith which the retreatants write on slips of paper; the questions are read by the spiritual directors and answered before the group. In this way, the retreatants can keep their silence and yet receive instructions.

In the question-box method of Friedman and Gerhart [129], essentially the same procedure is used. Members write questions or comments which are put into a box, opened by the therapist in front of the group, read aloud, and then answered. This method appears to be most applicable when the members either are frightened by the situation or are antagonistic. It is also applicable when the members of the group presumably have little confidence in the integrity of the therapist or are reluctant to expose their attitudes to other members. Ideally, if this method is used, the box should be used less and less as the group progresses, for questions and discussions will eventuallly come from the floor.

Group Bibliotherapy. There is a flourishing field of self-help books designed to enable people to think more positively, wake up and live, make friends and influence people, and otherwise make the same kinds of gains intended in interactional psychotherapy. Whether these books have any great value is a moot point, but undoubtedly they are used in great numbers for what we have called autonomous therapy.

A number of workers, among them Powell [291], Willner [410], Blackman [48], and Klapman [200, 201], have suggested group reading for therapeutic purposes. Klapman's textbook-mediated therapy is probably the best known.

The story of Klapman's discovery of his particular technique bears retelling, since in miniature it contains the essence of the experiences of many group therapists. In the early 1930s, Klapman, a psychiatrist assigned to a mental hospital, concerned with the fact that he was not able to give enough attention to the many patients under his charge, and unable to establish satisfactory relationships with schizophrenics, got the idea that if he gathered some of his patients into small discussional groups, some useful end might be attained. He began his work without knowledge that any one else had done this kind of thing before, and it was only some time later that he learned of the work of Marsh and Lazell. However, he was soon discouraged, because the psychotics were not able to come to attention. They would get up and wander about in the room or would sink into characteristic attitudes of apathy.

Casting about for some procedure that would get them to cohere, he hit upon the idea of presenting to each member some printed material, which he could read aloud while they read silently. To his delight, the printed stimuli served to keep their attention, and when he asked a member to read out loud, the others, for the most part, followed along.

In the present form of this method, the members sit in a circle, each member is presented with a mimeographed textbook containing a variety of articles written in simple form [201]. Books are opened to a specific article selected by Dr. Klapman, and he begins to read. After reading for several minutes, he will ask another member to go on, while the other members follow along. After a time, the therapist, depending on his judgment, may interrupt the reading and ask, "What do you think of this idea?" or "Do you agree with what the writer is saying?" and in this way attempt to get from the person who read, or from any of the members of the group, comments about the topic under consideration. Or he may stop the reading to comment on the topic himself and thus invite further discussion. If there appears at the time to be little reaction, the therapist merely asks another member of the group to continue reading.

The textbook may be viewed as a kind of a crutch to encourage verbal interaction. If a group develops well, less and less use is made of the textbooks and more and more dependence is put on free discussion.

Mechanical Group Therapy. No method of group psychotherapy is so unusual as the one introduced by Schmidhoffer under the name of mechanical group therapy [336]. It may be said, paradoxical as it may seem, that in this variation neither a therapist nor a group is necessary.

The method consists of playing short recorded messages over the loudspeaker system of a mental hospital. The messages are highly repetitious. Examples are: "Pay attention! Pay attention! I can get rid of any symptom completely and in less than 1 minute. Pay attention!" And, "I am not overly dependent on medicines or doctors. Pay attention!"

The captive members of the "group" may be scattered all over the hospital, in wards, private rooms, etc. It appears that the theory, somewhat similar to the one held by Dr. Schmidt, depends on repeated messages, on the grounds that if an idea is presented frequently enough, it will be finally accepted. Some suggestions of Couéism are also apparent.

Directive-actional-deep Methods

This particular section of group psychotherapeutic methods is reserved for the family of procedures fathered by J. L. Moreno. All of them depend on spontaneous interactions between individuals. Moreno's therapeutic philosophy is based on the concept that man's original nature is spontaneous and creative, and that a maladjusted person has been robbed of his initiative, which he may regain by acting out significant early incidents or by experiencing reality testing in group interaction. A great many specific techniques may be used including the mirror technique, double technique, interchange of roles, etc. However, therapeutic role playing falls under two headings, in which any of the techniques may be used. They are psychodrama and sociodrama.

Psychodrama. Moreno, a master of reification, has used this term in at least three ways. First, and most generally, psychodrama is all of living behavior. All of us are continually engaged in the drama of life. In terms of this thinking, group psychotherapy is a part of psychodrama. Secondly, psychodrama has been used as a generic name for any kind of role playing, whether for therapeutic, instructional, or other purposes. Thirdly, and it is this definition that we shall adopt, psychodrama is a specifically therapeutic procedure which requires one or more people with problems of personality or behavior to interact with others, who take varied roles in the patient's "social atom."

Sociodrama. In sociodrama, the patients are the members of the audience. The drama is conducted for their benefit. They are supposed to experience "spectator therapy" at viewing situations presumed to have personal meanings for them. The dramas may be enacted by members of the group, for whom the particular situation has reality meaning, or by special assistants.

Description of Psychodrama. In the second half of this book, a more complete account of a variation of psychodrama as developed by the writer will be given. This variety will be featured because it is simpler, cheaper, and more suited for general clinical use when the more elaborate props and personnel of the classic method are not available. In this section, an account of Moreno's classic procedure will be given.

The psychodrama takes place in a theater which consists of a circular, three-level stage, somewhat similar to a three-layer wedding cake, rising one step at a time from the floor. Immediately above the stage there is a small balcony, which also may be used. The audience is seated on chairs circling the stage. An electrician is available to control the lighting, or it may be controlled by the therapist.

The therapist rises from the group and goes onto the stage, standing at first either on the floor level or on the first of the three levels. He may now do any of a variety of things. If the group is a new one, he will attempt to "warm" it up. This he may do in any of several ways. He may pick one member out and question him, asking him how many people he knows in the group, to pick them out, to name them, to tell how well he knows them, etc. If the members do not know each other, he may pick one person at random and ask him to look about and find one person in the group to whom he is attracted, who looks interesting, etc. This individual searches about, finds someone, identifies him, and then is asked by the psychodramatist to explain why he picked the individual. A free and easy tone is maintained, and usually the group begins to laugh. The person picked is then asked to comment on how he feels at having been selected, and he may be asked to look about and in turn pick someone else who attracts him. In this manner, the therapist tries to loosen up a new group and to get them warmed up to the next stage of the proceedings, which consists of having a member come up on the stage to participate in the psychodrama.

If, however, a person has already been selected for the drama, and if the group is well warmed up as a result of prior acquaintanceship, the "warm-up" is not necessary, and the therapist may proceed differently. It must be understood that the essence of Moreno's procedures is spontaneity and that no two sessions are alike.

The dramatist may begin by reviewing the case history of the subject. He may spend some time discussing the dynamics of the problem. He may decide to take up some philosophical issue, all for the purpose of setting the scene.

Assuming that the person to come up for the psychodrama has not as yet arisen, Moreno may begin to talk while the subject is still seated in the audience, asking him questions, warming him up while he is still in the group. Part of the tactics of this method is to proceed from one stage gradually to another. If the new member were asked to come up on the stage, he might balk, get stage fright, and refuse. However, in the security of the group, seated in the midst of others, he will ordinarily find little threat in responding to questions from the therapist, who might come up the aisle and talk to him at close range.

When the therapist believes this next step will succeed, he will ask the subject to stand up and come to the front of the room, near the first step of the stage. Moreno will continue to talk to the individual, himself facing the group with the member having his back to the group. At this point Moreno may lay hands on the subject, shaking hands, putting his arm about his shoulder, holding his arm, etc., if he believes that this personal contact will help give the patient more confidence.

Moreno may mount the first of the three levels, invite the member to discuss whatever problem he has, and together they will begin to unfold the drama. Soon, the generalized problem is made specific. "Where might this occur? Who will be there? Has it happened often? When did it last take place? How does this person look? What kind of a person is she?"

Once the outline of the plot is clear, the therapist says, "Let us play-act. Show us how the matter may go. Let us take someone to act the part of your mother." And Moreno may ask someone, either an amateur member of the group or a professional assistant, to take the role of some significant "other" in the patient's "social atom," to act as an "auxiliary ego."

The plot is outlined, the auxiliary ego is given any further instructions necessary, either by the dramatist or by the patient, and then the spontaneous interaction begins; the patient may stop it at any time if it is not going the way it ought. More members may be brought in as auxiliary egos, and the action is permitted to develop.

After one scene is finished, others may be devised on the spot. They may be suggested by the patient, the dramatist, or anyone else. Usually, the patient's permission is secured before attempting any new scene.

When the drama is over, the member returns to the audience, and now the dramatist may give interpretations, ask for comments, and lead a discussion. The subject may be recalled to reenact a new situation or to repeat an old one, or others in the group may reenact the same situation in order to show the member who was the patient how he looked to the participants. This last procedure is called the mirror technique.

The variety of procedures possible can only be hinted at in this section. One can almost say that in psychodrama anything can happen and often does. Without question, this is the most exhausting and demanding of group therapeutic procedures, calling for limitless optimism and energy on the part of the psychodramatist.

Description of Sociodrama. The techniques of sociodrama are identical to those of psychodrama. However, while the patient in psychodrama is one individual, or several individuals in the same social atom, for example a "love triangle," in sociodrama the patient is the group as a whole. An example may appear in industry.

An employer, let us say, has the problem of selecting one of several people to fill an advanced position. He is well aware that his choice will cause those not selected to feel unhappy. He is also aware that for the good of his company he must make a good choice. He feels certain that no matter who is selected, the others will resent the choice.

A meeting may be called, presided over by the sociodramatist. Seated in the circle, let us say, are the president of the firm, the vice-president, the personnel manager, and the six candidates. The dramatist may begin by pointing out that this situation that faces all those present is fraught with unpleasantness. A hard decision has to be made. He may ask three of the six applicants to sit in a circle, and he may ask one of them to take the role of the president, one the role of the vice-president, and the other the role of the personnel manager. They are asked to discuss the question of filling the vacant position. In this manner, these three individuals may learn how three other people emphathize with them. After this action, the true executives may repeat the action and indicate how *they* feel about the problem, perhaps discussing the six men, one by one. Then the executives may assume the roles of the men who are up for consideration. They may be asked by the therapist to act out a discussion between one of the candidates and his wife, etc.

An exchange of attitudes takes place for the purpose of relaxing the general situation, helping everyone to understand the others, giving the persons who are to do the selecting an opportunity to obtain further information about the candidates, and in general, clearing the air, so that whoever is chosen and those who are not chosen will comprehend individual feelings and the nature of the total issue.

Or, instead of using members of the group to act out roles, the sociodramatist may employ actors, not at all involved in the issue, to take the roles of the officers and the candidates, devising situations from suggestions made by the members of the group.

Directive-actional-superficial Methods

In this particular class of group therapies, the actions of the subjects, or the stimuli presented to the subjects, are directed by the therapist to a greater extent than in the methods just discussed.

Dramatics. It has already been stated that the Marquis de Sade, probably with no understanding of the therapeutic consequences, used dramatics with psychotic patients. About 1880 Miraglia began to use dramatics in mental hospitals in Italy as part of a program of psychotherapy. Since then theatricals have been employed by a number of psychotherapists, among them Curran [94], Reider, Olinger and Lyle [311], Lassner [218], and Davidoff and Buckland [97].

Three elements may be isolated with respect to the value of such dramatics. First, the general process of preparation, which includes discussions about the selection of the drama, the rehearsals, the preparation of the stage and costumes, etc. This project requires the various members to work together harmoniously. The second element has to do with the personality effects of getting on a stage and acting in front of an audience. And the third element refers to the reactions of the audience to the drama.

At this point one may ask what the difference is between going through these various steps in an institution where the major concern is to present a play in order to make money and in an institution where the major concern is psychotherapy. While it may appear that there are essentially no great differences, nevertheless, in the two situations the attitudes of those concerned with the presentation of the drama will be quite different. In one case, there is a focusing on the drama itself, even at the expense of the feelings of individuals, while in the second case, the drama becomes secondary. In the first case, personality damage might occur, while in the second case, the director, who is primarily interested in the individuals, will behave toward them in ways to enhance the development of their personality.

Puppets. The issue of formality or intentionality arises also with respect to puppets used for psychotherapeutic purposes. There can be little doubt that this method of entertainment, which has fascinated countless generations of children, has had beneficial personality effects. Psychotherapy is not confined to professional psychotherapists; nevertheless it cannot be distinguished as such unless it is done intentionally. Therefore, the same puppet show presented in two institutions may be entertainment in one and psychotherapy in the other, even though the effects are similar.

Here, as in sociodrama, the audience is the therapeutic patient. In planned psychotherapy, however, instead of the drama being selected for entertainment, it may be modified to dramatize real problems of members of the audience. One need only observe the expressions and behavior of the children to realize the amount of catharsis or "spectator therapy" that occurs in such groups. Among the exponents of puppets for psychotherapy with children are Hawkey [159], and Bender and Woltman [33].

Acting-out Techniques. There is some controversy among psychotherapists about the therapeutic implications of acting out. Generally speaking, followers of Sigmund Freud view acting out as an act of resistance. Problems ought to be solved, they appear to say, internally rather than out in society. Moreno, of course, takes exactly the opposite view.

A most unusual method of group psychotherapy was used by Ernst Simmel [352], a psychiatrist in the German army during World War I. He was concerned with the rehabilitation of severely psychoneurotic soldiers. Believing that to some extent their difficulties were due to repressed hostilities against their own officers, he gave the men bayoneted rifles and permitted them to attack straw-filled dummies dressed in the uniforms of German officers!

Meals and Summerskill [258] have followed along essentially the same lines, to all appearances quite without any knowledge of Simmel's earlier work. They gave aggressive children bean bags which they were permitted to throw at pictures of people whom they did not like. The resemblance of this procedure to play therapy, in which a child is permitted to vent his hostility on dolls who symbolize individuals in the child's social atom, is evident.

ABC. Earlier, the problem that Klapman faced in trying to carry out psychotherapy with psychotics was recounted, and his solution described. Jacobson and Wright [176], working with a similar population had, of course, the same problem of getting the attention of their patients. Their solution, quite different from that of Klapman, nevertheless has essential similarities in terms of tactics.

The group meets in a room where there is a blackboard. The therapist attempts to have the members of this group of apathetic noninteracting persons stand close to the blackboard. He picks up a piece of chalk and writes the letters ABC on the board and then gives the chalk to one of the patients and indicates that the patient should continue to complete writing the alphabet. If the patient refuses or appears not to hear, he may ask another, or he may place the chalk in the hands of a resistant patient and even guide the patient's hand to the blackboard. As soon as a patient finishes writing the alphabet, the therapist may erase it, or he may have another patient do so. Then he may start off again by writing ABC, or he may ask another patient to start off, and then will try to have another patient complete the task. Consequently, the first step in this method of group psychotherapy with psychotics is to get them to work with the therapist at a simple task.

When the members have reached the point at which they will write out the alphabet, the therapist may introduce any of several variations. Chalk is given to two patients, and they both write out the alphabet, alternating letters. Now these two are engaged in an interaction, since one has to wait until the other has finished to begin. Or they may write to a count. The therapist may count rapidly or slowly, or he may vary the tempo of the count. Later, the patients may be instructed to write as fast as possible, or as slow as possible, as small as possible, or as large as possible. They may write the alphabet in competition, each one trying to finish it before another patient does.

The major purpose of this method is to rouse the patients' interest in something and to encourage them to work cooperatively. As the patients get into the mood of the activity, they begin to verbalize; the therapist is careful to fan into life, by encouragement, answering questions, asking questions, making comments, etc., any spontaneous attempt to communicate. It can be seen that the procedure is calculated to bring about interaction by the patients first on a nonverbal level and then on a verbal level. Ideally, the final step is to wean the group away from the blackboard so that all communications can take place by language rather than by action.

NONDIRECTIVE METHODS
Nondirective-verbal-deep Methods

The Client-centered Method. Followers of the therapeutic philosophy of Carl Rogers have used the group method employing essentially the same kinds of interaction used in the nondirective individual method. Gorlow, Hoch, and Telschow [142], and Hobbs [164, 165] have discussed this procedure and its rationale in detail.

The therapist operates on the primary principle that every person has the capacity to solve his own problems. He serves as a catalyst, helping the individual to come to fuller understanding and greater self-appreciation by attempting to create an atmosphere of security and support for the patient who is trying to find solutions to emotional and behavioral difficulties. The therapist does this by taking a strictly nonjudgmental attitude, expressing acceptance of the individual, and by acting as a kind of mirror, reflecting back to the client the essence of what he is saying.

The therapist who works in a client-centered frame of reference sets limits on his own behavior. For example, he may not even take the initiative in asking the various members to identify themselves, which ordinarily in the analytic groups is the first thing that the therapist does. He leaves this step to the initiative of the group. He may only set the limits of the group with respect to the length of time that *he* will remain in the room, or the number of periods per month that *he* will be able to meet with them. Even in these respects, he may, if possible, attempt to ascertain the wants of the members, so as to give them conditions that they will feel are optimal.

In the second half of the book a fuller discussion of the client-centered method of group psychotherapy will be found.

Leaderless Therapy. Bion and Rickman [46] have used a group method, primarily for research purposes, discussed in detail by Bion [45] in a series of articles, that is even more nondirective than the client-centered group method. Put into simplest terms, the therapist enters the group with the intention of becoming another member and of assuming no responsibility beyond that of anyone else. He sits in the group and watches what happens. He interacts only if he feels like it.

Nothing is more anxiety-provoking for a group than to have no understanding of the rules and limits of behavior, no explanation of what is to be done, no leader, no support, no encouragement. Baffled by the completely formless situation, the members, who, like those of all groups, probably enter the situation with the intention of being silent and passive until they understand the structure of the group, find that there is nothing to do, nothing to observe, no explanation.

The therapist sits, watches, listens—and waits. Some member may finally ask, if even *this* is not known, whether there is a leader, and the therapist may, if he feels so inclined, not even answer this question. If he is identified as the therapist and is asked a question, he may refuse to answer, or he may divert it. Eventually, the baffled members, out of sheer desperation, since the therapist may sit in silence the whole session or even for many sessions, begin to talk. As may be expected, their early statements represent feelings of anger, wonderment, and hostility. Usually, some member begins to assume leadership, but often the other members will resent this, and a division will occur with respect to this assumed authority. If, as a result of conflicts, the therapist is appealed to, he may indicate that he understands that the members of the group appear to have some concept of his role in the group which does not accord with his own.

This description of leaderless therapy, which has not, to the writer's knowledge, been used in this country, and about which relatively little is known in terms of possible effectiveness, indicates its unusual nature.

Round-table Psychotherapy. The method of group psychotherapy, introduced by Willis McCann and Albert Almada [251], is quite different from any method discussed so far. It may be considered group therapy without a therapist. In the leaderless method, the therapist is in the group but is inactive; in the round-table method, the therapist may not even appear in the group. In the writer's opinion, this revolutionary method has such important implications, especially for use in mental hospitals, that it deserves detailed analysis.

It must be understood that in mental hospitals patients often see themselves as prisoners who are detained beyond limits of necessity by the staff. Staff members, who have the responsibility of making decisions for release, usually take a conservative view and are reluctant to expose patients to the tensions and dangers of the environment to which they were unable to adjust, unless the evidence for their probable adjustment is fairly conclusive. This situation, irksome to psychiatrists and to other staff members, puts them into conflict with certain patients who feel they are ready to be released; it results in strained relationships and poor morale and is not conducive to good interpersonal communications.

In the round-table method, the therapist selects 25 patients to join the group. Six patients form the round table, the other 19 form the audience. They meet in two rooms, arranged in the manner of a radio broadcasting studio. The 6 members go into one room, in which there is a round table with a microphone. In an adjacent room, separated from the round-table room by heavy glass, are the other 19 members. The two groups can see each other, but the 6 in the round-table room can not hear the 19, while the 19, through a microphone in the round-table room, can hear over a loud-speaker what the 6 are saying.

The 6 members of the panel have several tasks to carry out, making decisions by majority vote. One task, the major one, is to recommend one of their members for presentation to the hospital staff. A second task is to decide which one of the 19 in the other room should be asked to sit in with the remaining 5 if one of the original 6 is released. A third task is to send back to the room of the 19 any member of the 6 who is considered unable to function in this group.

A patient may be selected by the therapist to enter the group. He is placed in a room with 18 others. From this room he can see and hear what 6 members do. One of the 6 may be sent to staff; if he is released, making a vacancy in the round-table room, the new patient will hear the remaining 5 members discuss the 19 and decide which one of them will be asked to enter the round-table room. This patient may be the one chosen to join the 5; he will then engage in discussions concerning which one of the 6 is ready to be presented to the staff. If a member is sent out to staff and released, the patient then has the task of arguing for and voting on one of the 19 to be invited into the group of 6. He may himself be selected for presentation to the staff. On coming to the staff, he may or may not be released. If not released, he reenters the group of 6, where he may discuss the reactions of the staff. If he should relapse and be unable to participate in the group, the other 5 may send him back to join the 19 in the other room. From there, the whole procedure may be repeated.

The therapy, as can be seen, proceeds without further intervention by professional people, except that the members may be seen individually. For research purposes, both groups may be observed by experimenters through one-way screens.

The implications of this method are that it may be possible, without expenditures of personnel time, to organize part of the typical mental hospital in such a way that group therapy of this kind will take place autonomously. It is possible that the psychological tensions created in the patient by the compulsion to make adjustments among his mates and to impress fellow patients with his own readiness for release, and freedom from the feeling that release depends only on the judgments of professional people, will result in more rapid improvements. Such appears to be the case from some early findings reported by McCann [250].

One may wonder if this procedure is suitable for regressed and non-communicating patients. McCann * cited one patient, who had been dissociated for a long time and was put into the room with the 19. He immediately turned his back to the window and sat hunched over, appar-

* Personal communication.

ently oblivious to what was being said. However, as sessions went on, he began to sit up and to turn about so that he could see what was going on. Finally he, too, was selected by the remaining 5 in the round-table group to join them; he was eventually voted on to go to staff and was released.

McCann has experimented with recording sessions and playing them back, believing that if patients hear what they have said they will gain increased insight. His major theoretical premise is that if a patient can lose himself in the problems of others, he interrupts the vicious circle of self-preoccupation that nourishes morbid thought processes. A second principle follows from the first: he who would help himself must begin by helping others. It may be seen, in terms of the nine major mechanisms discussed earlier, that McCann places primary emphasis on altruism.

Nondirective-verbal-superficial Methods

The three procedures discussed under the above heading have doubtful status, perhaps, in terms of a strict definition of group psychotherapy. Regardless of whether, in terms of their social effectiveness, they may be so defined, they ought to be seriously considered and understood by students of the topic.

Social Clubs. The method known as social-club therapy, introduced and developed by Joshua Bierer [41, 43], together with various colleagues, in England, resembles in some respects round-table psychotherapy but has important differences. Members of the clubs are selected by the professional staff. They are given quarters where they may meet and conduct their affairs, but they operate autonomously and are principally concerned with engaging in social activities among themselves and organizing entertainment activities for the hospital as a whole.

The professional members of the staff select the members of the clubs and are ready to offer their services when needed, but they are not permitted either to attend meetings or to express their opinions in the clubs, except on invitation. They may dissolve the clubs, but they cannot run them.

While the ostensible purpose of the clubs is to provide recreation for the members, the more important reason for their creation is to give members an opportunity to socialize and to regain their initiative through unhampered social interaction.

Alcoholics Anonymous. In terms of number of members, Alcoholics Anonymous [22], which is said to have as many as 70,000, is the most important group engaged in psychotherapy. A.A. is unusual, since in many respects it is a self-help group, not directed by any of the usual theoretic schools; it is in effect a kind of religious movement. One of its basic principles is that a person cannot break himself of alcoholism on his own but must depend on a higher power. Another basic idea is that an alcoholic is a definite personality type who cannot take alcoholic beverages at any time or in any amount. Both these ideas are unique in principle, not being contained in any formal system of psychotherapy.

The procedures used in Alcoholics Anonymous vary over the country very little. The major element of meetings consists of testimonials by members and subsequent discussions. In terms of mechanisms, altruism is a major element in helping to keep former alcoholics dry, since members are prepared to help others in diverse ways.

Although professional psychotherapists have had some negative attitudes concerning the value of A.A., there seems to be little doubt that this organization has done good work with a very difficult group. Psychotherapists are often reluctant to deal with the alcoholic, believing that he is usually too unstable and too likely to return to the bottle to do well in formal therapy.

Public Speaking. Although public-speaking training of the kind done by Dale Carnegie is not generally considered psychotherapeutic, there appears to be little doubt that the kind of training conducted by persons who give others practice in more effective ways of dealing with people in groups falls within our area of discussion. Among those who have discussed this issue formally and have used this method is J. I. Meiers [261].

The theory of this procedure goes somewhat as follows: in learning to stand up and talk before a group one obtains self-confidence, which radiates beyond the specific situation to one's other activities.

Nondirective-actional-deep Methods

Only one method appears to belong to this particular family of the group therapies. It combines the permissivism of nondirective methods and the spontaneity of psychodrama.

Psychodramatic Group Therapy. A number of group therapists, including Shor [350], Boring and Deabler [53], Lassner [219], and Corsini [84, 85], have made adaptations of Moreno's classic psychodrama, described earlier, by having the group meet in a circle, using members as auxiliary egos, and depending to a great extent on the spontaneous suggestions of the members for the specific procedures. One variety of this particular method, as used by the writer, will be discussed in the second half of the book. A variety of this method, leaderless psychodrama, has been reported by members of a group that met without a therapist for the purpose of employing psychodrama for self-improvement [221].

Nondirective-actional-superficial Methods

It may be worthwhile at this time to examine the concept of superficiality in group psychotherapy. In some ways this term is ambiguous, since if a person with a serious problem may be helped by simple procedures which do not penetrate deeply, then that method is proper for the condition. In using the concepts of deep and superficial, the major consideration is whether or not the individual in the therapy is permitted to discuss his very sensitive and often forgotten memories. Another criterion for determining the depth of psychotherapy is the amount of distress that a member may have as a result of procedures. It is evident, for example, that two methods that have a superficial resemblance—psychodrama and public speaking—differ considerably in potentiality for depth. In one psychodramatic session a member may operate at a very superficial level, reenacting, let us say, some difficulties he has in making purchases, and in a public-speaking session a member may desire to discuss his night terrors; but generally speaking, the two methods have quite different potentialities with respect to depth.

Activity-group Therapy. This particular method, developed by S. R. Slavson [354] at the Jewish Board of Guardians, while it has elements found in Rogers' nondirective method, Bion's leaderless method, and Moreno's psychodrama, is nevertheless a distinctly unique procedure. Slavson developed the method about 1934, apparently, like Klapman and others, without knowledge of the psychotherapeutic group work that others were engaged in at the time. Although Slavson professes adherence to Freudian theory, it appears that the procedures described below do not necessarily depend on this frame of reference. Indeed, it appears that the line of thought initiated by Rank and developed by Taft and Rogers is more in line with activity-group therapy than is psychoanalysis.

The method is considered best for youth in the so-called latency period, i.e., the teens. The group is first composed on paper, by analyzing the personalities of potential members and attempting, by balancing traits, to create a group that will function optimally. If the group is not properly selected, eliminations, additions, or substitutions may be made until the proper structural combinations are found.

The locale of the therapy should be a room where a great deal of noise and violent activity can be tolerated. The room ought to have tables and benches where the youth may work at a variety of handicraft activities, play games, etc. In addition, there should be provision for the making of simple lunches, for at the end of the sessions the group sits down and has a snack.

The therapist greets new members, shows them around, and makes introductions. After that he tries to leave the members alone, observing them but not controlling them, not intervening in any of their activities, no matter how boisterous, aggressive, or destructive, unless a possibility develops of serious damage to the building (such as a fire) or of danger to a member (such as an attack by one member on another with a dangerous tool). He usually will not interfere in a fist fight, in teasing, in minor destruction of property, or similar antisocial behavior, permitting the group itself to handle such situations.

While he is primarily an observer, he does not hesitate to assist a member who asks for help, and he may, at his discretion, even offer to assist. He may play games and in other ways behave as a member of the group, but he will not interfere in social situations that he regards as the proper concern of the members.

Near the end of the period, the therapist begins to prepare a simple meal, such as frankfurters and Coke, and the group eats and talks. Here, too, the therapist declines to take the initiative; he will not, as an example, reprove a member for using violent or scatalogical language.

In activity-group therapy, as in Bierer's social groups, the members assume their own obligations. While in Bierer's method, the therapist is not present in the group, in Slavson's procedure, the therapist is present. He prevents the group from becoming a gang, and he serves to set limits. In this procedure, the youth have the opportunity to interact, in a democratic manner, with an understanding and permissive adult, and they have the chance to form new and better relationships with their peers.

Music Therapy. Music has been used in mental hospitals for the purpose of calming patients, making them more accessible to verbal psychotherapy, and giving them an opportunity, by singing or playing instruments, to express themselves [264]. Altshuler [15] is a leading proponent of the values of music, claiming that it affects the creativity of individuals and helps them in their homeostatic processes.

There can be little doubt that listening to music may stimulate various moods, and familiar music may evoke memories. There is also no doubt that ensemble playing encourages cooperation. Further, it is likely that singing or playing in front of auditors is a social experience of some value.

Auroratone. Rubin and Katz [325] have introduced Auroratone films, which are abstract color patterns synchronized with soft, sad music, as a means of relaxing patients so that they will become more accessible to more usual means of verbal discussions. Auroratone serves the same purpose as music therapy, employing visual as well as auditory stimuli.

CHAPTER 7 *Applications of Group Psychotherapy*

Many are the uses to which group psychotherapy has been put. An examination of the literature on the applications leads to the conclusion that very few aberrations of mind or behavior have not been treated by some variety of the group method. It will be the purpose of this chapter to survey some uses. To do so will require a frame of reference. The following items will serve as a guide for discussion:

1. Diagnostic uses of group psychotherapy
2. Applications to somatic conditions
3. Uses in institutions for defectives and the mentally ill
4. Correctional uses
5. Major behavioral pathologies, noninstitutionalized
6. Minor behavioral problems
7. Miscellaneous uses

DIAGNOSTIC USES OF GROUP PSYCHOTHERAPY

A diagnosis in psychology may either be a classification of an individual or a group at the present time, or it may refer to etiological conditions which brought the present condition to fruition. Despite advances in diagnosing, a reaction against formal typing has occurred. Whereas the psychiatrist of several decades ago was primarily interested in labeling his patient, since there was little else he could do for him, the psychiatrist of today, who understands the gross unreliability of diagnostic labels and has a greater degree of optimism (as a result of advances in psychotherapy and somatic methods in the treatment of the psychoses), is not greatly concerned with differential diagnoses and tends to view the whole person on a continuum of illness or discomfort. Although the present tendency appears to be to devaluate labeling, diagnosis is still undertaken, and new techniques for more accurate classifying are still being introduced.

The datum that the diagnostician uses comes from various sources: it may come from case histories prepared by a social worker who obtains information from several places; it may come from test results; it may come from observation of the patient as he interacts with others; or it may come, and most often does, from an interview. Ideally, of course, a diagnosis is based on material from all these sources.

It has been suggested by many persons that the group situation gives a diagnostician a unique insight into the individual as he interacts with others in unstructured situations. Among those who have written on this point are Bell [31], Gula [147], Redl [308], Symonds [382], Atterbury [17], and Bierer [42]. The various arguments go somewhat as follows: the patient in a group is more natural and less guarded than in an interview, i.e., he is more himself; observing individuals in groups with their varied tensions gives greater insights into areas of strain; whereas individual observation is generally of short duration, the same amount of time per man allows the diagnostician more time for each member of the group; those individuals who have periodic flare-ups can be seen more readily over prolonged observation; people who do not verbalize well may be seen in behavioral interaction.

Diagnosing comes directly from medical tradition; it is a generally maintained principle in medicine that treatment is contingent on diagnosis. But in psychotherapy, diagnosis may not affect the nature of the treatment, that is to say, people with diverse diagnoses may get essentially the same kind of treatment. Actually, psychotherapy *is* diagnosis, and an individual analysis may be considered one long diagnostic interview.

APPLICATIONS TO SOMATIC CONDITIONS

One of the several applications of the group method which merged into group psychotherapy as it is known today is the treatment of somatic conditions. When J. H. Pratt started his first group he was interested in instructing patients in the efficient management of their disease; he appears to have been entirely innocent of any concept of what is today called psychosomatic medicine. Other workers, however, saw different possibilities in the group method and began to apply it as *the* therapeutic agent. On the one hand were some enthusiastic ministers, who, feeling that the church had a healing function, began to treat a variety of diseases through group activities: prayer, sermons, and hymns. On the other hand were some physicians who, perhaps misreading Pratt's papers, felt that there might be some therapeutic quality to groups. Among these were Smilie [301], who used group therapy for diabetics; Harris [157], who experimented with cardiac and prenatal cases; Buck [60], who worked with hypertension; and Emerson [114], who treated undernourished children.

It became evident that group psychotherapy per se had little if any effect on the course of a strictly somatic disease, but that it might be of considerable value for four separate purposes: (a) helping people with somatic disease to make adjustment to the disease itself, (b) affecting attitudes of relatives of patients with disease, (c) bringing about improvement when the condition is totally or partially based on psychosomatic reactions, and (d) relieving symptoms of a hysterical nature.

Adjustment to Disease

Deutsch and Zimmerman [101], and Randall and Rogers [306], who worked with epileptics, illustrate the use of group therapy in helping sick persons to make better adjustments to their disease. If epilepsy is based on somatic conditions, it is evident that the seizures cannot be controlled by psychological means. But even if seizures cannot be stopped, a person with epilepsy may still make an adequate adjustment to the environment. In short, the therapy does not affect the epilepsy but may help the epileptic patient.

Reports have been given by Day, Day and Hermann [98], and by Barnes, Busee, and Dinken [23] with reference to multiple sclerosis; and by Turnbloom and Myers [394], Corbin [82], and Blackman [50] about aphasics. It is possible to get patients to adjust to physical disease and to meet their ailments with better attitudes. Perhaps the best example is seen with senile persons. Surely group therapy will not affect physiological changes that are the result of aging. However, Smith, Bryant, and Twitchell-Allen [362], Silver [351], Linden [229], and Case [69] have reported on the use of group methods with those so aged they had to be hospitalized.

In the Smith et al. report, 43 women were observed in their ward in a mental hospital. Four were blind, several were partially disabled, and many were feeble. The morale of the ward was low, the patients had little to do of a constructive nature, and they were described as indifferent to their surroundings. Interactions between the patients were few and often of a hostile nature. A new program was instituted for these elderly women which included parties, group singing, handiwork, and games. As a result, the character of the ward was changed for the better, according to judgment based on continuous and periodic observation. For example, the first of three parties was characterized as *suspicious*, the second as *relaxed*, and the third as *gay*. Communications between patients increased and there was a decrease in problem behavior and a general improvement in morale. When the program was stopped, however, conditions went back quickly to the previous equilibrium.

Relatives of Patients

Group psychotherapy has been given to relatives of persons with various mental and physical diseases in the hope that the parents or husbands and wives, as the case might be, would get comfort from communication with relatives of other persons similarly afflicted, and might learn better how to deal with the patients. Wendland [408] discusses a group of husbands and wives of poliomyelitic patients; Gordon and Bowman [139] discuss group therapy with husbands of psychotic women; Bice and Holden [38] depict group counseling with mothers of children with cerebral palsy; and Ross [324] describes group therapy with relatives of psychotic patients.

Treating Psychosomatic Conditions

It is known that some diseases have predisposing psychological components, stomach ulcers, colitis, and allergic conditions being prime examples. It appears reasonable that if these diseases have their origin in psychological tensions, relief of these tensions should lead to improvement, if not cure, of the condition. The evidence for this point of view with respect to group psychotherapy is meager but impressive.

Ulcers. In one of the earliest but best investigations of psychosomatic conditions, Chappell, Stefano, Rogerson, and Pike [71] formed two groups of carefully matched patients who had subjective and objective symptoms of peptic ulcer. One group was given a course of treatment which included group psychotherapy, while the control group had no group psychotherapy. Results were impressively in favor of the experimental group, a majority of patients losing subjective and objective symptoms.

Allergies. Baruch and Miller [27], a psychologist and an allergist, have used group therapy with allergy patients who had a variety of conditions, including hay fever, asthma, and gastrointestinal disturbances. They used a permissive form of group therapy, eclectic in nature, which featured the analysis of projective drawings. In one of their papers [26] they state that 22 out of 23 patients improved, 6 to the point of complete remission of all symptoms. It may be noted that all 23 patients had allergies that had been confirmed by positive skin reactions to tests; none had benefited from medical care; and none had gotten any help from other procedures.

Overweight. Grant [143] calls obesity America's No. 1 problem in preventive medicine. Certainly, if the advertising that promises to help people lose weight serves as a criterion, the 40 million people in this country who are stated to be overweight do have a great interest in shedding excess poundage. Overweight may be due to many causes, but compulsive overeating appears to be the most important. The major problem for a person with such a compulsion is not to reduce but to remain at a lower weight once he has lost poundage.

Individual psychotherapy has been used to control weight, and according to Nicholson [278], "Psychotherapy leads to a higher percentage of successful cures in reducing weight than any other method."

In 1949 the U. S. Public Health Service in conjunction with the Massachusetts Public Health Department initiated a study on the effectiveness of group psychotherapy for the control of obesity. Reports by Grant [143] and Kotkov [216] subsequently appeared.

Results appeared to be good. Grant states that of 103 patients, 15 of whom attended 15 or 16 of the 16 scheduled meetings, 55 had weight losses after a 1-year follow-up. Twenty had lost no weight, and 27 had made weight gains of 5 per cent or more. These figures cannot be accepted at face value, since they include patients who attended only one meeting.

Two years later, Kotkov reported from the same clinic on 26 patients who completed the 16-week course. Originally, these members averaged 58 pounds overweight. At the end of the 16 weeks, changes in weight varied from a gain of 2 pounds to a loss of 48 pounds. At the end of the year, the group as a whole averaged 13.7 pounds less than when it began group treatment. Kotkov concludes, "Although no amazing overall weight loss occurred, it is concluded that group psychotherapy served as an invaluable relationship experience for the maintenance of weight loss in 48 per cent of the patients who did not succeed by other methods."

Hypochondriacal Symptoms

Pratt, in 1930, started a clinic at the Boston Dispensary for individuals who although they had no demonstrable symptoms, nevertheless had somatic complaints. He stated [302] that a study of 2,000 consecutive admissions showed that 36 per cent had unjustifiable complaints as far as physical examinations could ascertain. This time, instead of dealing with frank disease, as he had in 1905, he was concerned with neurotics who simulated illness.

In the Thought-control Class, as the clinic came to be known, the purpose is no longer to teach people how to manage their disease but rather to get them to give up unfounded symptoms. Members are referred to this clinic when it appears on physical examination that symptoms can not be supported or corroborated. New members are given individual interviews, and the purpose of the group is explained. When new members enter the session, they notice that the members sit classroom style. New members are asked to sit in the front row. The oldest members sit on an "honor bench" with the therapist, facing the rest of the group. The director calls the roll, and in this way members get to know each other by name. A secretary passes slips on which members write about any progress they have made. The collected slips are read by the director without mentioning names. Those who do not report improvements are interviewed privately.

A relaxation period takes place during which everyone is to close his eyes. This lasts from 5 to 7 minutes. The director then gives a short inspirational message. Following the message, testimonials are solicited from patients.

Pratt reports that the rate of improvement varies from 60 to 90 per cent, and he states that patients that attend this group do m ~~`h h~~ r than patients who see him privately.

MENTAL DEFECTIVES AND THE MENTALLY ILL

Perhaps the most important application of group psychotherapy has been with those persons who are institutionalized because they are socially incapable of making adequate adjustments. More than 600,000 people in this country are in mental hospitals at the present time, and more than 100,000 in institutions for the feeble-minded. The social importance of rehabilitating this huge population should be evident.

Mental Defectives

Mental defectives may be classified into three groups: the endogenous, who were born deficient; the exogenous, who became deficient mentally because of injuries or disease; and the pseudo defectives, who appear to be mentally inferior but are not. Only the last of the three groups may be helped with respect to improvement of intelligence. It is possible through group therapy to help the feeble-minded make better institutional adjustments. Fisher and Wolfson [120], Cotzin [93], Lipnitzky [232], Mehlman [259], Sarbin [330], and Taylar, Stickland, and Lindsay [384] have discussed use of group methods with mental defectives. In general the findings of investigators are that mental defectives are readily affected by such group experiences, and that as a result of treatment they frequently are able to make better adjustments to institutional conditions.

Psychotics

The earliest workers with therapeutic groups in mental hospitals appear to have been Marsh and Lazell. Neither of these pioneers, who began their work about 1910 and who, according to Pratt,* probably were not influenced by his work, had any intention of "curing" schizophrenia or any other mental disease. They wanted to bring some cheer and joy into the lives of the mentally ill. Who was the first to conceive of group psy-

---

* Private communication from J. H. Pratt to the writer.

chotherapy as a specific treatment for the insane is difficult to tell. The most probable explanation is that a concatenation of the work of Schilder, Burrow, Marsh, Lazell, Wender, Moreno, Klapman, and Low resulted gradually in the acceptance of the idea that psychotics could be expected to improve with group therapy as the primary treatment agent.

Many techniques have been used with institutionalized psychotics: the repressive-inspirational method, group analysis, psychodrama, textbook-mediated therapy, round-table psychotherapy, mechanical group therapy, ABC, and others.

Rhythm Therapy. Altshuler, an enthusiastic proponent of the value of music in psychotherapy for psychotics, has used a method which is a direct descendant of Lazell's earlier procedure.

Groups are formed of from 35 to 50 patients. The theory of the method, according to Altshuler [14], is to establish a parent-child relationship, later to be dissolved, between the therapist and the patients. The mechanisms are stated to be *catharsis, transference,* and *substitution.* The objective of the method is, "The development and strengthening of rapport, the stimulation of self-confidence, the creation of opportunities for self-expression, the cultivation of work habits and education of the reason coupled with training in morals and ethics. . . ." The ultimate aim of the method is, ". . . to offer reality so attractively and abundantly that the ego will lose its desire to remain in seclusion with the subconscious. . . ."

The method goes somewhat as follows. Each patient is given a small set of wooden blocks. An instructor invites the patients to clap the blocks in time to the music of a stirring march. This is to develop the attention span and to get the members to do something in common. Then song music is played, and the patients, who tend to congregate around the piano, are invited to sing. Chairs are put in a circle around the piano, and group singing continues. Following this, 30 minutes of discussions "attacking the emotional sphere" and 30 minutes devoted to "intellectual activity" take place, opportunity being given for the patients to express themselves. Among the specific activities are reading institutional news, commenting on world affairs, giving gifts to patients on their birthdays, etc.

It may be noted that music served Altshuler in the same way that textbooks served Klapman in his textbook method, and the blackboard and chalk served Jacobson and Wright in their ABC method—as a means of gaining the attention of highly distractible patients.

Discussional Groups. A quite different system was reported by Geller. Geller states [132], "By enabling patients, even in groups, to talk about their conflicts, reassurance and explanation would be possible; and further, many problems touched upon by one patient would probably apply to others, thus enabling such problems to become verbalized, and conscious to some extent for all involved."

Groups of from 10 to 15 were found to be optimal. Selections were made by physicians on each ward on the basis of their judgments of who was most likely to benefit. Each patient selected was interviewed by a psychiatrist who attempted to explain the nature and purpose of the groups. Sessions lasted for 1 hour and were held weekly. Individual interviews were also given at irregular intervals.

Procedures involved discussions and interpretations along dynamic lines. Analyses were carried out not only by the therapists but also by the patients, who were encouraged to participate. The therapist might agree or disagree with any interpretation. The therapist took a permissive attitude and allowed a maximum of initiative for the patients. It may be seen that this method is essentially similar to that initiated by Burrow [64] and used also by Schilder [334] in dealing with neurotics.

The following results were noted. Expressions of resentment and hostility toward the hospital and its personnel were common. New patients who entered already formed groups tended to be silent at first, but when they did begin to participate, they generally were critical. Such expressions were regarded as a "testing" of the group. Hostile feelings subsided quickly, either as a result of ventilation, or because the therapist tended to answer all complaints and to explain the situation complained about. Favorability of attitudes was not confined to the group: other patients on the wards also began to change their attitudes as communications were spread throughout the hospital. Feelings of acceptance and of security began to develop. It was noted that patients were affected more by the opinions of their mates than by those of the therapist. Anxiety was reduced by discussions of symptoms. A sense of unity began to develop in the group. Although Geller states that results in terms of any single person did not approach the depth to be found in individual analysis, in some cases remarkable insights were obtained.

In addition to these therapeutic groups, other group activities were established in which educational and recreational activities predominated. A convalescent-status orientation group was assembled for patients who were about to leave, designed to help them make the precarious adjustment to the world outside. These meetings, held daily, consisted for the most part of lectures with opportunities for questions.

Therapeutic Social Clubs. We have already discussed the social clubs used by Bierer in England, but the method is discussed further here because of its revolutionary implications for the administration of mental hospitals. Bierer's basic postulates, which stem out of Adlerian philosophy, are the following: (*a*) patients should be treated as normal, no more being done for them than is absolutely necessary; (*b*) treatment is under "field" conditions, or, as Moreno puts it, "on the spot," (*c*) situational treatment is considered to be aimed at a result intermediate between insight and fulfillment, or between intellectual and emotional changes, (*d*) asociability, or loss of contact with others, is the most common maladjustment, (*e*) treatment depends not on transference but on the full range of social tensions and attractions, (*f*) the personality and experience of the psychiatrist determine the success of the treatment, (*g*) the club can serve as a prophylactic instrument, and (*h*) the method is socially efficient and available to many.

Bierer's basic attitude is that psychotics have motivations; and that institutional personnel can be victimized by patients who will accept help even when it is not needed. The major purpose of the clubs is to aid patients in recovering their initiative under democratic circumstances. The therapy is hidden, or indirect, since there are none of the usual activities seen in therapeutic groups, such as interpretation of symptoms, analysis of past history, and direct advice.

This method may be compared with Moreno's early philosophy of every man being the therapeutic agent of the other. It may be recalled that in 1931 Moreno suggested that prisoners be classified into groups of such composition that the interactions between the individuals would be beneficial to all members. Bierer's procedure is similar to McCann's method of round-table psychotherapy in that in each case the therapist is absent.

CORRECTIONAL USES

One may look at correctional institutions—jails, penitentiaries, training schools, reformatories, prisons—from the point of view that they are intended to be therapeutic. Prisoners are sent to these institutions not only for punishment but also for correction. That little correction actually takes place is another question. It may be worthwhile to consider the concept of punishment, in order to understand a fundamental problem with reference to the treatment of people who commit crimes.

Criminals are stigmatized. Those who view them with sympathy are usually derided for their soft-headedness. But even though it may appear "natural" to regard the criminal as "bad," it may be recalled that the insane, the feeble-minded, tubercular, luetic, and epileptic patients, the deaf, lepers, alcoholics, and gamblers were once looked on as "evil," or filled with the devil, and were treated cruelly and inhumanly. Deeply ingrained in our laws and mores is the concept of the evil of the criminal offender. This feeling is sustained and developed by the common media of information, which publicize the relatively few crimes of professional criminals, who, as a matter of fact, rarely go to prison. If we can consider the criminal as sick, it may be that advances can be made in treating criminosis, just as advances have been made in treating psychoses.

A basic question is whether it is possible to punish and to correct at the same time. While this question may seem academic and may appear to be answered affirmatively by personal experience, it is to be doubted that a prisoner who feels himself scorned is in a state of mind to benefit from psychotherapy. It has already been noted that a basic prerequisite of psychotherapy is love, expressed by acceptance, but in a prison there is little acceptance of inmates, who are forced to wear degrading uniforms, are herded into groups, marched to dinner and to work, made to eat in silence, given cell and work assignments without regard for preference, and are locked in cells from which through several layers of bars they can see guards stalking the walls ready to shoot them down if they try to escape.

The literature on individual psychotherapy in prisons is almost nonexistent. The accounts given by Lindner [230] and Karpman [192] do not manage to overcome Brancale's [54] pessimism about psychotherapy in prisons. Perhaps the major reason for the failure of individual psychotherapy in prisons is the "unsymmetry" of individual therapy, using Moreno's terminology. Two common undesirable aspects of individual psychotherapy are resistance and dependency. If an insecure person is put into therapeutic association with a secure person, it is quite likely that the weaker, who is supposed to confess to the stronger, may resist the process, even if he is paying for the privilege. Later, as the association continues, the weaker may feel he needs the stronger person, and a dependency relation develops. Fidler states [118] that the deeper levels of personality can not be handled until anxieties and hostilities, which are other names for resistance, are settled. Lipschutz says [234], "... I believe I can safely state that the majority of failures in psychotherapy are essentially due to the factor of resistance."

It is not to be wondered at that individual psychotherapy, as ordinarily practiced by psychoanalysts and those who assume semiauthoritarian roles, has not been successful in prisons, since it must be evident that in such circumstances, the resistance generally encountered in patients who come to therapists of their free will in a free situation is multiplied by the nature of the institution. However, the capacity of group psychotherapy to reduce resistance appears to be well established. Lipschutz, quoted above, also states, "It was found that the usual resistances met in psychoanalytic therapy are more readily broken with the aid of group therapy." On this same point, Wolf et al., also representing the psychoanalytic point of view, state [414], "It is largely the interactive atmosphere of a group session, deliberately cultivated by the therapist but increasingly acted upon by one patient after another that enables those more blocked to engage in the emotional give and take ... even these severely immobilized analysands can frequently be reached by the explosive atmosphere of the group."

The following conclusion seems warranted: if resistance is a problem in psychotherapy, and if resistance to therapy is greater in a prison than outside, then if in a free situation resistance to therapy is lowered by the group form, it might appear that group therapy will be more successful in correctional work than individual therapy. And such, indeed, seems to be the situation, since practically the entire literature of successful therapy in correctional institutions is about group methods.

Defective Delinquents. It is difficult to conceive of a group more resistant to psychotherapy than delinquents who are also mental defectives. Yonge and O'Connor [418], who engaged in group therapy in a British correctional institution, have summarized an experiment utilizing two matched groups of boys, ranging from sixteen to twenty-one in age. One

Table 4. Reactions in Percentages of a Group of Defective Delinquents during a Period Which Included Group Therapy

Reaction	Quarters of period under observation			
	1	2	3	4
Positive attitudes to authority figures	21	27	54	29
Positive attitudes to nonspecific authority	2	1	1	8
Positive attitudes to group members	8	3	3	16
Appreciation	7	13	4	25
Masochism	48	43	40	1
Feasible aspiration	8	22	20	50
Critical attitude to self	4	10	11	5
Critical attitude to mates	12	7	20	19
Unsatisfactory work behavior (boys in workshops):				
Experimental group	48	34	31	15
Control group	39	10	27	44

group was made the control and was treated exactly like the other, except that the experimental group had 1 hour of group therapy once a week for 32 weeks. The two groups were observed in their various activities in order to obtain the data discussed below. The method used was a variant of the circular discussional method, originally employed by Burrow but based on the writings of Foulkes, who was originally introduced to group psychotherapy by Schilder.

The two groups were periodically rated with respect to a number of categories. Table 4 indicates the reactions of the therapeutic group to various factors over the four quarters of therapy. The results for the control group are not given, since they showed no systematic changes over the 32 weeks. The table also shows results of similar observations of boys in workshops.

It will be noted that changes were in some cases quite rapid, and in general the trend is favorable.

Although the statistical significance of these results is not given, the trend is unmistakable. As indicators of changes for the better in self-perception and other forms of perception, the data do seem to bear out the efficiency of group psychotherapy.

Training Schools

Bad boys and girls go to training schools, which are given a variety of names, such as protectories, reform schools, industrial schools, parental schools, etc. The inmates of these schools may be as young as ten and as old as eighteen, but the bulk of the population is found among the early teens. The crimes may vary from such minor infractions as disobeying parents or playing hooky to the serious crimes of robbery and murder. Group therapy has been employed in several of these schools with some success.

Lassner [218], in one of the earliest reports, used dramatics, in much the same manner as that employed by Curran and Schilder [95] with youths in a mental hospital ward. He reports that clinical improvements in behavior were noted.

In a more complete report, Thorpe and Smith state [390] that while the boys reacted well to the group in the beginning, in a short time hostility developed, which showed itself in negativism and criticism. This phenomenon has already been cited in discussing Geller's report on analytic groups in a mental hospital. However, this negative reaction is interpreted quite differently in "correctional" settings. More detailed discussion of this subject will be given later.

The most adequate report concerning group therapy in training schools is by Gisela Konopka [212]. Miss Konopka, in spite of the advantage of her sex and the fact that she was not a regular member of the staff, nevertheless found the inmates difficult to deal with, primarily because of the autocratic nature of the institution. This point needs further discussion, because, although seen most clearly in juvenile institutions, it is a problem in all correctional institutions and represents a clear-cut philosophical conflict between the ideologies of therapy and those of "correction."

It was mentioned earlier that an essential aspect of psychotherapy is the existence and demonstration of a noncritical attitude, called *acceptance* or *love*. It was also made clear that the official attitude of a correctional institution, based securely on the demands of the public or at least on the interpretation of these demands by the administrators, is the opposite of this, as witnessed by the many and often ridiculous rules. Thorpe and Smith, who were concerned with negative attitudes, and Konopka, who found her work difficult because of the autocratic nature of the institution, illustrate the problem in specific detail.

A personal example may well fit in here, to show the nature of the problem.

At a particular institution for juveniles, smoking was forbidden except at certain times and certain places, and even then the cigarettes were carefully rationed out to the older boys. All employees were cautioned to watch for unauthorized smoking and were required to report any infractions of these rules. Despite this, and maybe because of it, secret smoking took place all the time, and some employees closed their eyes to such violations of the rules. The superintendent had periodic drives against smoking and made an issue of the whole matter.

A group was formed in this institution for the purpose of therapy. It met in a secluded room under the supervision of a psychologist and a psychiatrist who had discussed in detail beforehand the philosophy, theory, and practice of the therapy. At the first session, one of the therapists was laying down the ground rules, stating, "In this group you can say or do anything whatsoever without getting any punishment, any warnings, or any reprimands. We will keep everything you say and do a secret. We want you to feel free to express yourself in any way you wish. If we desire to set up rules, we will do it democratically. We will be like a little independent island. . . ."

At this point one of the boys took out a cigarette, deliberately lit it, and took a great puff, slowly exhaling the smoke through his nose, looking right at the speaker. The other boys fastened their eyes on the greatly desired butt and began to beg for a puff. As the therapist went on, the cigarette moved from mouth to mouth, and no attention was paid to his fine statements.

The therapists were put into the situation of having to either ignore the cigarette or do something about it. If they ignored it, then they were being insubordinate, since the superintendent had established a firm "no smoking" rule. If the therapists commanded the boys to stop smoking, then this would have been a direct contradiction of their permissive philosophy. If they had tried to get the boys to stop smoking during the therapy by democratic vote, at least in the early life of the group, the vote would have been 12 to 2, with the therapists in the minority. The therapists did nothing about the situation, except to indicate in the vaguest terms that everybody should keep secret what happened in therapy, but very shortly other inmates began to ask to enter the group, stating quite frankly that they wanted to enter so that they could smoke. At this point, the therapists dissolved the group.

Reformatories

The second stage of correctional institutions is represented by reformatories, which generally take inmates from the age of sixteen to thirty. Curiously, in these institutions very little in the way of group psychotherapy has been reported, and what does exist is generally of a comparatively superficial kind. Probably the most distinguished effort is that at Highfields, New Jersey, where an entire segment of a reformatory was transferred to a private estate with the intention of engaging in "guided group interaction" under the direction of Lloyd McCorkle. This project has been favorably reviewed by Weeks [397], but little is yet known of its effectiveness.

Plowitz [287] has experimented with group therapy at the reformatory at Elmira, New York, and reports favorable results in its early use. Gula [147] has used an institution for the main purpose of evaluating youths held in detention, and also for therapy. A doctoral thesis was published by Gerstenlauer [136] with reference to the use of group therapy in delinquency.

One of the more informative and hopeful of reports in this area is by Kennedy [195], who was in the position to reorganize an entire institution through creating a number of overlapping commissions to inquire into various aspects of the institution. One of the commissions investigated the potentialities of group therapy, and later such a program was put into effect. One of the results of the total reorganization was a decided drop in institutional infractions and an improvement in morale.

Prisons

It would appear that the major use of group therapy in correctional work is found in the prisons. The first report in the literature about group methods with adult offenders seems to be by Abrahams and McCorkle in 1946 [3]. Their procedure, called *guided group interaction*, has been described, as used at various times with military and civilian prisoners, by McCorkle [254, 255, 257]. In essence, it is, as its name implies, a circular discussional type of therapy in which the inmates initiate and discuss issues under the general direction of the therapist. It is quite similar to the procedure used by McCarthy [253] and Lerner [225] with alcoholics.

Psychodrama in prisons was first used by Lassner [219] at San Quentin. On the basis of his observations and follow-ups, Lassner concluded that psychodrama was of considerable value in helping prisoners. Further reports of the use of psychodrama at the same institution were published by Corsini [83], who felt that this method was uniquely valuable for the rapid dissolution of resistances and the attainment of "immediate therapy" [85]. Using a combined lecture-testimonial method, Corsini [87] also tried a unique experience in treating inmates who were at first actively hostile to group therapy. Despite initial resistance and after some early struggles, the members of this forced group began to function and apparently got some value out of the proceedings.

Bromberg and Franklin [56] report the use of psychodrama in a correctional setting in a mental hospital. In view of what has been said about the difficulties of carrying out group psychotherapy in an authoritarian locale, the following excerpts from their report may be of value.

For several weeks tension had been mounting in the hospital and community, because of the increasing socialization of sexual patients. A surge of hostility feeling was expressed in local groups, P.T.A. groups and among the hospital staff. Particularly irritating to the local public (medical and lay) was the observed reduction in feelings of degradation by the sexual patients. The demand for strict restriction of sex patients under treatment was overwhelming. The culmination of this trend was an administrative order to lock up all sex patients ... with the vengeful restriction of privileges for all patients classified as criminal or psychopathic. The immediate reaction to this action was a stronger jelling within the group with increased loyalty to the therapeutic ideal which had been freely discussed throughout the sessions.

Apparently the opposition of outside forces aided the group, for Bromberg and Franklin continue, "The finality of opposition to the sexual therapy program consolidated the attitude on the part of the patients which held the therapist and staff in a realistic role: the therapist was no longer completely identified with authority."

Among others who have discussed group psychotherapy in prisons are Fenton [117], Janney and Bemis [180], Hadden [152], Clarke [73], Cavanagh and Gerstein [70], and O'Brien [279]. Hadden more or less summarizes general opinion about the value of group methods in adult correctional institutions in saying, "Group psychotherapy has been studied sufficiently to be appreciated as being more effective than any other method in the treatment of certain neurotic states. Some of its dynamics are unique properties which make it highly effective in penal situations." Referring to the problems of conducting what is essentially a democratic form of treatment in an autocratic environment, Hadden goes on to say, "Psychiatric services in a prison can be effective only when prison personnel is cooperative and sympathetic."

One of the relatively few critical comments about group psychotherapy is found with reference to prison use. O'Brien deprecates its value, considering it only a supplement to individual therapy. However, O'Brien's understanding of the term seems to be quite different from its usual definition, since he equates it with any kind of group work, including academic classes and recreational teams.

Parole

The parolee has just come from prison, where he has been on the one hand subjected to all the disadvantages of mono-sex associations and on the other hand carefully conditioned to lose all his initiative, since any display of uniqueness of behavior is a signal for trouble in prison. With no recent experience in meeting social problems and with a crushing understanding of how the rest of the free world regards him as an ex-convict, he is thrown into a society full of dangers and temptations. His parole officer, who is sometimes unsympathetic and always overworked, is usually regarded with some fear and suspicion, especially since he can return the parolee to the institution.

To the writer's knowledge, no one has made any attempts to conduct *official* therapy groups made up of parolees. In some states, since ex-convicts on parole can not associate with each other, conducting therapeutic groups for this population may actually be a violation of the law. King [198] has suggested group therapy as a means of helping parolees make a better social adjustment, and so has Fuller [130], but it was Yablonsky [417] who made the first attempts to treat parolees with psychodrama through a community agency.

Jails

Jails are a unique kind of institution, primarily holding prisoners in temporary custody. For the most part, no programs of any kind are held for men or women in jails. One of the very few reports in this area is given by Lerner. Using a discussional method quite similar to that of McCorkle, he has dealt extensively with alcoholics. He presents extended transcriptions of remarks. Illing [173] has also discussed group psychotherapy in jails.

Predelinquents

In every community, the police and others, including schoolteachers and community leaders, know of youths who are definitely heading for correctional institutions. Many juvenile courts, as a matter of policy, tend to return youths found guilty of infractions for the first time to the custody of their parents. Among those who have discussed the use of group methods with predelinquents are Schulman [337], Buck and Grygier [58], Hill [160], and Gersten [135]. Actually, in many community agencies, such as those described by Slavson [357] and Dreikurs [105], a sizable proportion of the youth express their disturbances by antisocial behavior.

The predelinquent finds the world a hostile place. On the one hand, he is desperately seeking to find his place in a society, wanting to become an adult, and on the other hand he is often treated by his parents and adults as a child who should be in school and whose major task is to conform. The inadequacy of programs for afterschool recreation of such youths, especially in crowded sections of cities, is well known. Many of these youths simply do not have any place to discuss their problems or any person who will listen to them seriously; they have no opportunities for real communication with others.

MAJOR BEHAVIORAL PATHOLOGIES

What may appear to be a most difficult condition to one person may appear quite otherwise to another, and so to differentiate pathologies as major and minor, especially in view of an infinite series of gradations of seriousness for any class of conditions, must remain the prerogative of the classifier. In this section, sexual aberrations, alcoholism, and drug addiction will be considered major behavioral pathologies.

Sex

Two sexual conditions that have been reported on deal with anorgastic women and homosexuals. With reference to the first condition, Stone and Levine [378] and Van Emde Boas [395] have found that sexual adjustments in marriage may be improved through group therapy.

Stone and Levine used the following approach. Wives met for three 2-hour sessions, and later the husbands came for one 2-hour session. One of the therapists conducted the group, the other acted as an observer. The therapist started with a short lecture, answered questions, and then led a discussion. The discussions, according to the authors, were, from the first, amazingly free and frank. By the third and last session, any evident feeling of constraint had disappeared. However, anxiety and other emotional reactions were found.

To evaluate the results of these 8 hours of therapy, a 6-month follow-up was held for members of either sex. Significant changes in attitude were noted by these clinicians. Some of the wives had achieved orgasm for the first time. Some couples reported that they were now capable of talking to each other, for the first time, about sensitive matters. In addition, the members stated that they had lost a sense of feeling isolated from others, and that the release of feelings in being able to talk about sex before others without condemnation or disapproval had created a sense of greater ease. Considerable insight was engendered by these few hours: understanding occurred for many with reference to the background causes of the behavior, and the understanding led to better attitudes toward their mates and towards sex.

Homosexuality

Probably no other condition has been so seriously misunderstood as homosexuality. The multiplicity of theories and plain distortions of fact about sexual inversion, the emotional attitudes of so-called normal persons, and the exhibitionist tendencies of some transvestites have created a folklore about homosexuality which modern authors, such as Ellis [113], have vainly attempted to correct. A person with a sexual liking or preference for one of his own sex usually suffers because of this liking, since there is a strong desire on the part of all people to be accepted, and since those who are known to be homosexual are regarded with almost unvarying contempt by others. While there may be biological determinants of this condition, it seems most likely that homosexuality is learned, and what is learned can be unlearned.

Two writers have discussed group therapy with homosexuals: Taylor [385] and Eliasberg [112]. The latter reports on two groups, each consisting of six men on probation. One of the 12 was considered schizophrenic but not institutionalizable. The men were white and colored, single and married. One of the married men was the father of three children. In order to protect the participants, no names were mentioned: each individual was given an arbitrarily chosen name which was indicated on a label which the patients wore.

The method of treatment was analytic—that is to say, members commented on whatever seemed to interest them, and an attempt was made by the psychiatrist to interpret the meanings of remarks. Various members discussed how they started their practices and what their reactions were. Eliasberg permitted the patients to function as analysts, attempting to decipher each other's dreams. Dr. Eliasberg's attitude about the value of the procedure may be seen from his concluding sentence: "Whenever treatment of homosexuals is considered, for social, legal or religious reasons, analytic group treatment is the method of choice."

Pedophiles

An account of group psychotherapy with pedophiles (adults who seduce or criminally attack children) was written by Corsini [87]. The members of the group, when interviewed individually, refused to participate. Two questions arose: whether it would be a violation of ethics to force treatment on these adults, and whether it would do any good. The answer to the first question is that there is plenty of precedence for treating people against their will: mental hospitals are a prime example. The answer to the second question came from the experience. Although the majority of the group was initially hostile, by the end of the term of the group, all but one had participated in telling about their crimes, and several asked for the group to be continued.

Alcoholism

It may appear that relatively little has been said of any practical use with respect to the treatment of persons with various kinds of conditions. The reason is that the outward manifestations of maladjustment may differ radically among persons with similar problems. At the time of writing this book, the author is treating three patients, each of whom has essentially the same problem but expresses it in his own unique way. The purpose in this chapter is to show not how specific disturbances can best be treated, but whether they have been treated, in what way, and, if there is any evidence, with what results.

In terms of alcoholism, the work of Alcoholics Anonymous is perhaps best known. A good account of this organization is given by Bales [22]. Among the others who have worked with alcoholics are Pfeffer, Friedland, and Wortis [286], Allison [12], Mueller [275], McCarthy [252], and Lerner [225]. The reports of the last two may be of greater interest, because they contain long transcriptions of actual sessions. One learns from these reports that alcoholics are like everyone else, and that they express themselves in much the same way as other persons do.

Drug Addiction

There is little to add with respect to the problem of drug addiction except to say that, like alcoholism, it may be looked at as a particular form of symptom which some persons, for unknown reasons, assume. Although drug addiction appears to be growing in importance, actually it is decreasing statistically, at least in terms of use of the worst habit-forming drugs. Among those who have discussed the problem of group psychotherapy with narcotics addicts are Buck [59], Johnston [183], and Thorpe and Smith [390].

MINOR BEHAVIORAL DISORDERS

The list of specific disorders that might be cited is probably so long that a simple accounting might fill this book, since it is likely that no two people have exactly the same problems. Nevertheless, there are classes of problems that occur with great frequency.

Neuroses

At one time, during his undergraduate years, the writer understood rather clearly what a neurosis is, but this clarity of understanding has now escaped him. As used here it refers to any problem not otherwise clearly identified, which is neither normal, psychotic, nor psychopathic. It is impossible to attach the label of neurosis to any particular deviant expression, however, for, on reflection, it appears that alcoholics, as an example, may be normal, psychotic, psychopathic, or neurotic. Actually, the writer's feeling about this kind of labeling is quite negative. Probably the most sensible approach to the issue has been suggested by Sheldon, who states that one should consider disturbed people as being on a continuum of disturbance and not as falling into neat categories [349].

In private practice, for example, as well as under other circumstances, the group therapist will run into a great many people with all sorts of minor feeling and behavioral problems. People who are fearful, insecure, laden with guilt, burdened with hostility or with feelings of hopelessness, unable to get away from powerful mothers or deal with demanding wives, unable to assert themselves, anxious, timorous, and people with hundreds of other similar kinds of problems come for psychotherapy. Some of these people may be found in mental or correctional institutions; some may express their problems via alcoholism or drug addiction; and some may manage to avoid institutionalization or gross labeling, and to function with some adequacy, although with a great deal of difficulty.

The Family

This large area of problems connected with the family may be separated into marital problems, child-parent relationships, and problems of children in the home. Special concern with this area derives out of theory and logic. Almost all later problems of life have their origin in the home. If every family followed the principles of mental hygiene implicit in all group therapy, then it is possible that the incident of mental disturbance would be very much smaller than it is at present.

Marriage. It is evident that every family begins with a father and a mother, who are husband and wife, and who were lovers before marriage. Since in our culture people are free to marry whom they wish, and since this important decision is usually made with great consideration, it is surprising and shocking to learn that approximately one-half of all marriages can be classified as unsuccessful, i.e., they end in divorce or desertion, or husband and wife live together without further communication or live together in a state of misery.

The causes of marital infelicity have been examined, and they are various, extending from cultural differences to differences in personality patterns. Sometimes a single shocking event in the family, such as unfaithfulness on the part of one of the mates, may upset a marriage's equilibrium to such an extent that it is never again the same. For many years, centers have been in existence, and private counselors have functioned for the purpose of helping couples compose their differences and learn to live together in happiness.

Moreno [271] has described psychodrama in the treatment of a marital conflict of the triangle sort; Redwin [310] has used the behind-the-back technique; Ruskin [327] has used analytic group therapy; and Solby [364] has used psychodrama.

Child-Parent Relations. The observer of the social scene may well be forgiven if he considers children and parents in our society locked in a death struggle for supremacy. In clinics one learns more and more about the independence shown by some children, the lack of respect to parents, the winning by children of battles with parents, and one learns of almost shocking forms of behavior by parents to win over their children or to punish them. Some parents become completely lost, they feel that the battle is over, they no longer have any self-confidence. For these cases, group therapy, which enables parents to meet together and come to feel that they are not unique in their family problems, is a means of relief, first because of the universalization effects, and second because of learning new and psychologically effective techniques for handling children.

The methods used in child-guidance or parent-guidance centers vary somewhat, but most of them tend to be of the circular discussional type (for small groups) or of the lecture sort. A rather unique method is that initiated by Alfred Adler and developed by Rudolf Dreikurs; it has already been described and is further explained in the second half of the book. Among those who have written on the topic are Lowrey [242], Amster [16], Buchmueller and Gildea [57], and Kahn, Buchmueller, and Gildea [190] (a rare article since it describes a failure of the method in a Negro school), Kadis and Lazarfeld [188], Kolodney [209], Konopka [211], and Spotnitz and Gabriel [373].

Children. Therapeutic groups for disturbed children have been reported by many. The procedures are usually of an activity kind, taking place in playrooms, on trips, in playgrounds, etc. Hawkey [159] made use of puppets, as did Bender and Woltman [33]; Papanek [280] used a democratic social club kind of procedure, reminiscent of the later procedures used by Lewin, Lippitt, and White [228]; Lippitt and Clancy [233] have used psychodramatic techniques with children in the kindergarten and nursery school levels; Rosenthal [321], Burlingham [63], and Wineman [411] have offered further descriptions of methods of dealing with disturbed children in groups.

Speech Difficulties

How a person expresses maladjustment may have little to do with precipitating causes, and even if precipitating causes are different that has little to do with how treatment is given. In taking up the issue of group psychotherapy of persons with speech defects, it is always understood that such defects are functional, not structural, as is evident when a person speaks perfectly in one location, such as his home, but is completely unable to talk clearly anywhere else.

Attempts to improve speech by direct attack come under the heading not of group therapy but of education. It is when the patient is considered a whole individual, and concern is not just on a symptom, that a therapeutic relationship is established. The fact that all members of the group happen to have the same symptom does not mean that discussions need center on that symptom. It may be that some members may make gains in other ways; for example, one person may continue to have his speech defect but become able to accept this impediment with greater ease. Others may improve in their speech and also, concomitantly, in their social relationships.

A review of the literature, including articles by Backus and Dunn [20], Beasley [29], Brody and Harrison [55], Cypreansen [96], Haas [149], Honig [167], Lenert [223], and Pohlmann [288] in which methods such as monodramas, psychodramas, lectures, debates, and circular discussions have been described, leads to the impression that considerable advances, beyond those of straight rehabilitative training, may be made in certain cases by therapeutic group work.

Reading. Why Johnny does not read is currently a subject of some concern. Flesch argues [122] that the cause of reading retardation lies in the current use of whole-word methods of reading to the disregard of phonetics. This is only partially true: some people may learn better in one way, and others may learn better in another way. For some people there may be no difference, and even if they are taught in an inferior way they will learn just as well. Others may not learn in one way at all, but may make progress if taught in a different way. But still others will not learn in any way whatever. It is here that psychotherapy comes in, as a last resort.

The evidence that has come to the attention of those interested in this problem is that in some cases marvelous improvement in reading comes about when the nonreader is put into a group in which he is able to feel accepted. Mildred Berl [34] describes the School Guidance Center, an educational clinic in Washington, D.C., where group psychotherapy is used with children who have emotional difficulties shown in their incapacity to maintain normal learning rates in terms of their mental abilities.

The groups are small, consisting of from four to five children. Games, drawing, puppets, and play acting are used. An amusing anecdote is told by Miss Berl. A mother telephoned that her child was sent to the center to learn to read, "not to play games." In such cases, parents are invited in for conferences so that they will learn that their children's lack of progress lies in the emotional, not in the intellectual, sphere. In the case of the boy referred to, although he was on the failing list in the school, "playing checkers" somehow helped him not only to pass but to be advanced. An eleven-year-old with thirteen-year-old reading capacity as based on intelligence test results, he had had 1 year of "reading training" but could read only at second-grade level. After one semester in group therapy lasting 4 hours a week, he advanced to the sixth grade.

College Work. Exactly the same kind of thinking may be expressed with reference to college work. There is no question that a good deal of difficulty in maintaining good work at a college level is a function of emotional maladjustments, and not, as all too commonly believed, a function of methods of learning or teaching, regular habits, or will power. The classic experiment by Landsman and Sheldon [217] tells its own story: students themselves *at first* preferred the lecture methods, which turned out to be relatively inefficient, resisting therapeutic procedures and seeing little in them. Among those who have discussed group psychotherapy at the college level are Hinckley and Hermann [161], who present a full-scale discussion with transcriptions of sessions, Pepinsky and Pepinsky [284], and Torrance [393].

MISCELLANEOUS USES

By this time it must be evident that the earlier statement with reference to diversity of uses of group therapy is true, and yet the specialized uses that have been made of this method have not yet been mentioned. Since some school problems have been discussed, it may be well to indicate that some workers have begun to suggest that the content of school classes be minimized and that personal relationships be maximized [145]. Any change in traditional methods of teaching causes a considerable disturbance among parents, but it does look as though schools will continue to emphasize social and emotional aspects to the minimizing of the three r's. And it may be that greater progress will be made in basic subjects as a result! Among the various reports about attempts to establish a therapeutic atmosphere in schools are those of Jacobson [175], Grunwald [145], and Seidler [342].

Mrs. Grunwald, using Adlerian principles, tried to turn the class into a democratic situation where cooperation would replace the usual principle of competition. Such concepts, entirely foreign to most schools, where individuals are in constant conflict with teachers and fellow students, may well represent a new era in educational thinking.

Relatives of Disabled. Parents and mates of schizophrenics have been gathered into therapeutic groups by Bauer and Gurovitz [28], Kahn and Prestwood [191], Peck, Rabinovitch, and Cramer [282], and Ross [324]. The logic behind such groups is simple: the schizophrenic individual came from a particular family, and presumably the relationships in that family were such as to affect the individual adversely. Consequently, if personality patterns of families could be changed, a better environment might be provided for the disturbed family member. Although it would have been better if optimal conditions had been established earlier, so that the psychotic break might not have occurred, working too late is better than not working at all, in terms of beneficial results for the patient and of possible prophylactic effects on other members of the family.

Coleman [80], and Weingold and Hormuth [398] have reported on similar groups for parents of mentally defective children. The purpose of these groups is to get parents not only to understand and accept their children but to accept themselves as parents of abnormal children. DeFries and Browder [99] have discussed group therapy with mothers of epileptic children; Wendland [408] with mates of polio patients; Gordon and Bowman [139] with mates of schizophrenics; and Bice and Holden [38] with mothers of cerebral-palsied children.

Industrial Uses. It is quite a leap from parents and relatives of mentally and physically disabled persons to industrial concerns. The term group therapy is no longer used, because of the sensitivity of people concerning names; the terms role playing, training discussions, etc., are substituted. Among the various reports one may find in the literature on the use of therapeutic techniques in industry are some by Speroff [370], Laughlin [220], Franks [125], and Stahl [374]. It seems, on reviewing some of the literature, that a common problem in industry has to do with communication: how can messages with reference to attitudes be transmitted vertically, from top management down to the workers, and vice versa, with greatest dispatch?

Stahl [374] has summarized data from a nationwide survey of role playing. When questionnaires were sent to 600 training directors of industries in 1951, 71 sent returns which were usable for statistical purposes; but in 1954, out of 445 directors questioned, 107 indicated use of or experience with role playing in their companies. The purposes of role playing were to train people and to help reach solutions of specific problems. Problems included improving morale, teamwork, and attitudes, increasing productivity, adjusting to new jobs, training in specific skills, developing human relations techniques, and handling grievances. Most attention was given to "middle management," or line supervisors. Although the procedures were not considered more expensive than others, there were some objections to them on the grounds that they were too time consuming, failed to present material in true perspective, and produced some embarrassment, and that it took too long to get a group to feel at ease. These objections, according to the author, result mostly because of inexperience in handling role playing properly. Among the advantages noted were that the method helps develop human relations skills, generates increased interest, sharpens insight, makes for greater group participation, makes problems seems more real, and helps change attitudes. The optimal number of group members, according to reports, ranges from 11 to 20. Role-playing groups appear to be larger than circular discussional groups.

In Churches. According to Jackson [174], the sermon is the oldest form of group psychotherapy. A new attitude on the part of some ministers seems to be that in addition to the older procedure of sermons, in which the burden of communication falls on the minister, some interaction with the congregation is necessary. The Quakers permit discussions, prayers, and sermons by any member who feels moved to speak, but most churches operate in such authority-bound ways that the congregation serves only as an audience.

Cope [81] invited several psychologists to conduct group therapy in his church, and a rather sophisticated report of the experiences is given by Coffey, Freedman, Leary, and Ossorio [76]. Kew and Kew [196] have discussed group therapy in a church setting. Leslie [226] has written on pastoral group therapy, and Boisen [51] has discussed the therapeutic significance of the traditional method of religious services.

Social Attitudes. Ackerman [8] has discussed the use of group therapy in the treatment of minority problems, and Sommers [369] has experimented with mixed racial groups. In our society, composed of mixtures of people with diverse origins, social adjustment to color and to nationality is a continuing problem which at local levels is capable of solution through group methods.

Outdoor Group Therapy. A number of therapists have taken their groups out of homes, institutions, and agencies into the great outdoors on trips, vacations, etc., so that they could experience better relationships as socially independent groups and with greater freedom of action. In leaving the protected confines of a room and entering the world in which others are in interaction, group therapy becomes less artificial and more real. Among the various accounts of such procedures are descriptions by Sadie Dreikurs [108], Levy [227], Moss [274], and Schiffer [333].

CHAPTER 8 *Procedures and Processes*

Group psychotherapy has no definite procedures or unvarying rules. It is the therapist and the group who determine what is to be done and in what manner. In short, group psychotherapy is an art, based on the one hand on ethics and theory and on the other hand on experience and knowledge. The present chapter deals with a variety of practical problems that the group therapist will face, and indicates some solutions. The following material should be considered not as a set of directions but rather as material that needs to be studied and may be used or rejected.

FORMATION OF A THERAPEUTIC GROUP

A group means three or more persons. How do these persons get together to form a therapeutic group? There are many ways in which a group may be formed, but some are preferable to others, since the very process of recruitment may have implications for therapeutic gains. In general, there are autocratic and democratic ways of constructing a group; and the group may come from a natural or from an artificial source.

If Dr. Jones decides he wants to do group therapy at Alpha Hospital, selects a group of patients by examining the records of patients, and assembles the group, the selection was autocratic and the group came from a natural source, the hospital. If Dr. Jones decides he would like to carry out group therapy with hospital patients, and he posts a note to that effect and gets self-referrals, this is an example of a democratic group from a natural source.

If Dr. Smith has patients sent to him by social agencies, this is autocratic and artificial. If Dr. Smith announces his intention of conducting a therapeutic group, and if patients come from various places by self-referral, this group is democratic and artificial.

These words "artificial-natural" and "democratic-autocratic" have other connotations, but in the sense used here, neither is necessarily better than the other. A democratic group is self-selected; an autocratic group is made up by others; a natural group comes out of one environment; an artificial group comes out of several. Four possible combinations exist, but there is no evidence that any one is better, necessarily, than any other. Undoubtedly, there are special problems connected with running each of the four types, and there are some differences among the four with respect to the problem of getting started.

Although, as stated above, none of the various methods of assemblying a group is superior to any other as far as is known, nevertheless there probably exists a suspicion that a group composed of volunteers is preferable to one composed of forced participants. Some may even raise an ethical issue and ask whether it is proper to force people to participate in groups; others may wonder whether such groups can attain any benefits.

Both these issues, mentioned briefly under Pedophiles in Chapter 7, should be examined. On the ethical side, there appears to be no question. Society has traditionally forced treatment on those who may endanger the rest of the population. Psychotics may be forced to go to mental hospitals, tubercular patients may be restrained in an institution, criminotics, of course, are sent to correctional institutions, which have walls to make certain that the persons "treated" will not escape. The psychotic may not desire shock treatment or lobotomy, but they may nevertheless be forced on him. Consequently, it appears that if the public weal is concerned, no ethical issue is involved in forcing a person to participate in group therapy. The question is whether it will do any good.

The answer cannot be an unequivocal no. Some evidence exists that a person can be driven to psychotherapy and that he will benefit. One may take one of two views. The first, as exemplified by the San Quentin procedure described in Chapter 6, involves repeating again and again the same message, hoping that eventually, as the result of many repetitions, the desired message will be understood and accepted. Much the same philosophy seems to be inherent in mechanical group therapy, in which the same message is sent over a loud-speaker system to patients in a hospital [336]. The second view, illustrated in certain studies, notably the writer's experience with elderly pedophiles [87], is that persons originally hostile to the group may, if proper procedures are followed, change their attitudes, begin to participate freely, and make gains. Is the overt hostility of such patients any different from the covert reluctance of new members of groups to begin participating? Both reactions are the result of fear of a new situation, and both can be overcome.

Selection of Applicants

In some cases the therapist has an embarrassing number of applicants, and he feels that he may pick and choose whom he will accept. Some may set certain critical limits to reduce the number of applicants, others may make selections on the basis of interviews, etc. Still others may take the first ones to apply. A great variety of procedures for selection has been employed. In groups constructed for particular purposes, say weight reduction, or helping parents of psychotic children, the criteria for inclusion are evident. In other cases, the therapist may set certain broad limits, or areas, for inclusion and exclusion. The most common agreement seems to be that patients in the group should be at the same level of intelligence. Dreikurs [105], Bach [19], and Wender and Stein [407] agree on this point. Dreikurs believes, in addition, that group members ought to be at the same age level. Wender argues for similarity of social levels. But the most controversial issue is whether patients ought to have the same kind of problems or the same kind of diagnoses.

The nondirective school of psychotherapy, in general, seems suspicious of the value of giving people diagnostic labels. Joel and Shapiro state [181] that there is no need for group psychotherapists to employ diagnostic labeling. In general, however, people trained in the medical tradition take a contrary view. Moreno, for example, says that, as in other fields of medicine, therapy cannot be prescribed without diagnosis. Hulse argues that scientific group therapy is based on careful selection of patients whose diagnoses have been established [169]. Cavanagh and Gerstein [70] believe that members have to be selected carefully. Renouvier states [313] that in group therapy treatment and diagnosis go hand in hand.

However, for the most part these statements appear to be concessions to tradition, not articles of behavior, since there is almost nothing in the whole literature of group therapy with reference to specific treatment for specific diagnostic conditions, and very little with respect to how patients may be selected. The most complete account is given by Bach [19], who uses an extremely complicated method of selection.

Bach, through an interview, decides whether or not the patient really needs psychotherapy. Then he decides whether his particular method is suited for the particular person. Then he decides whether the combination of the other members of the group is such as to indicate that this particular patient will make gains in that particular group. To come to these conclusions, Bach believes, as do Powdermaker and Frank [290], that three characteristics of the patient should be understood: (*a*) the nature of the patient's authority problems, (*b*) the patient's ability to reveal himself to a peer group, and (*c*) his ability to express aggression and his tolerance for hostile expressions.

To evaluate the patient Bach uses, in addition to an interview, tests of personality, including projective tests such as the Rorschach Test and the Thematic Apperception Test. But even satisfactory showings on these tests are not sufficient to enable one to join the inner circle. The applicant who passes the therapist must now be approved by the group, and so the candidate "visits" with the other members, who size him up and decide whether or not he should be permitted to join.

Homogeneity

Probably the most contested issue in selection has to do with homogeneity. Some therapists assume that a homogeneous group is superior, and they set standards with respect to age, intelligence, social status, diagnosis, etc., to ensure that the group members are alike with respect to certain factors. The issue may be of some importance. There are two questions involved in this matter: (*a*) is homogeneity-heterogeneity an important aspect of selecting a therapeutic group, and (*b*) if so, what should be the elements of determination for homogeneity?

The most complete statement on this problem has been made by Furst [131], whose opinions will be restated here. According to him, the arguments for homogeneity are the following: (*a*) identification occurs quickly, and transference is rapid, (*b*) reeducation and insight take place quickly, (*c*) psychodynamics are bared quickly, (*d*) duration of therapy is shortened, (*e*) attendance is more regular, (*f*) interference, resistance, and destructive behavior are lessened, (*g*) intramural cliques are uncommon, and (*h*) a rapid recovery from symptoms occurs. But homogeneity has certain defects: (*a*) such groups are difficult to assemble, (*b*) the level of therapy is largely superficial because of absence of interactive factors, (*c*) although symptoms may be removed quickly, the essential character structure is untouched, (*d*) opportunity for reality testing is lessened by the absence of interaction which would occur in heterogeneous groups, and (*e*) the opportunity to develop multiple and shifting transferences is lacking.

It may be seen that the question of selecting homogeneous groups is complicated, that homogeneity has advantages and disadvantages. The same is true with respect to heterogeneous groups. According to Furst, in such groups (*a*) therapy is deeper, (*b*) character structure, as well as symptoms, is affected, (*c*) reality testing is more thorough and adequate, and (*d*) intragroup transferences are formed readily. Also, such groups are more readily assembled. But there are arguments against heterogeneous groups: (*a*) recovery is slow, (*b*) interaction and tension problems are magnified, and the problems of therapy are increased, (*c*) group identification develops slowly, and (*d*) attendance is more irregular.

On the basis of these arguments, Furst recommends that groups be homogeneous when (*a*) an intensive therapy is not desired, (*b*) when the therapist is not trained or prepared to go deeply, (*c*) when time and money are important factors. But heterogeneous groups should be established when (*a*) deep therapy is desired, (*b*) changes in character structure are wanted, (*c*) the therapist is willing and able to go to deeper levels, and (*d*) time and money are not too important.

Eliminations

The question of who belongs in group therapy may be approached negatively: who does not belong in group therapy? There is a variety of opinions about this question, some in contradiction to others, but the contradictions are only apparent, since the writers are discussing selection of cases from the point of view of their methods and their experiences. What is one man's meat is another man's poison; the very patients that some therapists avoid are the ones that others prefer. For example, no group may seem less appealing than lobotomized schizophrenics, and yet it is with this group that Dr. J. W. Klapman has done most of his work. However, it may be instructive to obtain an idea of preferences.

Bach [19] would not include in his groups those with insufficient reality control, with culturally deviant symptoms, with dominating characters, and with psychopathic tendencies. Now, this does not mean that Bach believes that such persons do not need or cannot benefit from psychotherapy; all it means is that they are not desired in a group of private patients in intensive therapy. Sternbach [377] seems to be in essential agreement with Bach, stating that,

... when the individual patient's condition is one of too strong hatred and suspicion of authority, as in severe cases of primary behavior disorders and antisocial psychopaths, he will be unable to benefit from a regular therapeutic group which depends on voluntary meetings and regular hours. ... His strong hatred will also either disrupt the group and lead it to rebellion or the group will exclude him quickly.

Sternbach would exclude not only psychopaths but also the psychotic: "Narcissistic patients who have regressed from the capacity to object libidinal relationships into isolation out of pathological anxiety will not be able to accept competition in the relationships to the therapist. ..."

Even among the nondirective therapists with a client-centered orientation we find some criteria for exclusion. Hobbs, as an example, states [164], "In general, we feel it best not to include in the group the extremely hostile and aggressive personalities, whether psychotic or not, because they make it difficult if not impossible to achieve the atmosphere of acceptance and freedom from threat that is essential to the success of the group."

The writer and Dr. Lundin [89] surveyed some forty institutions in the Middle West to ascertain the experience of various group therapists, and learned that there was relatively little agreement as to who benefits most from group therapy. The most general conclusion is that a person who does not benefit from individual therapy is not likely to benefit from group therapy.

ARRANGEMENTS

Someone has to decide where the group shall meet, when it shall meet, how often it should be together within any period of time, and the size of the group. Usually, the therapist makes these decisions; sometimes the group participates in making them.

Location

There is very little in the literature on the question of the proper locale for group therapy. Moreno requires a special stage for the most effective use of psychodrama, and Slavson needs a special room which can stand abuse by children in activity-group therapy. But little has been written about location with respect to the more usual needs of discussional groups.

The most important consideration is two-way privacy. That is to say, the group must be assured that no one else can hear or see them, and they must not be able to see or hear others.

The size of the room is important. It should be small rather than large, and distracting elements such as pictures and desks should be eliminated if possible. A room should not appear to be a living room, and yet it should not look like a clinic. Seating should be flexible and varied. A classroom would be an example of an unsuitable room. Acoustics should be excellent, so that low voices can be heard distinctly. Very bright lights are not called for.

Once a group becomes accustomed to a particular room, it should be retained if possible. All distractions during the sessions should be avoided. Messages and telephone calls ought not to be admitted. Any disturbance of the group's routine should be guarded against.

Size of the Group

Therapeutic groups have consisted of as few as 3 members, as in Dreikurs' multiple therapy, and as many as 400 in the repressive-inspirational technique. However, for the more common discussional group therapy, the general rule was stated by Trigant Burrow in 1927: "The number of persons composing a group session has come to be limited empirically to 10." Some opinions on this issue may be of interest. Hobbs [164] believes that 6 is the optimal number, while Goldfarb [138], and Pfeffer, Friedland, and Wortis [286] believe that 8 is sufficient. Cavanagh and Gerstein [70] argue for 10. Other suggestions are 6 to 8 by Kelman [194] and Joel and Shapiro [181]; 5 to 10 by Kew and Kew [196]; 7 to 8 by Foulkes [123]; 8 to 10 by Ebaugh [111]; 8 to 12 by Altshuler [14]; 6 to 20 by Wender [401]; and up to 20 by Dynes and Hamilton [110].

The method used, among other factors, has a direct bearing on the size of the group. With a nondirective discussional group or an interpretive group, Burrow's suggestion of a maximum of 10 is wise. However, with a psychodramatic group, 15 may be close to the optimum. With a lecture type of group, 40 may be desirable. On this point, Geller [134] feels that the analytic groups may range from 3 to 10 persons, groups for specific methods from 8 to 15, repressive-inspirational groups from 30 to 50 persons, and that for guidance groups more than 50 people at a time may be accommodated.

Cholden [72] believes that groups below 5 in size are inhibited, while groups over 10 are blocked. It goes, of course, without saying, that any therapist may have his own preference about size, some being more comfortable, within any method, with a group of a certain number.

Number of Sessions

How often should a group meet within any period of time, and for how long? On the basis of a survey of practices in the Middle West [89], it was found that some groups met five times a week and other groups met once in every 2 weeks. The modal frequency of sessions for 40 institutions was twice weekly. Among those who report this frequency are Loeser et al. [238], Cavanagh and Gerstein [70], Joel and Shapiro [181], Foulkes [123], and Taylor [385]. The optimal frequency of sessions, and whether it can be related to the nature of the group, in terms of membership or method, are unknown.

How long should a group session last? While this also is a question that has not been settled by experiment, the usual length of time is 90 minutes. The writer has found that 1 hour is too short and 2 hours is too long for the usual group.

Concerning the question of whether a group should have a limited number of sessions or whether it should continue indefinitely but change its membership, practices vary. Some therapists argue for a semester type of therapy group with fixed beginning and ending dates, while others feels that an "open" group with no fixed ending is superior. Cotton [92], for example, set his group time limit at 6 to 8 weeks; Wender and Stein [407] ran closed groups for 6 months. Bach [19], on the other hand, has an open group, and some members have been in it for several years.

STARTING A GROUP

Well begun is half done, says the proverb, and this is true in group therapy. From the very first the therapist sets the pattern for the group, and his early behavior is of the greatest importance for the future development of the group. If the beginning is bungled, members may drop out; if the therapist is uncertain, members may lose confidence in him; if the therapist makes unnecessary changes, the members may become confused; and if the therapist is too powerful and overbearing, the members may assume dependency attitudes. In any case, how to begin is a problem which every therapist, no matter how experienced, has to meet in every group.

The average member of a therapeutic group starts with the intention of watching and listening and not participating until he is sure of the situation. Most patients are fearful and somewhat suspicious at first and are unwilling to expose themselves. They look to the therapist for guidance and assistance, even though later they may be willing to assert themselves. The therapist realizes this, but he also knows that only through participation will benefits occur; consequently it is his task to lead the members to voluntary interaction as quickly and as painlessly as possible. How this is to be done depends on the therapist's judgment of the nature of the group.

A usual way to begin is for the therapist to greet members, to ask them to tell their names, to ask each member what he expects to get out of the group, and then to state his (the therapist's) own intentions and expectations. This may be called the *introduction*. But during the introduction, immediately after it, and frequently during the early sessions, periods of silence will occur. How the therapist handles silence is a prime measure of his ability.

If when an awkward pause occurs, the therapist can remain silent, waiting patiently for someone to contribute, smiling in an expectant manner, and then reacting to any comments in a natural, easy way, he helps the group to explore itself. If, however, he cannot stand silence and feels the need to fill in a vacuum, he may soon find that he is doing most of the talking.

An Example of a Bad Beginning

In an institutional setup, the writer once had the opportunity to watch a psychologist, inexperienced in group therapy, start a group. The disastrous session went somewhat like this:

T.: Well, I am glad to meet with you. My name is Dr. Thomas. Do you want to tell me your names? . . . [The therapist wanted to start off on a democratic footing, without any ordering.]

T.: Well, anyway if you won't tell me your name, at least you know mine. [Therapist did not wait long enough for anyone to respond. His second statement may have blocked future responses.]

T.: Well, what do you think we should do? Or maybe you think that I should know what we should do? [At this point the therapist appeared to realize that he had made some kind of error and that he was talking too much.]

T.: Looks like I am doing all the talking. That isn't too polite, so maybe you people ought to say something. I mean, perhaps some of you would like to say what you would like to get out of the group? [The therapist did not wait long enough again, his anxiety and confusion mounting.]

T.: You, there. I wonder if you would tell us your name.

J.: Jones.

T.: Well, you *can* talk. [Therapist stops, realizes that the remark may sound critical and sarcastic, but although he tries to repair the damage he makes things worse.] I mean I knew all along you could talk. I just wanted to hear you talk. I guess I tried to make a joke out it. I hope you don't mind, Mr. Jones. Is there anything else you might like to say, like why you came here, what you expect out of the group, or anything else like that?

J.: No, sir.

T.: Well, then how about somebody else? We are in therapy and it is important that we all talk and have confidence in each other and that sort of thing. Has anyone anything to say? [The therapist is now desperate, and he loses his head. He feels the group's hostility. First he tries the "sympathy" routine and then takes a "tough" attitude. But by this time he has either alienated or frightened the members.]

T.: Look, I need help. I don't know what I should do. I feel that I perhaps gave you the wrong impression. If someone would talk then I would know what is on his mind. [He waits a very short time, and then gives himself the *coup de grâce*.]

T.: You there. Would you mind telling me what is the reason you are in the group?

P.: I was told to come here.

T.: But what do you want?

P.: I don't know.

T.: Of course you know. Jones, you know Peters, what is wrong with him that he won't say why he is here? Don't you think he should tell us?

J.: That's his business, sir.

An Example of a Good Beginning

T.: I am glad to be with you tonight, and I hope this will be the beginning of a fruitful and meaningful experience. As you may know, my name is Dr. Saul, and I am the nominal leader of the group. But I'd like to say that I am interested in learning who you are and what you would like to get out of the group. [Therapist stops, smiles, and looks about the group. He waits about 60 seconds.]

T.: I can imagine that we all feel uncomfortable. I know I do. [Here, he talks about his own feelings and empathizes with the members. He waits another 60 seconds. The members are still silent.]

T.: Well, perhaps I should talk a bit. I see the group as an opportunity for me to learn more about people, and as an opportunity to contribute to the learning of others. That is, I hope I can tell you things that are valuable, and I hope and expect that you will tell me things that are valuable. [Notice that the therapist has not managed to get any response from the group, but he does not show any anxiety or anger. He tries to talk mostly about himself and does not demand anything from members. He waits a relatively long time between statements.]

A.: How long do we meet?

T.: I guess you are asking me the question?

A.: Aren't you the doctor?

T.: But I think that in your question you imply that I have to make that decision.

A.: Isn't it so? [Notice that the therapist is "pulling" the speaker into a discussion by not giving him an answer but by replying to questions with either questions or incomplete answers.]

T.: I don't think that I should make the decision that affects all of us. [Note that he has not put anyone on the spot. Here he begins to indicate his philosophy. He waits, and another patient responds.]

B.: Do you mean that we can set our own time?

T.: Well, let me think about that. [He is not going to have all the answers right away.] I can speak for myself only. I would like to arrange the hours so that they will be convenient to me, but I wouldn't set anything without knowing how you feel about it. Are there any particular feelings about hours? [Note that in asking this question, which is one that has been led up to and which is relatively innocuous and not directed to any individual, the therapist does not threaten the group.]

B.: Makes no difference to me.

T.: Good. I assume almost any arrangement will be O.K. with you.

B.: What'll we do here?

T.: I think that depends on what we decide. [He waits, and finally he gets a reaction.]

C.: Isn't this supposed to be group psychotherapy?

D.: Of course it is, you knew it when you signed up, didn't you?

C.: Yes, but what *is* group psychotherapy?

D.: Maybe the doctor will tell us.

T.: I assume you are asking me to tell you. I'll be very glad to tell you what I think it is, but maybe we ought to get some opinions. I don't mean that I don't have an opinion, but wouldn't it be interesting to know opinions of others?

E.: Well, I think it means telling what is bothering you, like my head-aches.

F.: I think it means we will tell you our symptoms and you tell us how we get them and how we can get rid of them.

From then on it is clear sailing.

This particular example is not given as *the* approach to use. Every therapist will develop a method that is compatible with his own personality. The therapist ought to have a very clear understanding of the limits he will set on himself, and as complete a comprehension of the individual members as possible. To avoid undue difficulty, it is wise for the inexperienced therapist to have individual interviews with prospective members and to begin with relatively small groups. In the first sessions, he must be careful to stay calm and to pause before making any responses. If the therapist is able to assume an attitude of humility, based not on a strategic plan but rather on a true feeling of democracy in the group, and if he is willing to discuss his own feelings, his approach will help the others. However, the major element in many beginnings has to do with anxiety developed by awkward pauses. Bion [45] meets this problem by keeping quiet and saying nothing. Presumably he would be ready to stay the whole hour in silence if necessary, since he feels no compulsion to take an active part.

Instructions

The therapist usually has some communications to make to the group, or he has some issues that he believes ought to be discussed soon. The problem is to prepare the group for these instructions or notices and to have the group accept whatever messages are given. One matter may be with reference to the procedures the therapist would like to follow.

The ground rules of the method have to be expressed early, otherwise the group members will make their own. Ordinarily, the therapist, if he wishes to assume a democratic role, may suggest procedures as a member of the group. Usually the other members will be happy to have him do the leading in this respect.

The question of confidentiality invariably arises, and the therapist may ask members to use their own judgments about what to say and do, and how far to go. Very little difficulty has been found or reported with respect to the matter of security of information, but this is an issue which concerns some members. The therapist would be wise not to bring this issue up too early nor to make any unwarranted statements about secrecy of meetings.

PHASES

Any particular session may operate in a flexible manner, varying according to the immediate demands of the members, or it may follow a pattern. Family counseling and psychodramatic group therapy are two rather rigidly determined systems, with provisions for certain steps which usually follow in invarying order. In analytic therapy and in client-centered group therapy such controls are absent. Which of the types is better is unknown; there are advantages to both.

But there is another aspect of phases, i.e., the movement of the group as a whole. It is evident that certain events occur during the life of a group, and that in general a group at the end of a long period of psychotherapy is quite different from the group at the beginning. What are the natural phases that the group goes through?

Stoute [379] discusses three phases: (a) resistance, (b) gradual discussion of deep problems, and (c) friendliness and freedom. Cholden [72] also finds three phases: (a) self-conscious searching to understand limits, (b) attention to events in the group which provoke anger, worry, and fear, and (c) discussions of the origins of emotions, causes, and effects. Thorpe and Smith [391] say groups (a) test the therapist, (b) begin group-centered operations, and (c) become group-acceptant. Taylor [385] states the three phases as (a) candid self-revelation, (b) transforming personal problems into group problems, and (c) group interpretation.

Wender [400], Dreikurs [105], and Abrahams [2], however, identify four phases. Wender calls them (a) intellectualization, (b) patient-to-patient transference, (c) catharsis, and (d) group interest. Dreikurs states that the following are the phases in group therapy: (a) establishment of relationships, (b) therapist interprets dynamics, (c) patients begin to understand themselves, and (d) reorientation. And according to Abrahams, the phases are (a) relationships in terms of the past, (b) interaction, (c) lessening of resistance, and (d) development of a therapeutic attitude of mutuality.

These seven descriptions may appear confusing, but it is evident that acceptance of any one does not invalidate any other. We come again to the problem of describing what exists, but doing so in different terms. An eclectic statement of processes or phases might go somewhat as follows:

1. There is a stage of hesitant participation, in which the individuals operate as separate units, each concerned with himself and his own problems. The members are testing out the group and the therapist. Attitudes of fearfulness and suspicion exist. Operations are at a surface level, but there is a beginning of mutuality and friendly relationships.

2. A second phase follows this first one, merging into it imperceptibly,

in which the members begin to discuss sensitive matters, including the dynamics of their own and others' behavior and of their own group behavior. During this phase the members begin to feel that the others are like themselves. There is the gradual development of a group spirit.

3. In the third phase, solutions appear. A feeling of freedom and friendliness develops. The group feeling becomes stronger, and concepts are acted upon, the members making gains in their personalities.

Understanding by the therapist of these characteristic phases gives him confidence that the group will, in due time, move from step to step. Comprehension of the dynamics of therapeutic groups enables him to have greater flexibility in his own behavior.

CHAPTER 9

The Group Therapist

Group therapists vary widely among themselves with respect to many dimensions, including training and background, personality, conceptions of their roles, and aims and intentions. Some are well trained in group techniques, but they are in a minority. Most individuals who practice group therapy have been trained in cognate areas, such as medicine, psychology, or social work. Some may have had considerable relevant training, but some have had very little experience in dealing with groups. Some group therapists have retiring personalities, are mild and gentle; while others are forceful and aggressive. Some have well-defined philosophies which their group work supports and emphasizes, but others take a pragmatic mechanistic approach and are concerned with "improvement of personality" or "relief from symptoms" or "amelioration of behavior" without special axiological connotations. Some see themselves primarily as teachers who have something to contribute to the group members, who are to be relatively passive auditors and spectators; others see themselves as clarifiers or analyzers; and still others see themselves as enablers or catalysts, helping people to find themselves. Some group therapists take a very modest view of their efforts, hoping to assist people in limited ways, while others take the grander view that they reconstruct the entire personality.

It may be of value to examine group therapy from the point of view of the therapist, trying to understand what he does from his particular standpoint, and trying to see his problems as he sees them.

REQUIREMENTS

Who is a group therapist? May he be anyone who is doing therapeutic group work? May only people within certain professions be so labeled, or are there no such limitations? This is a point which, perhaps fortunately, has not been the subject for much discussion, probably because group therapists are too busy with other things to worry about such matters.

From a legal point of view, anyone may call himself a group therapist. From a professional point of view, probably only those who have been accepted as members of one of the major national societies of group therapists should so label themselves. The various societies usually restrict full membership to members of the psychiatric, psychological, and social work professions, although exceptions can be made in unusual cases. These three professions, incidentally, in the American Society for Group Psychotherapy and Psychodrama are found in the proportions of 5:4:1, respectively.

In a survey by Corsini and Lundin [89] a majority of group therapists felt that the most adequate training for a group therapist included training and experience as an individual therapist. Historically, most group therapists had experience in individual work before entering this more difficult and demanding field.

No evidence exists to indicate that members of any particular profession are superior, by virtue of their training, in therapeutic group work. There is no evidence, when we come down to it, that psychiatrists can do better than teachers, psychologists better than counselors, or social workers better than sociologists. Nevertheless, some people feel that it is soundest to restrict such work to persons who have had training and experience in cognate lines, especially in individual therapy. Hadden [155], for example, believes that too many unqualified persons enter this field, but he has not specified what constitutes qualification. About the only definitive statement with reference to qualifications comes from Clinard [74], who believes that sociologists are particularly well qualified for group psychotherapy.

The writer, who has had experience in training group therapists in each of the three helping professions listed above, has found that some individuals, otherwise well trained, just do not appear to have either the interest or the capacity to do this work, while others take to group therapy naturally and eagerly. Handling therapeutic groups requires, it would seem, not only interest and technical knowledge, but also direct experience in dealing with common difficult interpersonal situations. Such experience can best be acquired by supervised practice. On the issue of various professions, Spotnitz, himself a psychiatrist, states [372], "A gifted lay individual psychologist or social worker may do much better work with certain groups than a physician who may lack intuitive understanding of the individual in the group or of group dynamics." The writer recalls an elderly psychiatrist who took a position in an institution and who was impressed into doing group therapy. He was observed lecturing to his semi-illiterate audience on brain pathology, in the belief that this was group psychotherapy.

At the present time it can be said that not enough knowledge is available to decide which kinds of training are most valuable for group psychotherapy. With respect to restricting group therapeutic work to those with particular kinds of training, one may feel that this is a conservative and wise procedure until more is known about the subject, or one may feel that restrictions are unnecessary since we don't know enough about the matter.

It may appear that group psychotherapy is less difficult than, say, a full-blown psychoanalysis. However, quite the opposite seems to be the case. Two psychoanalysts may be quoted for evidence of the difficulty of group psychotherapy. Foulkes makes the statement [123], "It is an instrument so delicate and yet so powerful that its skilled handling demands more from the therapist than the most difficult analysis." Wender states [404], "Group therapy as I practise it is a form of therapy predicated upon psychoanalytic thinking and similar to individual psychoanalysis both in its objectives and methods, except that the elements involved are much more complex."

Where can one get training, and what kind of training is the best? Most group therapists of the present generation are self-taught and picked up their knowledge by trial and error, which may be why we have so many different brands of group psychotherapy. In some respects, self-teaching, i.e., organizing and working with one's own group, supplemented by literature, may be the best method, although it may be hard on the therapist and the group. The next best way may be to learn through participation and supervision, although this has the danger that the therapist may learn one particular method not too well suited to his own individuality. Another way of learning, and for some people possibly the best, is to enroll in courses on group psychotherapy, which are rare. The various professional societies often give comprehensive courses, and they conduct periodic meetings for members. Some universities give courses in this area.

Which of these various methods is best for any individual person is difficult to decide, but it does appear best that the group therapist be experienced in individual therapy. Once he has the requisite skills for individual work and a solid grounding in the particular theory he believes in, transition to the group should not be too difficult. For those therapists who do not have access to instruction and must proceed on their own without much or any help, two expedients may be helpful. The first is to begin with a simple method, such as lectures, and then gradually shift to more complex procedures. The second expedient is to begin with a group of two or three members, gradually adding to it until it reaches optimal size.

PERSONALITY OF THE GROUP THERAPIST

Relatively early in the history of group psychotherapy the question of the importance of the therapist's personality arose. In 1908, Pratt wrote [298], "Success depends on gaining the friendship and confidence of the members." Pratt's theory was based on Déjérine's belief [302] that, "Psychotherapy depends wholly and exclusively upon the beneficial influence of one person on another." A more recent statement by Pfeffer, Friedland, and Wortis [286] probably fairly represents current opinion on this issue, "... as yet undefinable aspects of the therapist's personality may be more important for his results than the technique he says he uses."

The question of the personality of the therapist is one that has as yet not been explored. There are two ways of examining this issue—statically and dynamically. One may study the kind of person the therapist is or the kind of person he acts. The first way of looking at this issue is to consider the character structure of the therapist, his uniqueness as a person, using perhaps a series of adjectives for the purpose of description. We may feel that kind, considerate, sympathetic people may be better therapists than brusque, impatient, or insensitive people. The other way of thinking of personality is in terms of the role the therapist plays in the group. This distinction may seem somewhat artificial if one believes that one acts as one is. But the issue is not simple, since a group therapist may be able to assume a particular role in conformance with his conceptions of how the ideal therapist should act which may not resemble to any great extent his usual manner of social interaction.

Probably both issues need to be explored, and it may be that the latter is just as important as the former. It may be argued that while psychotherapists vary in much the same way as nonpsychotherapists with respect to essential personality, nevertheless good therapists operate in more or less the same manner. If this were not true, then there would be little point in having training.

The Ideal Personality

Is there a generalized ideal personality for group therapists? Do certain methods call for specific personalities? Probably both questions should have an affirmative answer. According to Slavson [356], the therapist should be friendly, generous, tolerant, accepting, and quiet. If we study these requirements we are forced to conclude that Slavson is defining a gentleman, or an ideal personality in terms of our culture. Others may set up different personality criteria for the therapist who has to deal with groups. The following are the major essential personality characteristics of the group therapist as seen by the writer.

Patience. The first quality that comes to mind is patience. Above all the therapist must have a high tolerance for boredom, frustration, and delay. He must have the ability to proceed doggedly in the face of disappointments and failure under conditions that induce anxiety, anger, and unrest. Patience should be the resultant of a deep conviction, amounting to faith, in oneself, the group, the method, and the theory. The patient therapist combines a feeling of assurance, security, determination, confidence, and hopefulness about himself and others. He must have an optimistic outlook on life.

Courage. Somewhat related to the concept of patience is that of courage. The therapist must have the capacity to act on his convictions and not be swerved by immediate events. He needs faith to hold on with great tenacity to his convictions, to follow with determination his line of attack, and to meet in a serene manner the opposition, which at times may explode with some violence. Courage is needed to penetrate, sometimes blindly, into new areas, or to meet crises with aplomb. The therapist must have inward qualities of fortitude of the kind possessed by martyrs.

Flexibility. Courage does not mean rigidity, for while the therapist must hold on to basic principles with tenacity, he must nevertheless be able to modify tactics without changing strategy. He needs extraordinary flexibility to go rapidly from topic to topic, emotion to emotion, from person to person, keeping meanwhile a sense of the needs of the group as a whole. He must be sensitive to the moods of the group, and to the needs of the individuals, but he must also be alert to the demands of society, the desires of patients' families, and ethical issues.

Warmth. The ideal therapist is a warm person, with a genuine liking for people, who really wants to see others improve. While he may have preferences among the patients, he must value them equally as striving individuals in trouble. He must be ready to give of himself fully.

The Therapist in Action

How does the ideal therapist behave in the group? How does he demonstrate by action the qualities listed above? Actually, we have almost no information from the literature. However, a notable example comes from Gordon [140], who writes from a client-centered frame of reference. He says:

It is . . . a reasonable hypothesis that . . . changes are facilitated by the . . . therapist as he consistently demonstrates that he respects the worth of each member. The therapist provides for the group a kind of model—a person who attends carefully to the words of each member; who never interrupts; who does not evaluate, criticise or judge; who never takes sides; who does not subtly manipulate others.

This particular view of the ideal group therapist would probably be acceptable to those who follow Carl Rogers' philosophy of therapy, but would most likely be violently opposed by those therapists who believe that interrupting, criticizing, judging, etc., are essential in group therapy. Probably most therapists would agree that the therapist does serve as a kind of model for the group, that members pick up from the therapist certain clues for their own behavior. The therapist's behavior, therefore, may be considered either crucial or unimportant, depending on whether members of the group imitate behavior or essential personality, if the two can be separated.

Personality and Method

It was stated earlier that the method that a group therapist comes to use is a function, other matters held constant, of his own personality. It is difficult to think of a really introverted therapist using psychodrama with any success; and it may be just as difficult for a really aggressive, outgoing person to contain himself within the limits of the nondirective procedure. If we accept the argument that the best method for any person is one that accords with his own nature, and that a person can do his best work with a procedure that is natural for him, we may be freed of any hierarchy of values with respect to methods. Pratt makes his maximum contribution with the class method, Moreno with psychodrama, Rogers with nondirective therapy, and Dreikurs with family counseling. One need only think of Freud attempting psychodrama to realize the incongruity of the situation, especially when it is apparent that Freud's method—use of the couch, sitting behind the patient, etc.—was a function of Freud's own personality. We have direct evidence on this point from Freud himself, who said [128], "I must, however, expressedly state that this technique [free association] has proved the only method suited to my individuality. I do not venture to deny that a physician quite differently constituted might feel impelled to adopt a different attitude to his patients and to the task before him."

Others have made similar remarks. Spotnitz, for example, says [372], "The personality of a therapist may determine whether the group has an active or passive type of therapy." Kline comments [206], "It is probable that the dynamics of different groups actually do differ radically with the personality of the therapist." Kline not only makes this point but gives a personal example: "... I have always emphasized that within limits the organization of the group and the role of the therapist should be dependent largely on the personality of the therapist himself rather than on rigid techniques. This conviction was derived from my initial unsuccessful attempts to emulate the procedures of Dr. Paul Schilder...."

The therapist needs absolute freedom to follow his own judgment. No one can tell him how to do what he must do. For the purposes of research, Powdermaker and Frank [290] tried to get therapists to operate in a uniform way, and even though the therapists wished to follow this established pattern, nevertheless they managed to make subtle changes, in each case making modifications suited to their own personalities.

It is in the spirit of this freedom for the therapist that the present book is written, in the hope that explicit denotations of a variety of attitudes and methods will help a therapist make a better choice of methods, or will help him have the courage to strike out on his own.

THE ROLE OF THE THERAPIST

The therapist should operate in a way natural for him, but nevertheless there may be a kind of etiquette of behavior for group therapists, and it may be profitable to consider the outlines of such an etiquette. In life there are many conventions that must be followed. One does not eat in the same way at a picnic, at home, in a restaurant, or at a banquet. The individual is still himself in these various places, but he adjusts to the situation. We play different roles on the street, on the beach, at a party, or in the office. If we were to act in precisely the same manner, no matter what the occasion, we would demonstrate a lack of flexibility to adjust to different environments and circumstances. The same is true for the group therapist. While what is indicated below is not intended as a guide for action, it does indicate some of the conventional sides of the role the group therapist plays.

Ethics

Probably the major reason to demand that the group therapist be a member of a responsible profession is that he may then be expected to adhere rigidly to the proprieties. Many ethical issues may arise in therapeutic groups, and while a well-intentioned person of any background may meet them adequately, it is likely that a person who has had professional training in proper behavior with patients will be able to deal with such issues with greater security and satisfaction.

The therapist has a duty to help people. He can help them if they will cooperate with him, and therefore he must engender confidence in himself; but he must be scrupulously careful not to misinform or misrepresent. He should not present an exaggerated account of the benefits to be had from group therapy.

Patients may desire to discuss matters that the therapist feels are unsuitable for group discussion. For example, they may wish to criticize the therapist's supervisor or other staff members. The therapist may decide that he does not wish to participate in such discussions. For him to put a stop to such discussions may be unwise; it may be equally unwise to let the group proceed. Were a member to make sexual overtures to another, the therapist might feel that the problem was no longer one that involved only the participants but that it involved also himself, the group, the other members, and the institution, as well as his profession. The therapist may be asked questions about himself, other patients, or other people which he could answer but feels he ought not to. His refusal to answer may affect the group unfavorably. But there are limits to all human interactions, and it is the therapist's ethical responsibility to establish them. He must act in conformance to his conscience, the ethics of his profession, and the laws of society. Nevertheless, even with these limitations, there is usually plenty of latitude for expression.

Privileged Communications

With respect to sensitive material, the therapist must consider the possibility that such information may harm the patient if it is transmitted by other persons. For this reason, the therapist will do well, if it is necessary, to warn the members that the other members may be fallible and may leak out information to outsiders. To attempt to handle this problem by forcing a compact of silence is probably foolish.

It is a magnificent testimony to human nature that in the writer's experience in a number of prisons, prisoners, who are probably the worst gossips in the world, were able in almost every case to keep all information divulged in therapy to themselves. In over 10 years, only one case of revealing of information came out—and it was reported by the guilty one himself!

Attitude to the Group

What general attitude should the therapist take toward the group? A number of suggestions are found in the literature. Berlein [35] suggests that the therapist ought to handle himself without excessive sentimentality or authority. This means he should take a reasonable attitude, meeting situations in a common-sense manner. Cotton [92] feels that a therapist ought to be relatively passive and operate as a quasi member of a group. Mullan [276] believes that the therapist cannot operate as an ordinary member. He states that the therapist should be careful to use the patient's own metaphor and should take a permissive attitude.

According to Cholden [72] the leader facilitates and stimulates communication between members. He serves as a kind of bridge, or communication pathway, between members. Acting in such ways as to pick up predominant feelings, being aware of the group as a whole, noticing when it is disturbed, helping withdrawn people into discussion, and separating himself from an authoritarian role are ways in which he can do this. Abrahams [2] points out that the therapist is at one and the same time a leader, a participant, and an observer. Some have tried, as have Powdermaker and Frank [290], to eliminate the therapist as an observer by having present a person whose special function is to observe and summarize, either to the therapist or to the group as a whole, what happens in the group. Blackman [50] feels that the therapist may participate in the group even to the extent of becoming a patient in the group himself. He is somewhat suspicious of the value of interpretations. Kotkov [213] states that the therapist should play a passive role, letting the group settle its own agenda and participating only when the discussion is circular. Wender [403] feels that the therapist should be an arbitrator and an observer.

We note that these various roles are functions of particular methods. In Dreikurs' conception of psychotherapy, which is primarily educational, the therapist is very active, struggling along with the various members, criticizing, evaluating, interrupting, being a prime mover of action. In Klapman's procedure, the therapist takes the entire burden of motivating and directing the group, making assignments and otherwise controlling activities. In a procedure of the kind used by Lerner, McCorkle, or McCarthy, the therapist waits for opportunities to clarify, and he may do some directing. In the analytic procedures, the therapist permits the group to operate as it will, but, as he sees fit, he may interpolate remarks directed at clarifying dynamics. In the nondirective approach, Rogers would comment only to the end of helping others learn that he understands and accepts their statements.

Authority

What authority should a therapist have? This is, of course, a function in any specific case of the therapist's personality, his theory of psychotherapy, and the nature of the group. Some therapists are irrepressible and seek to dominate any group they are in. Other therapists are more reserved and, regardless of method, will try to let others have their way. Some methods demand that the therapist make decisions, while others eschew such a procedure. And finally, some systems of psychotherapy, especially those with a cognitive basis, call for the therapist to assume authority, while those with affective aspects as the major element, deny the therapist use of authority.

But there are two or even three distinct kinds of authority. The first kind calls for someone to decide when and where and for how long the group will meet. It also refers to decisions about the relationship of the group to the environment. Generally, the therapist assumes these responsibilities as a matter of course. A second kind of authority is that of technical leadership. Someone may assume the responsibility of starting the group, deciding the agenda, acknowledging members, cutting off discussions, asking for questions, etc. And the third kind of authority, the one that is mostly at issue, refers to comments with respect to interpretations of events. The two polar views are presented by Rogers [316] and Klapman [200]. Rogers does not agree that the therapist's interpretation is more correct than that of any member, and he would not agree that the therapist should use his authority to force his opinion on others. Klapman [200], on the other hand, takes the view that authority is called for at times, and he gives as an example his experience with psychotics. Pratt, it may be recalled, prohibited patients from even discussing the possibility of failure, while Chappell et al. [71] prohibited their patients from discussing their symptoms even with family members. In considering this issue of authority, Jacques came to the conclusion that "technocracy," or doing things to people, results in hostility; while "collaboration" leads to self-solutions and no hostility [178].

REASONS FOR GROUP PSYCHOTHERAPY

Group therapy, by way of definition, has the purpose of effecting subjective and behavioral changes of an ameliorative kind. However, the reasons for instituting such groups may be examined from the viewpoints of agencies, patients, and therapists. Some differences in these points of view may be found.

Viewpoint of Agencies and Institutions

The supervisor or head of an institution, while he is concerned with the individual progress of a patient, has in addition much more to think about: the institution as a whole, its relationship with the community, the agency's budget, personnel problems, etc. When the question comes up of starting a therapeutic group, he may wonder how the group will affect the institution as a whole, how much it will cost, how the other personnel will react, etc. The value of group therapy may be unknown to him, but its potential value has to be balanced by other considerations. How will it affect other patients not in groups? How will it affect other staff members who do not run groups? Any new procedure may well affect the climate or tone of the whole institution. His responsibility is not only to individual patients and staff members but also to the organization. A major argument for establishing group therapy, even though it may not be entirely valid, is economic, since the administrator is usually concerned with shortages of trained help, anything that looks like a timesaver is welcomed.

In attempting to establish a new program, it is important to give attention to two matters. First, a climate favorable to the establishment of a new program should be created, i.e., there should be no strong objections to it; and second, the personnel concerned should be sold on the presumed greater efficiency of the group. Again and again the literature has statements to the effect that in a particular institution group psychotherapy was started for economic reasons. A good example of this comes from Simon et al. [353], writing from the Army's largest neuropsychiatric hospital.

Unlike treatment in a civilian psychiatric hospital, time is essential and of the utmost importance in a military psychiatric hospital. These time limitations circumscribe both the aim and scope of treatment and the forms of therapy which must include only those methods which can be expected to be effective within a reasonable period of time. . . . One of the major difficulties in psychiatric practice anywhere, and one which is sharply emphasized in military neuropsychiatry is that there are not, and have not been, sufficient psychiatrists, social workers and psychologists. Individualization of treatment for patients when thousands are involved is most difficult. Wherever possible, methods and techniques of treatment must be organized for applications to groups. . . . Group therapy, therefore, is recognized at this hospital. . . .

A further argument for the institution of group psychotherapy that will appeal to administrators is that such programs usually help morale. Discontent in institutions is often due to poor communications, and in groups open discussions help to resolve tensions. The tensions of persons not in groups are also minimized when the members communicate to other patients, inmates, etc.

It does no harm for the potential group therapist to be a practical psychologist in selling a program to an administrator and to emphasize these issues rather than the more important issue that the group may help patients.

Viewpoint of Patients

Every member of a therapeutic group is an individual with his own troubles, concerns, and wishes. In entering a group most patients are somewhat fearful, but at the same time they are hopeful. A good many of them hold on to a cognitive theory and expect that good results will come from their receiving knowledge.

The therapist, who may have different ideas about what therapy is all about, is faced with the problem of communicating his own concepts. Some therapists do this by bluntly telling the members that this is not what psychotherapy is; others let them find out by themselves. Some patients feel greatly disappointed when what they get is not what they expected. Such persons tend to leave the group in its early stages unless this problem is handled well. How this is to be done, of course, depends on the ingenuity of the therapist. The writer mentions the problem because he feels that the therapist has a responsibility to the insecure patient, who is likely to quit a group unless he is reassured from the beginning.

Viewpoint of Therapists

A therapist's major purpose is to effect ameliorative personality changes. However, therapists may have a variety of other reasons for establishing therapy groups, some of which are:

For efficiency: to affect more people per unit hour
To prepare patients for individual therapy
To make selections for individual therapy
For purposes of diagnosis
To evaluate patients who have been treated individually
To taper off individual therapy
To supplement individual therapy
To provide a bridge between individual therapy and social living
To train cotherapists
To teach group therapy to members of the group
For dissolving resistance, transference, or dependency
For research purposes

Variety of Therapeutic Aims

Earlier, it was mentioned that the effecting mechanisms of group psychotherapy could be divided into three general groups: *cognitive, affective,* and *actional.* It is also possible to separate the intentions or aims of the therapist in the same manner.

Intellectual. A major purpose of group psychotherapy is to help the client to learn more about himself, about others, and about himself in relation to others. Many therapists believe that one of the major purposes of psychotherapy is to gain "insight." Insight is a complex term but is usually meant to refer to an understanding of one's behavior in terms of the effects of past events, or in terms of unconscious motives. Not all therapists agree as to the importance of insight. Hobbs [163], for example, calls it an epiphenomenon which accompanies but does not necessarily lead to behavioral changes. Gorlow, Hoch, and Telschow [142] students of Hobbs, found that less than 1 per cent of remarks they analyzed in nondirective groups were of the insightful variety. However, in their study insight was associated with progress, for "more profited" people did respond with more insightful remarks than the "less profited." Cotton is another therapist who doubts the value of insight, stating [92], "I do not feel that insight is the essential goal for adequate group therapy. In fact, I believe that overenthusiastic attempts to instill theoretic formulations or insight are frequently very detrimental to the group and to individuals making up the group." However, Cotton is speaking of insight in a special way; he is considering it not as the result of an autochthonous process, but rather as the result of interpretations forced on patients by therapists.

Insight has many defenders. Among those who cite it as one of the purposes of group psychotherapy are Cavanagh and Gerstein [70], Sacks and Berger [328], Luchins [243], Burchard et al. [62], and Stone and Levine [378]. Glatzer and Durkin [137], for example, state that the function of the therapist is to make conscious to the patient the bases for his choices.

For purposes of illustration, here are some expressions of intellectual aims of group therapy and of effects considered worthwhile:

"Increases in understanding of self" [25]
"Education of reason" [14]
"Inaccurate conclusions lessened" [102]
"Understanding of reality" [379]
"Understanding of symptoms" [207]
"Gains in empathy" [327]

There can be little doubt that the experience of really learning something new is a powerful emotion, especially when the thing learned relates to an area that is causing distress. A patient in a group who obtains insight into some aspect of himself or others usually undergoes a strong emotional reaction.

Emotional. There is practically universal agreement that the purpose of group psychotherapy is to give the patient relief of emotional discomfort. Patients often come into such groups most keenly aware of their tensions, guilts, somatic complaints, feelings of unworthiness, anxieties, obsessions, and the whole list of unpleasant subjective sensations that appear to characterize our era. Below are listed some of the aims, purposes, or effects of successful group therapy in relation to these emotions:

"Relieve feelings of isolation" [346]
"Reduction of guilt" [25]
"Lose feelings of isolation" [50]
"Integration of hostile tendencies" [36]
"Learn to express feelings" [140]
"Alleviate guilt" [148]
"Strengthening of rapport" [14]
"Promote feelings of belonging" [314]
"Symptomatic relief" [331]
"Stimulation of self-confidence" [14]
"Diminish feelings of uniqueness and isolation" [377]
"Increase in self-esteem" [79]

"Strengthen super-ego forces" [183]

"Increase morale and feelings of security" [82]

"Emotional maturation" [377]

The above expressions reflect some of the aims of group therapists with respect to changes in the feeling tone of members which might be classed under the heading of emotional changes.

Behavioral. The third class of changes refers to new behaviors, i.e., observable reactions. These reactions may be classified into two types: those that occur in the group and those that occur outside the group. From one point of view, the latter may be considered the most important. Certainly to other people who have to deal with those persons who go to group therapy, behavioral changes are most desirable.

The three types of changes just mentioned may, in some cases, be merely different expressions of the same thing: they may occur in any sequence or at the same time. Thus, a person may (*a*) learn something fundamentally important which changes his perceptions, (*b*) feel differently, and (*c*) act differently. To attempt to disentangle relationships of causations or even to evaluate these differing processes is a task probably not even worth trying. Man is a whole organism, and any reaction has intellectual, emotional, and behavioral consequences. It may not be so important to try to decide which reaction, if any, comes first, but it may be decidedly important to learn which procedures cause ameliorative reactions. While this may be an anti-intellectual attitude, one may recall that many issues, such as the relationship of emotions to behavior, as in the James-Lange theory, have not been settled yet; and moreover, things often are not what they seem. It may be, for example, that a patient has "insight," then feels good, then improves in behavior. There might appear to be a clear case of progress from the intellectual to the emotional to the actional, but keen observations may indicate that prior to the emergence of the new understanding there were increased feelings of acceptance which may have helped the insight to come about, and also that the individual was already making new adjustments to situations prior to the emergence of the insight.

In terms of the four methods discussed at some length in the second half of the book, the matter may be somewhat simplified as follows. In the Rogerian method and in the analytic method, a major emphasis is put on the emotional factors, and the creation of an area of safety, security, and acceptance is of the essence. In the Adlerian method, there is a great emphasis on the intellect, on reason, logic, common sense. And in the method of psychodrama, argued for by Moreno, action comes first, and understanding and emotional factors come next.

The following are some expressions of therapists with reference to desired behavioral changes as a result of group psychotherapy:

"Help to face reality" [251]
"Socialization gains" [377]
"Relationship patterns" [6]
"Ability to face problems" [25]
"Increased sense of ease" [25]
"Feeling relaxed" [50]
"Enjoy friendly competition" [50]
"Freeing expressions" [32]
"Reduction in problem behavior" [362]
"Increased social communication" [362]
"Expressions of affection" [32]
"Adaptation to reality" [62]
"Tolerance of frustation" [379]
"Social integration" [413]
"Release of hostility and frustration" [412]
"Teaching individual to share" [404]
"Resume role as adequate and satisfactory member of society" [207]
"Eliminate undesirable behavior" [236]

The above behavioral changes may be viewed as end results. If one were to assume a purely behavioristic attitude and state that the value of therapy ought to be measured by facts and not by feelings, these then might be called the final aims of psychotherapy, in the group or in individual interviews.

Integration. Psychotherapists, like patients, have various ideas as to what is important. The term *amelioration* is, of course, personal. What to one therapist may be of the greatest value may well not be regarded too highly by another. A therapist may desire for his patients certain gains in which the patient himself is not interested. It is not unusual for a patient who is in distress to have no concern with the distress per se but only with its behavioral consequences. Luckily, however, amelioration usually shows itself in diverse ways; when gains are made they are demonstrated in affective, intellectual, and behavioral changes.

CHAPTER 10   *Evaluating Group Psychotherapy*

The progress of any method of therapy, psychological or somatic, depends on continued evaluation. To persist in the use of any method of treatment without understanding its effectiveness is unscientific. For this reason, almost every psychotherapist who has discussed this matter has commented on the great importance of scientific evaluation. However, it is one thing to desire measurement or evaluation; it is quite another thing to actually measure and evaluate when it comes to psychotherapy. As far as psychotherapy in groups is concerned, there are several reasons why it is difficult at this time to come to a satisfactory understanding of the value of the procedure: first, group psychotherapy is relatively a newcomer in the field; second, as has been stated, group psychotherapy is composed of a variety of methods and theories; third, procedures for evaluation are difficult, complex, and not unequivocal.

It is often necessary to answer questions such as "Do you think group therapy will be useful in this agency?" "I would like to refer a patient to a therapeutic group; do you believe he will benefit?" "I would like to join a group; do you think my kind of problem can be helped?" To answer these and other specific questions, which in essence are questions as to whether group psychotherapy can accomplish therapeutic changes, the practitioner should have as broad a knowledge of the field as possible; and he should be aware of current trends. In this chapter, some of the information available will be summarized to help lead to answers.

METHODS OF EVALUATION

There are six common approaches to information about the value of group psychotherapy. Each will be discussed briefly. Some people may prefer one of them over any of the others; some may think that some of these methods are better than others; but undoubtedly the combination is superior to any single one.

Theory. Some people will find themselves able to answer the question

136

of the value of group psychotherapy, either as a general concept and practice or in a specific case, solely on the basis of arm-chair speculation, calling into play common sense, prejudice, judgment, experience, principles, or philosophy. There is currently much suspicion of the essential value of such theorizing about matters of concern, but it must be kept in mind that some people believe very strongly in their capacities to make good judgments on minimal evidence, and it is certainly true that when a judgment has to be made in the absence of good information, it must be made on the basis of prior available information plus intuition. Therefore, we may indicate that theory, using it in a somewhat derogatory sense, meaning by it bias, is one method for evaluating group psychotherapy.

Testimonials. A second common way for evaluating group psychotherapy is the testimony of others. Actually, it is the most available method and may be at the present time the best. Testimonials may come from all kinds of people: from eminent psychotherapists, such as Paul Schilder, who are very much impressed with the potentialities of the field; from practitioners such as Foulkes, who report on their experiences; and from patients who indicate what the group experience has meant to them. Testimonials will vary in quality, and the person who is interested in secondhand evaluations will, of course, evaluate the testifier and will be interested to know to what extent any opinion reflects the common consensus.

Reports. A third method of evaluation depends on vicarious participation in a group through the reading of objective summaries of group sessions, whether transcriptions or reports of many sessions. Many such reports are available in the literature.

Statistics. A fourth procedure for evaluating group psychotherapy is to analyze statistics of improvement. Some people want facts and believe that numbers are the best kinds of facts. For such individuals, objective data are most impressive.

Research. For some people, the best kind of evidence depends on careful research in which hypotheses are examined and tested for an indication of their worth.

Personal Experience. For other people, personal observation through participation in groups is the best method. One may participate as an observer, a patient, or a therapist. In this way, one uses his own eyes and ears and does not have to depend on indirect or secondhand information.

THEORY

We may now ask this question: how do people react to the *idea* of group psychotherapy as a method of attaining real and worthwhile changes in personality and behavior? Unfortunately, there is not much information in print on this subject, and the writer can only mention the results of his own observation.

Patients. One source of theoretical evaluation of group psychotherapy, i.e., of opinions not based on facts, is the patient himself. The writer has had occasion, in the course of a dozen years or so, to talk about group psychotherapy to several hundred potential patients, introducing the concept to them in many cases. More than one-half of such people, perhaps three-quarters, react unfavorably to the idea of participating in groups, thinking that the experience would not be suitable for them, although rarely denying that it could be valuable for others. This kind of negative reaction may be dismissed as an expression of resistance, but in the sense that the term *theory* is here used these reactions may be counted as expressions of lack of acceptance of the idea on a priori bases. If it is kept in mind that the majority of the individuals discussed were already favorable to, and often wanted, individual therapy, it can only be concluded that persons with emotional problems tend not to accept group psychotherapy as a valid means of treatment. This is only one therapist's experience. Unfortunately, there is no information available in the literature on this particular aspect.

Psychotherapists. Some patients like the idea of group psychotherapy and even desire it more than individual therapy; it appears, therefore, that there are two opinions about group therapy among unsophisticated laymen. The same is true of sophisticated therapists. As already shown, some psychotherapists think very highly of individual therapy, rating it over group therapy, while others value group therapy more. But for the most part, the group supporters tend to have had experience with the method, while, as far as can be told, those who do not think highly of the group method base their view on theory alone.

The writer has had the privilege of discussing the group method with a number of psychotherapists who were inclined to take a negative attitude even without having had any firsthand experience with the method. A summary of some of their opinions follows:

1. Members of groups will not divulge important and sensitive material, since they will not trust the judgment or sincerity of the other members.

2. Group psychotherapy must remain much more superficial than individual psychotherapy for the above reason.

3. Patients may take advantage of other patients, may discuss their affairs with others, may try to seduce them.

4. A patient may be harmed in a group through hearing material that is upsetting or shocking.

5. Some aggressive patients may overwhelm the therapist and gain control of the group.

6. Shy patients will not get much attention.

But those who argue that group psychotherapy is theoretically correct argue along the following lines:

1. Psychotherapy need not be considered a private confessional. It can be carried out in the open community—it should be a part of life.

2. Life is primarily social; psychotherapy should then be a social experience.

3. There is less chance that the therapist will make consistent errors in groups, since he must bring out his ideas in the public forum.

4. Group psychotherapy is inherently democratic and consistent with the current values of society.

5. A group provides an individual with valuable interpersonal experiences with peers.

In conclusion, there is a variety of opinions, based on first principles or biases, about the value of group psychotherapy, and there is no clear-cut preponderance of judgments favorable or unfavorable to the *idea* of group psychotherapy, as far as is known.

TESTIMONIALS

In an earlier chapter a number of statements amounting to testimonials were given about the value of group psychotherapy. Each of those statements amounts to a judgment of group therapy procedures based on experience. Some further quotations may further illustrate the nature of testimonials.

J. H. Pratt, discussing his class method, made the following statement [303]: "Patients in the class usually have recovered more quickly than have my private patients."

Writing from the same clinic, H. I. Harris states [157], "Perhaps the most satisfying result obtained in a large majority of patients is the completely new emotional adjustment to life which they succeed in making."

Nicholas Hobbs, who started out using the individual client-centered method of Carl Rogers, states [165], "... it is probably important to note that group therapy is not a second-choice therapeutic procedure advocated for economy reasons. With growing experience we have realized that group therapy has unique possibilities and that it may offer more therapeutic advantages than individual therapy."

Simon, Holzberg, Solomon, and Saxe, who worked with military psychoneurotics, state [353], "... group therapy is selected [by patients] as the most valuable treatment in the hospital ... there is a consistently positive attitude towards group therapy...."

Paster, who also operated in a military hospital, has this to say [281]: "Instituted at first as a mere expediency to meet the magnitude of the problem, group psychotherapy proved itself of definite value ... it has many distinct and valuable features not encountered in other forms of psychotherapy."

But Sarlin and Berezin [331], who, like the two previous authors, worked in a military hospital, appear to come to quite different conclusions. They say, "If the standard for evaluation of the results of this work is to be established on the basis of patients returned to useful military service, then it is obvious that the treatment was entirely unsatisfactory."

A rather enthusiastic testimonial is provided by Rudolf Dreikurs, who comments [105a], "The understanding of the patient's psychodynamics is greatly facilitated by group therapy. . . . The facility with which the patient can gain insight through group therapy is remarkable."

A final statement by Geller [133] may represent current attitudes. "This is a method which is adaptable to the large scale treatment needs of the state hospital. . . . The effectiveness is proportional to the degree of illness of the patients under treatment, just as with any other psychotherapeutic procedure. . . ."

The fact that most of the reports quoted are favorable is not due to the writer's own biases, since most reports found are distinctly favorable. However, this does not necessarily mean that all experiences in groups are successes. There is a common tendency on the part of people to put into print only material that is favorable, and it is quite possibly true that a good many unsuccessful groups are not made known. When group psychotherapy comes to its full majority, there will be as much interest in failures of group treatment as in its successes, if not more.

REPORTS

Inherent in a testimonial is an evaluation: someone tells whether he thinks whatever he is testifying about is good or bad. A more objective procedure, at least on the surface, is the report, which to be valuable should be unbiased, reporting what happened, giving the facts. There are many reports in the literature, summaries of groups, details of experiments tried out in groups, case histories, etc. Like the testimonials, however, most reports tend to create a favorable impression. No one likes to write about failures.

Below, a number of reports are summarized. They fall into two kinds: case histories of individuals and histories of groups.

Individuals

A very good example of a case history is reported by Miller and Baruch [263], who worked with people who had allergic difficulties. The subject is a girl of twenty-three who had a skin condition, diagnosed by the allergist as neurodermatitis, which had been present from childhood and which had not responded to medical treatment. Dr. Miller, the allergist, suspected that the condition had a psychogenic origin, and the girl was therefore referred for group therapy.

This girl stated in the group that her major problem was that her parents overpowered her. It was noticed in a conference held with the girl and her mother that the mother dominated the interview. After every session, her father picked up his daughter. The mother phoned the therapist frequently asking that the therapist insist that her daughter sleep 8 hours.

For five sessions the subject did not participate in the group. At the sixth session she spoke only one sentence. At the seventh session she began to talk, complaining that her parents would not allow her to have music lessons. "They both try to take too much care of me. They don't think I am grown up. They try to keep me a baby."

Later, she participated in psychodrama, acting in an inhibited manner. She listened to others discussing their hostile feelings toward their parents. One patient stated that she wanted to poison her father. The girl saw how much acceptance the group and the therapist showed for such hostile feelings; and she saw besides how, even in the group, members were able to express animosity toward each other—and still obtain liking and acceptance.

She began to express her own resentments about her parents' treatment. As more negative feelings were expressed, more positive ones emerged. She was able to get her father to stop calling for her. She smoked, for the first time, in front of her parents. Members of the group commented that she looked happier and that her skin condition had improved. By the eighteenth session she reported that she had stood up to her mother and that she felt better. She also reported that whereas previously she had had difficulty holding a job, now she had been given a raise.

This report is typical of a good many "success stories" to be found in the literature of group psychotherapy. About one out of every three articles contains at least one such case history. There is a plethora of testimonies of individuals obtaining relief from problems through membership in therapeutic groups.

Another kind of report has to do with "critical incidents," that is, a particular event which occurred in a group and which appeared to be a turning point in an individual's life. A report of this kind is given by Corsini [84].

Manuel, a prisoner at San Quentin, accidentally learns of a group that meets to discuss problems, and he participates, as a visitor, in one session. After this, he asks the therapist if he may have individual therapy. He is told that this is not possible, but that if he wishes, he may join the group. He demurs, saying that he is in for a sex crime and so would not feel free to discuss his crime. He is told that he need not discuss anything he does not care to, and accordingly he joins. After several weeks, he brings up an incidental problem and acts it out in psychodrama. Later, he discusses his father, who it turns out is an absolute tyrant who made all decisions for Manuel, even after Manuel was married and had a family. Manuel acts out the situation and appears to be quite unable to stand up to his father, as acted by another inmate. The same scene is repeated, a week apart, for 4 weeks, and finally during the fourth repetition,

. . . Manuel suddenly lunged for his father, got him by the throat, threw him to the ground screaming. The rest of the group, after a moment's hesitation due to being startled by this sudden violence, separated the two men, having to drag Manuel off his father. He kicked and thrashed about, screaming hoarsely, "The bastard! I'll kill him! I'll kill him! The bastard!" We held Manuel down on the ground as he continued flailing about, screaming vile obscenities, and finally helped him to a chair, where he lay exhausted, panting, and sighing, showing great agitation. As soon as he appeared to be getting control, we turned to other business, leaving Manuel alone.

Following this incident, all the more dramatic because up to this point Manuel had insisted that he loved and respected his father, Manuel, at the next session and without any intervention, came to the conclusion that he had always actually hated his father and had desired his death, and that the reason he had committed his particular sex crime was to receive punishment for the death wishes he had entertained against his father. This is considered an example of "immediate therapy."

Groups

A type of report much more commonly found in the literature is the natural history of a group. An excellent article by McCann [250] may be taken as an example.

First, the author expounds the philosophy that determines the form of the group. He states that mental conditions are not problems, rather they are answers. However, often the answers are incorrect, and it is the problem of the therapist to help people to find correct answers. Therapy, then, is a procedure that enables people to find new answers to old problems.

Four wards in a state mental hospital were set aside for research: two for controls, the other two for the experimental evaluation of the round-table method. Patients were selected for the various wards in such a way that the groupings of types of illness were approximately equated. Then for a period of 5 months, no oftener than three times a week, patients in the experimental groups participated in the round-table procedure, which has already been described. Some partial statistics are quoted, since at the time of the report the experiment was still in progress. Five of 22 female patients showed a remission of symptoms, while only 2 of the 22 control female patients showed such remissions. Of 10 male experimental patients, 7 showed remissions, but this was true of only 1 of the 10 control patients.

McCann refuses on the basis of such partial statistics to make any conclusions about the value of the method, but he does report that, in terms of his experience, two principles emerge for wholesome living. The first principle is that he who would find himself must lose himself—in the problems of others, which appears to be about the same as the mechanism of altruism discussed earlier. And the second principle is essentially the same: he who would help himself must begin by helping others.

In reading case histories, critical incidents, and histories of groups, one comes to two conclusions: in all cases what appears to be quite impressive work is being done; but everyone accomplishes his work in a somewhat different manner and interprets his success in a different way.

STATISTICS

Suppose you read an article about the use of group psychotherapy in a mental hospital and discovered that 70 per cent of the patients eventually improved. This might create the impression that the patients improved because of group psychotherapy, but when it is known that approximately 70 per cent of patients recover from psychotic states without any treatment whatever, as seems to be indicated by the investigation made by Eyesenck [115], it is evident that this apparently high figure is actually quite low.

Some quotations of statistics of recovery on the basis of group psychotherapy are appropriate.

Pratt, writing about his clinic, states [303], "Among all patients attending classes, 187 or 68 per cent, reported having been helped."

Johnson, writing about the same clinic, reports [182], "Statistical studies indicate that 60 to 90 per cent are notably helped to recovery." Abrahams and McCorkle [4] found that 78 per cent of their subjects made satisfactory adjustment for 3 months in the military service subsequent to group treatment. Kahn, Buchmueller, and Gildea [190] state that 80 per cent of subjects in parental group therapy showed behavior improvement. Altshuler [14] states that his careful statistics indicate improvement in 72 per cent; Friedman and Gerhart [129] found that 60 per cent of patients claimed improvement; Lerner [225] cites 80 per cent of alcoholics as stating that they benefited from group therapy; Smith and Hawthorne [361] state that 80 per cent of relatives of people in group therapy claimed that their family members had improved.

Some more conservative statistics are also found: Wright [416] found 56 per cent improvements; Barton [24], 50 per cent; Jacobson and Wright [177], 49 per cent; Seguin [341], 48 per cent. It seems, then, that, using the therapists' or the patients' judgments, improvements are found in from 5 to 8 out of 10 people in the typical group.

Some other figures may be of interest. Schwartz and Goodman [338] state that all out of 19 patients who were overweight and had diabetes lost weight while in group therapy. Klein [204] reports that 7 out of 13 patients with skin disease were symptom-free at the end of therapy. Baruch [25] found that 15 out of 18 members felt that an easing of personality problems had taken place as the result of group therapy. Wender and Stein [407] state that 11 out of 14 patients who had group and individual therapy improved remarkably. Buchmueller and Gildea state [57] that 9 out of 13 children in one group and 9 out of 12 in another group showed improvements. Fisher and Wolfson [120] found that 8 out of 12 mentally defective children improved as a result of group therapy. Kotkov [216] found that 48 per cent of overweight patients who had not been able to lose weight in any other manner made weight reductions as a consequence of group therapy. Becker [30] reports that 17 out of 26 children with sibling rivalry resolved their problems through activity-group therapy. Solomon and Axelrod [367] discovered that 8 out of 11 girls who were withdrawn neurotics made rapid improvements.

The position taken by the writer is that these statistics in reality prove nothing but should be considered as evidence that the therapists who report them appear to find them impressive. The subjectivity of the patients and of the therapists is at issue. One may see what one looks for, and one may give answers that are expected. Moreover, therapists are ego-involved in their work, and it can hardly be expected that they will tend to take ultraconservative views when it comes to reporting their own successes. And yet, if the writer were asked to indicate the per cent of people in his own experience who have made improvements because of group psychotherapy, he too would feel inclined to say that the percentage is about seventy. But what per cent of improvement would have taken place without therapy is impossible to say, because the common garden variety of problems that come to therapeutic groups outside of institutions have not been studied sufficiently in terms of spontaneous cures.

RESEARCH STUDIES

In recent years an increasing number of well-designed research studies has appeared. Many of them are doctoral theses and are not generally available. In addition to the research studies discussed here, others are reported in other sections of this book.

Value of Topics. Does it matter what topics are discussed in group sessions? Talland and Clark [383] investigated this issue by questioning seven groups of patients at Maudsley Hospital in London. A list of items taken from an analysis of topics actually discussed was rated by the patients for their sensitivity and also for value. In addition, 35 psychologists rated the items.

There was general agreement that the most helpful topics were also the most sensitive. In order of sensitivity and helpfulness the topics went as follows: sex, anxiety symptoms, shame and guilt, childhood memories, quarrels, other members of the group, marriage problems, the therapist, physical symptoms, dreams, children, work problems, social position, outside people, and money problems. The writers conclude, "There is strong, though not conclusive indication that topics which cannot be discussed outside the intimate atmosphere of the therapeutic situation are thought to be the most valuable items in clinical discussion."

Play Therapy. Fleming and Snyder [121] report an experiment with nondirective play therapy. The subjects were seven children—three girls and four boys—residents of a progressively run children's home. Controls were 23 other children.

The children were given a series of personality tests before and after therapy. The therapy consisted of 12 sessions, each lasting one-half hour, and extended over a 6-week period.

The control group was found not to have changed with respect to the scores on the tests, but four of the children in the experimental group, the three girls and one of the boys, did make considerable gains on the tests. The authors conclude: "Measurable changes in adjustment do take place as a result of non-directive group play therapy."

Delinquents. Newburger and Schauer [277] present one of the most methodologically satisfying research studies in group psychotherapy. They started with a control and an experimental group, and then changed the groups from control to experimental and from experimental to control, meanwhile measuring changes.

The population of the study consisted of 60 delinquents, matched into two groups. Each group was given a sociometric test, to determine how many people in the institution were friendly with the various boys. One of the groups was made into the experimental subject, and the members of this group received therapy. At the end of 3 months, the experimental group showed a 7 per cent gain in sociometric choices, while the control group showed a 32 per cent loss. At the end of the period, the groups were reversed, the control group now getting the therapy, while the erstwhile therapy group became the control. At the end of 3 more months, the new control group showed a loss of 46 per cent in sociometric selections, while the new experimental group showed an increase of 5 per cent in being chosen.

The authors state, "Within these limitations, the following conclusions appear justified: group psychotherapy when started early in the period of institutionalization of this delinquent group fostered an increase in mutual choice and pair structures."

Psychotics. Feifel and Schwartz [116] used group therapy with acutely disturbed mental patients in a Veterans Administration hospital. The report concerns first a group of 34 patients who, during a 3-month period, did not receive group therapy but did obtain the usual services of a modern well-run mental hospital, including occupational therapy, corrective exercises, and special services, such as movies, dances, etc. This group served as the control. During a second 3-month period another group of 34 patients were equated with this first group, but, in addition to the various treatments and services, they had group therapeutic sessions. Each patient attended from 8 to 20 sessions. The method of therapy was analytic, the procedures described by Standish and Semrad [375] being followed as a model.

At the end of the respective 3-month periods, all patients were evaluated by three psychiatrists who were not connected with the group therapy and who had no idea what the purpose was for the ratings. The judges rated 17, or one-half, of the first group as "improved." In the experimental group 24, or 70 per cent, were rated as "improved."

The differences were not statistically significant, but the authors state, "Over and beyond the quantitative findings, the authors were strongly impressed by the qualitative differences between the groups." They continue, "The most striking aspect of the experimental group's development was its maturation from a gathering of individuals, most of whose members talked unintelligibly, to a coherently interacting group amiably discussing common problems and drawing upon one another for help."

Defectives. Mehlman [259] hypothesized that if mentally retarded children received group therapy they would improve not only in their behavior but also on intelligence tests.

Three groups of defective children were established. One was designated group play therapy, another group inactive, and the third, group movie. Each child was given the Rorschach Test, rated by an independent judge. The ratings were ranked, and every third child was assigned to one of the three groups. The children were also rated on a behavioral scale and on the results of a personality test and two intelligence tests.

Nondirective play therapy as described by Axline [18] was used. The children were in 29 sessions, which took place twice weekly over 16 weeks. Each session lasted 50 minutes. After the experimental period, the children were retested. Significant changes were found in favor of the experimental group on a behavior rating scale. The experimental group made a gain of 31.62 points, the movie group a gain of 21.48 points, while the inactive group showed a loss of 0.48 points. On the Rorschach Test, only the F per cent showed a statistically significant change. No notable changes were found on either the personality test or the intelligence tests.

Mehlman takes a somewhat cautious attitude about results, since he indicates that the behavior rating scale may have been contaminated by the possibility that the judges may have known which of the children were in the therapy group. The Rorschach increase in the F per cent could have been the result of chance; in any case its meaning is not clear.

In view of the somewhat negative results, one may feel inclined to wonder at the rather short periods of therapy reported on in this and other studies. Individual therapy not infrequently extends over years. It seems hardly fair to expect measurable changes to occur over short periods, amounting in many cases to not more than 10 hours of group therapy.

Delinquents. At the New York State Training School for Boys, Gersten [135] attempted to evaluate changes in behavior and adjustment of 22 boys, ranging in age from thirteen to sixteen, who participated in 20 one-hour, once-weekly sessions. The boys in the therapeutic groups were equated with other boys for intelligence and age. The IQs of the boys ranged from 71 to 105, and most of them were below par in this respect.

The 22 subjects were placed into three groups. During the first five sessions, interview therapy was attempted; this soon was modified to include handicrafts. Subsequent sessions were of a mixed handicraft-interview type, a rather curious combination.

The 22 experimental subjects and 22 control subjects were given a battery of tests before and after the therapy. Sessions were recorded, and Gersten states that the recording did not appear to inhibit the subjects. Gersten's approach was truly eclectic: at times he was directive, at other times nondirective, and he employed procedures borrowed from Moreno and Slavson.

Evaluation indicated that while the IQ of the experimental subjects increased 3 points, that of the controls did not change. The experimental group made a gain of 1½ years on scholastic achievement tests, while the control group gained only 3 months. On a behavior rating scale, the experimental group showed greater progress toward social maturity. The phonographic recordings indicated that the subjects had experienced emotional release, had made gains in insight, and had achieved greater emotional and social maturity.

Gersten notes that although Slavson " '[states that] nothing of real value occurs in the group before the 25th session,' nevertheless the results were gratifying and point to group therapy as a valuable adjunct in the treatment of juvenile delinquency."

Leaders. In therapeutic groups one not infrequently finds that some subjects emerge as leaders. Sears [340] was interested in evaluating such persons. From each of 10 therapeutic groups one was designated as a "leader" and another as a "nonleader." The terms were not more precisely defined, such definition being left to the judgment of the therapists.

The therapists were asked to examine the behavior of leaders and nonleaders. No differences were found of any significance with respect to intelligence, education, age, marital status, occupational status, or life success. Leaders were judged to be sicker, on the average, than the nonleaders and were frequently described as hysterical, psychopathic, or paranoid, in contrast to the nonleaders, who were more often diagnosed as anxious with somatic features.

Differences between the two groups were considered to be qualitative rather than quantitative. Differences were a function of the type of defense used against anxiety. Leaders tended to externalize anxiety, while nonleaders internalized it. Leaders were more communicative and had father-rejection histories to a greater extent than nonleaders. They also had more rebellion patterns than nonleaders.

Zimet and Fine [419] describe an experiment that, while not involving therapy in a group, nevertheless gives confirmatory evidence of the superiority of discussional procedures over lectures.

Fifteen school administrators met for 16 five-hour sessions. At first, 2 hours were spent in a structured lecture situation, followed by a 1-hour lunch period, and then a 2-hour discussion period conducted nondirectively. At the end of the eleventh session, the first 2-hour period was changed to a group-centered operation.

The two modes were evaluated in several ways. It was found that in the lecture approach the leader participated 26.6 per cent of the time; in the nondirective approach, the leader contributed only 10.7 per cent of the remarks. Several significant changes were found in the discussional approach for each of the four quarters of the 16 sessions, but no significant changes were found for the lecture sessions. Zimet and Fine state that the quality of participation improved, more positive attitudes were displayed, and changes toward greater democracy were found. He notes, also, that a greater early defensiveness was found in the beginning of the nondirective sessions.

This greater reluctance or resistance toward the more democratic group-centered procedure over lectures was also mentioned by Landsman and Sheldon [217], who worked with college students. This is probably to be explained by the greater familiarity people have with lecture groups over democratic ones. However, after the initial discomfort of nondirective or group-centered groups has passed, members find them preferable to lecture groups.

A Comparative Study. Baehr [21] was concerned with the comparative effectiveness of individual, group, and combined individual-group therapy.

He worked with 66 veterans, self-committed to a Veterans Administration hospital but not considered psychotic. Subjects were separated into individual-therapy patients, group-therapy patients, and combined individual–group-therapy patients on the basis of the Baehr Discontentment Scale, a questionnaire which measures the nature of and degree of patients' complaints. The reliability of the scales is said to be 0.84 over a 24-hour period, and this scale has a validity of 0.47 with estimates of ward physicians' estimates of patients' disturbances.

The 66 patients were separated into three groups: 17 who were to receive individual therapy, 16 who were to receive group therapy, and 33 who received combined individual and group therapy. The groups were given equal amounts of therapy and then were retested with the Discontentment Scale. It was found that the amount of change on this scale between those who had individual and group therapy was nonsignificant, but that those who were in the combined group–individual-therapy group did significantly better than the other two groups.

While the implications of this small study must be tentative, it does appear that no differences in significance were demonstrated between group and individual therapy; they were presumably of equal value. However, the combination of the two yielded superior results, which may resolve the issue of comparative value in an interesting manner. Both, applied at the same time, may be better than either alone.

PERSONAL IMPRESSIONS

Some evidence for the validity of group psychotherapy as a procedure for attaining desired ends of improved intra- and interpersonal states and relationships has been presented through theory, testimonials, reports, statistics, and research. The final avenue of exploration is through personal impressions. Of course, this means that every person who investigates this subject must come to his own conclusions. The writer would now like to summarize his own impressions.

Need. Anyone who is in one of the helping professions mentioned early in this book finds that he is subjected continually to demands from people for help. One hears continually of personal unhappiness, feelings of inferiority, fears, somatic complaints that have no organic origin, anxieties, compulsions, social maladjustments, family conflicts, etc. There seems to be a never-ending supply of personal and social maladjustments.

But whether one is in the private practice of psychotherapy, in a social agency, or in an institution, it seems completely impossible to meet the demand. Individual psychotherapy, as is well known, may take many years. It is often impossible, in view of the time available or for economic reasons, to fill the need for individual therapy. Group psychotherapy

seems to be a solution which enables one to allocate his time more efficiently. Even if a group method were demonstrably inferior to individual
therapy for any single individual, it might still have a place if individual
therapy were completely impossible for this person and he could be given
some relief through group therapy.

Therefore, the first conclusion to be drawn is that on economic grounds
alone, group psychotherapy is a valid procedure since it *apparently* meets
a social demand. That is, people who want attention can get it in this
manner when no other possibility exists.

Problems. It has already been stated that in the writer's experience, a
great number of persons who demand psychotherapy do not react favorably to the idea of group therapy. When these attitudes are explored, they
seem, generally, to be based on the idea that since the individual's problems are unique, other members of the group will not understand them.
There is also a fear that others in the group will have a low opinion of the
individual when he does express his particular problems.

However, when a group is assembled, after the initial hesitation is
overcome, the members almost always come to the concept of universalization. Such statements are common: "My problem is like yours." "I
am surprised to find that you think as I do." "It seems to me that we are
all in the same boat."

Group members experience a great and evident relief when they finally
expose their sensitive areas and find that the others in the group can
and do accept them in spite of their previous fears that they would not
be highly valued when they told about themselves. A patient often finds
it difficult to believe that others can have tolerance and respect for him
when they know him. He also finds it quite difficult to understand that
others can be so upset over problems that seem relatively minor to him.

Processes. In therapeutic groups various stages occur. At first there is
generally a reluctance to participate. Then there is an expression of
dissatisfaction; then follow attempts at solutions. The group may combine
and recombine into cliques; attention may be given at various times to
various persons; some persons may incur the displeasure of the group;
and the members may experiment with various techniques of handling
group problems. The therapist serves as the agent of each individual and
also of the group as a whole, helping the individuals to express themselves
and the group to persist toward its goal of individual advancement.

One may view the group movement as a movement of individuals, each
of whom proceeds toward vague goals; the more any individual advances,
the more he helps others to advance. There sometimes seem to be levels
in the group: as one patient advances to a particular level of feeling or
accomplishment, others get courage to go ahead. In any event, it is impossible for the therapist to evaluate all that goes on in the group. A

rather quiet member who seems to be making little progress may suddenly report startling progress, crediting it to the group, and no one, including the therapist, may see how the change was accomplished or what part the group played in it.

Achievements. The final purpose of group psychotherapy is to improve the individual. As stated before, improvements are of two kinds: subjective and objective. Some of the subjective improvements that have occurred in the writer's groups may be worth examining.

John states that he cannot look at people's faces, that he has the habit of always looking at the ground. He feels most uncomfortable with people and cannot tell why. During the course of the group he talks about coming on his mother while she was in the sexual act with a strange man. He and the mother looked full into each other's face, and then the subject—aged ten at the time—ran out of the room. After he tells this distressing memory and listens to the group discuss it, he reports that he feels better. At the next session he reports that he no longer feels any difficulty in looking at people.

Frances states that on her job she does not get along with other women. There is one woman who smells bad. Frances has to work next to her but cannot stand her odor. She does not know what to do. After she explains her problem, the discussion goes to something else. No solution is given to Frances, but at the next session she informs the group that she complained to her supervisor, who told her that he was aware of the problem and transferred her away from the woman. Frances feels exceedingly proud that she has been able to solve her own problem and soon reports that she likes the other women and that they like her. She attributes her new attitude to the group's effect on her.

Jim reports that he hates his brother so much that he daydreams continually of killing him. At the next session he reports that he no longer thinks of this but is planning to write to the brother so as to reestablish relationships with him.

Anne says that she cannot find an honest man. Every man is out to take advantage of her. She repeats this assertion with varied and sundry evidences of the validity of her viewpoint. Finally she does meet a man who is different from the others. The group points out to her that she has also changed in the group.

Karl complains that he cannot study. He feels there is little purpose in life. He has contemplated suicide. He feels no one loves him. Others discuss him and offer him various proofs that they are interested in him. Later he informs the group that his grades are improving and that life seems worthwhile.

Alvin is unhappily married. His wife is unfaithful to him. He knows he must seek a divorce but cannot ask for it. In the group he obtains in-

formation that some of his own behavior is not above reproach, and it is
suggested that perhaps his wife is unhappy because of the way he treats
her. Eventually, he reports that things are going along much better, that
his wife has changed in her behavior.

Jake complains of chronic fatigue, which he cannot understand. In the
group he ventilates about business problems, and he comes to understand
that they are related to his subjective feelings.

Individual vs. Group. Evidence concerning the value of group and
individual psychotherapy also comes from patients who are in both
simultaneously, or who have been at various times in one or the other.

One patient said, "I liked individual therapy better in one way. I had
you all to myself, and I felt more comfortable in discussing very personal
problems. But, over-all, I felt that the group was more important, since
they were many people and they represented a transition to society as
a whole."

Another patient put it this way: "In individual therapy I feel I can
learn more about myself; in group therapy I can learn more about others."

Still another patient made this remark: "First, as I see it, I must make
a relationship to one person, then I have to make it to others. It is much
more difficult to learn to belong to a group than to one person."

And another patient, with rare insight, said, "I am the kind of person
who is always out to confuse and fool people. I think I can fool you, but
I can't fool other people in the group. They don't let me get away with
things. They represent social reality."

A Philosophical Viewpoint. The writer is against psychotherapy. He
wishes that it did not have to exist. How much better life would be if
everyone practiced mental hygiene and were so treated that no one would
have those problems we call neurotic! But since there is a need, the best
thing to do about the need, it seems, is to educate people so that they can
take care of their own problems, and so that they in turn will treat other
people in such a way that psychotherapy will not be necessary for those
with whom they interact.

What appears to be of the utmost importance is the dissemination
of attitudes that will affect people in general. In this sense, psychotherapy
is education. Group psychotherapy is a particularly effective kind of psychotherapy, since new ways of living are given not to individuals but to
groups. In this sense it is more economical.

Also, group psychotherapy is more democratic than individual therapy.
The therapist in the group tends to be another member, and he must
contend with others on the basis of equality. In the group the authority of
the therapist is diluted. Members tend to learn their own strengths. They
see the therapist in relationship to others. The therapist, continually
brought down to earth by the members, can hardly succumb to the delu-

sion of godliness, which is almost an occupational hazard of individual therapists.

Over-all Evaluation. On the basis of all the writer has read, listened to, and experienced, there seems to be no question whatever that group psychotherapy is a valid method of treating individuals for internal and external problems. It is a procedure applicable to any kind of problem that is also treatable by individual psychotherapy. It is a more complex way of working with people, and yet, curiously, in some ways it is much easier, since the therapist's responsibility is divided among others. In a very real sense, every member becomes a therapist, and this duality of roles contributes a great deal to the progress in the group. We get by giving.

However, what is needed is further information. Such questions as those listed below need to be answered:

1. For what kinds of problems is group psychotherapy indicated?
2. What is the optimal size of groups?
3. What are the optimal compositions of groups?
4. When should a member be accepted in a group?
5. When should a member be removed from a group?
6. If group and individual psychotherapy are prescribed for a person, what proportions should be used?
7. Which methods are preferable for individuals with particular problems?
8. What are the reasons for successful and unsuccessful treatments?
9. How can the presumed greater economic efficiency of the group be increased still more?
10. How can all formal psychotherapy, of any kind, be liquidated?

PART TWO

*Some Major Methods
of Group Psychotherapy*

CHAPTER 11 *Introduction*

A complete understanding of the values, uses, and limitations of group approaches to psychotherapy, of specific indications for individuals and groups, and of how a therapist may make best use of his personal qualities and resources comes from exploration of the literature on psychotherapy, from an understanding of an integrated theory of personality growth and development, from exposure to various approaches, including participation in groups, and finally from personal experience as a therapist. A book such as this can only serve as preparation, giving the therapist some understanding which may facilitate his clinical performance, assisting him by providing a frame of reference for his unique personality, theory, and situations. A therapist learns mostly by experience, not from books or courses.

In order to supplement the highly concentrated material presented up to this point and to create a sense of differential processes in groups, it may be useful to present protocols of typical sessions of group psychotherapy using some of the major methods. In a search for material of maximal value for the typical reader of this book, the writer surveyed the literature, examined various protocols of actual sessions, and, in addition, listened to various phonographic recordings of meetings of therapeutic groups, but he did not find protocols that he believed would meet the reader's needs. The sessions reported are either fragmentary or they are much too long for reproduction here; besides, the discussions often do not manage to contribute an understanding of the essential and differentiating elements of specific methods. The reader who is interested in reading some transcripts of sessions would do well to investigate those published by Moreno [268, 271, 272], Lerner [224], and McCarthy [253].

Just as an artist may, by judicious selection of visual impressions, emphasizing some aspects and neglecting others, provide a more satisfactory portrait of a person than the more exact process of photography, so too it is possible by presenting modified reports of group sessions, edited to

157

bring out the significant aspects of a particular method, to give a more exact and satisfying impression of the unique procedures involved than could be given by actual transcripts.

The various accounts presented here are based on real sessions but have been edited to indicate the ideal performance of the therapist within a particular method and philosophy. The purpose of these accounts is to contribute to the reader's understanding of the various methods, especially by emphasizing the therapist's responses. The therapist will be known as "T.," the male members will receive letters from "A." to "M.," and female members will be labeled from "N." to "Z."

In general, the report will be as follows: the group, the therapist, the situation, and the locale will be described. When indicated, parts of several sessions will be reported. In order to illustrate typical interactions, the long narrations that sometimes occur in group sessions, during which one member may speak without interruption for up to half an hour, will not be reported.

The Methods. The methods to be illustrated are those which are at the same time the most familiar to the writer and the most popular. Probably 90 per cent of therapeutic groups are run in general accordance with the principles of these four methods: analytic, nondirective, counseling, and psychodramatic.

The analytic procedure is followed, of course, by Freudian and Adlerian psychoanalysts as well as by many other therapists who do not adhere to the theoretical demands of these systems. The essence of this method, which differentiates it from the others, lies in the basic presumption that the function of the therapist is to analyze behavior and statements of members, giving explanations for individual reactions. The therapist becomes a kind of detective, trying to puzzle out clues, finding them by "listening with the third ear." He links various clues, thereby creating a comprehensive, connected picture of the individual as a functioning person. The analytically oriented therapist pays a great deal of attention to unconscious processes.

The nondirective procedure depends to a great extent on the creation of a group climate of safety, in which individuals can feel able to express themselves with maximal freedom. The therapist refrains from interpretations, but, by rephrasing ideas in a neutral manner and by otherwise not indicating any disapproval, he does attempt to help the individual to understand himself. The therapist attempts to free himself from any values, does not put any limitations on the expressions of individuals, never corrects, and strives to attain personal understanding and acceptance of his clients.

The group counselor, on the other hand, takes a very different basic approach from that of the analytic or nondirective therapists. He is concerned with improving immediate behavior, not with digging away at deeply hidden motivations. He operates in a common-sense manner, attempting to understand the problem, looking for workable solutions, trying to help the counselee to understand the errors he is making, and urging him to attempt new solutions. By enabling the patient to meet immediate problems successfully, he hopes to inculcate in him a general understanding of principles through education and action rather than through exploration of attitudes.

Psychodrama depends a great deal on the effect of acting out problems. The therapist tries to re-create, within the group setting, problems of significance, and has the member reenact situations of sensitivity in a neutral emotional setting. Then through discussions by the group as a whole, the member is expected to gain new insights as well as new modes of behavior.

How to Read These Protocols. The reader must keep in mind that the principal reason for the presentation of these protocols is didactic. He ought to try to follow the reasoning of the therapist, and he should contrast the various approaches. *Only enough material will be presented to illustrate various typical reactions.*

It may also be worthwhile to note the reactions of the members to the therapist's reactions. That is to say, in the interactions, the therapist sets the pace and the mode of operating and the group members adjust to him, to some extent.

CHAPTER 12 *Analytic Group Therapy*

This particular group consists of three men (A., B., C.), three women (X., Y., Z.), and the therapist (T.). The therapist is a psychoanalytically oriented psychiatrist. The meeting place is the therapist's office. He arranges chairs in a circle, seating himself behind his desk. He knows each of the members, having had them in individual treatment for from several to several hundred sessions. The group is to meet twice weekly, for an hour at a time, and is "closed," i.e. no new members will be permitted during the life of the group. The members do not know one another when the first session begins.

SESSION 1

T.: This is our first session in an experience that I hope will be helpful to each of you. None of you know each other, and I would like to introduce you. To my right is Mr. A.....

Now that we are through with introductions, I would like to explain how I think we should operate, and make some remarks which I hope will help us in getting the greatest value out of group psychotherapy.

Each of you has been in individual therapy with me. But we are starting here afresh. I will not reveal in the group any information that I may have about you which I have obtained prior to today. In general, the same rules will hold as in individual therapy—that is to say, you will speak about whatever may be in your mind, and I will try to tell you whatever I see in your statements. You may try to analyze one another if you wish. I expect that each of you will respect each other's confidences. While I cannot give you any guarantees about the other members, I know each of you rather well, and I have every confidence in the integrity of each of you. But at the same time you will do well to use your good judgment on what to talk about.

I don't expect to talk in the future as much as I will today in the

160

first session, but let me continue a bit more with some further information. First, psychotherapy is psychotherapy, no matter in which mode it is found. Essentially, it is a problem of self-understanding, learning what unconscious motives excite us to behavior. We want to attain insight, so that we will understand what is behind our behavior and our reactions. The goal of psychotherapy is increased satisfaction with ourselves and greater improvement in social behavior. Second, you may be somewhat suspicious about this method, and you think, as I know from talks with each of you, that it may be difficult for you to reveal yourself to others. I think you all share this feeling. However, if you will be able to defer judgment and share in the discussions, you may find that the group method will be valuable and more useful than you believe now. Thirdly, the experience of being in the group per se may not be of value, unless you participate. As trite as this may seem, you will probably get no more out of the situation than you put in. And finally, we may experience all sorts of positive and negative attitudes about one another. These transferences are an essential part of psychotherapy, and you should not be upset if you go through these experiences.

I think that I have said enough, but let me conclude by saying that I am very optimistic about the potentialities of what we are doing, and that I have great hopes we shall all benefit. And so, let us now start.

[In these various accounts, dashes will be used to indicate periods when no one speaks. Each dash will represent a period of 10 seconds. Thus, – – – means that 30 seconds went by with no one talking.]

T.: Well, who will begin? – – – –

A.: I guess no one wants to start.

T.: Of course, it is difficult to begin. I am sure all of you feel, "I hope somebody else begins." This may be our first lesson, that we are all alike in being afraid of a new situation. The fact that you, Mr. A., spoke first is probably no accident. What do you think it may mean?

A.: I am a somewhat impulsive person, and it is typical of me that I will take the initiative. As a matter of fact, this is a problem for me. I want to learn how to allow others to have their say, but I tend to be too bossy, too impulsive. If I can learn greater control from this group I will appreciate it. I think people resent my being so aggressive.

X.: However, it seems to me that you did react appropriately. No one wanted to say anything, and the fact that you spoke up made me feel pretty good. At least you broke the ice.

A.: But an icebreaker suffers a lot of damage; and sometimes he gets stuck in the ice.

Y.: I'd like to respond to something that T. said. He had to argue with me to join this group, and I did feel quite reluctant to join, and I still am not 100 per cent convinced that this will do me good.

T.: Is it possible that you may not want to improve?

Y.: Does that make sense? I am here, after all.

T.: But how reluctantly!

Y.: Well, you said yourself it is understandable.

T.: Yes, but there are degrees of resistance.

Y.: Do you think I am extraresistant?

T.: Well, I wouldn't like to give a complete answer, but let me say that I did come to the opinion that even though you did engage in therapy, your defenses are so strong that you find it hard to break through them.

B.: How can you tell about the strength of defenses?

T.: By my judgment. I think very shortly all of us will begin to have an idea of the defenses of others. Defenses, after all, serve a very valuable purpose in life. They represent modes of resistance to change. We all do want to change, but at the same time we are afraid to change, and we do have some unconscious hope that we will not change.

B.: It seems as though we have first of all to affect the strength of defenses. How can that be done?

T.: I'd like to answer that. Research indicates that school children pay more attention to the opinions of fellow students than to the teacher, and maybe members of a group such as this will pay more attention to the opinion of fellow members than to my opinions. You are here all therapists.

X.: And maybe I ought to get paid!

T.: That is another story! But we were going to talk about how to reduce resistance. . . .

X.: Well, you have to form a transference, that is to say you have to have love for your therapist and confidence in him.

B.: Whom do we have to form a transference to in this group? To the therapist? Between us, I feel a bit angry with the therapist, since before, I had him all to myself, and now I have to share him with others. I feel that perhaps I won't get a chance to discuss myself freely and frankly enough. Actually, I feel a bit jealous and resentful of the group.

T.: Can you relate this feeling to another?

B.: You mean did I ever feel this way before? Sure, frequently, whenever I have to share whatever I value with another. It is jealousy.

T.: When did it first occur?

B.: I imagine in childhood, when I had to share things with my brother.

X.: Were you insecure?

B.: I imagine I was. How would you like it when all the attention you get is suddenly transferred to someone else, and the other person becomes the family favorite?

X.: I felt the same way about my kid brother, and more than that, I began to resent the fact that I was a girl and I couldn't have the privileges that he had.

SESSION 10

T.: Well, I guess we are all here and ought to begin. I wonder how things have been going with Miss Z.? She seemed to be right in the midst of a problem when we stopped last session.

A.: I was wondering about that, too. I hoped that she was able to make out.

Z.: Well, I thought quite a lot about what we discussed, and I am glad to say that I think I made progress. I realized that I was fighting with my mother because of resentment I had to her, and that I really did not love her as much as I thought. Then, it came to me, I was really too dependent on her and it would be much healthier if I were able to deal more realistically with her. After all, it wasn't good for her either.

Y.: Then you think you really don't love your mother?

Z.: I wouldn't say that. What I think is true is that I am overly dependent on her, and that my resentment of her was really a resentment of myself because, because ... no one really loves me. [Begins to cry.]
— — — —

X.: I feel that Z. is wrong. People can love her, just as anybody can be loved, but in order to be loved, you have to love others. — —

A.: Even in this group, Z. seems to keep aloof and won't let others get too close to her. — — — — —

Z.: It is as though my mother and I formed a combination against the whole world. My father left her, and so she depended on me, and I was frightened of the world by her, and so the two of us were alone together, and I had little to do with anyone else. It is a pretty bad situation.

T.: Let us try to understand this. I think you are touching something of great value. Both you and your mother formed a cabal against the world. I think you resent her complete possession of you. But now you are aware that it isn't only love you have for your mother, but also hatred. However, you begin to understand how you came to depend on your mother, and also how she came to depend on you. Finally, you are able to see how you have been emotionally enslaved by her. But it must be difficult to experience such emotions, and you must feel alone.

A.: It is difficult to fly away from the mother.

Z.: Who else have I got?

B.: The world is filled with two billion people I am told. I can't see what is wrong with you that you can't get married like anyone else, and settle down in your own home.

Z.: But how about my mother? How can she get along without me?

A.: That is just plain stupid in my opinion. She'll learn to get along. The young have to think of themselves. How old are you anyway?

Z.: I am twenty-three.

A.: And how old is your mother?

Z.: She is fifty.

A.: Well, I would advise you to leave your mother, take a room somewhere, and live your own life.

T.: You must remember, A., that you are a different person from Z., and what may be a reasonable solution for you might not be a good one for Z.

A.: She has to learn to live, and she isn't living. She will be absolutely no good for anything unless she breaks the silver cord.

T.: You are probably right, but maybe she has to work it out in her own mind somewhat before she starts to act. Too violent actions may bring on repercussions.

Z.: I couldn't leave my mother. Not without some preparation. I am afraid. Who will take care of me?

Y.: Don't you think you will learn?

T.: This reaction on the part of Z. illustrates a lack of security of the self, undue attachment, and also there are signs of ambivalence. After all, she is now aware of something that had not come to consciousness up to this time, and I do think that she is making progress. Let us not crowd her, let her solve her own problems. I think that as she begins to have new attitudes she will communicate them to her mother, and her mother will understand them and adjust to them. We mustn't see the mother as an ogre; she is, after all, a person with problems of her own.

SESSION 20

T.: Well, how has everything been going?

A.: I'd like to report some success. I was able to sleep without waking up for a couple of nights.

T.: I imagine you are happy about that.

A.: I sure am. I was almost resigned to the fact that I was going to be a perpetual insomniac.

Z.: What do you think was the reason for your being able to sleep and not wake up your wife?

A.: I don't know.

T.: I think some of us know. What do you others think?

B.: It is obvious to me. He was waking up because he wanted to disturb his wife.

A.: What an idea!

B.: Last week you told us you really did not love your wife, that you wanted a divorce, and that her attitudes to you were not too good. You were able to express your hostility to us, and bang—now you sleep. How else can you explain it?

T.: That's what I think. Hostility when repressed shows itself in diverse ways. You were waking your wife up, getting her to worry about you. How did your mother act when you couldn't sleep?

A.: She'd sing to me.

T.: Maybe that is what you want your wife to do, to take your mother's role.

A.: That would be immature as hell.

T.: Well, aren't you?

A.: I guess so. I guess there must be some connection. But I must agree to it on logical grounds.

T.: Of course you don't want to see it. If you do, then you have to say you are immature, hostile, childish, and so forth. Such opinions do not accord to your concept of yourself. Your superego says, "I am a nice guy," but now your ego becomes aware of the fact that you aren't so nice. And so you don't want to hear of it.

A.: It sure sounds logical. You must know.

T.: Don't you?

A.: I guess you are right, but what should I do now, have it out and tell her what I think of her? I'd break her heart.

Z.: Maybe she knows, and maybe because she suspects it hurts her more.

A.: Well, I don't exactly hate her.

Z.: When I told my mother what I thought of her, I thought she would cry and get upset. On the contrary, she told me she knew, and she told me a couple of things too, and now we are on a much better footing. Incidentally, I do want to let you know that I had a date with Jim and had a wonderful time, and I have another date with him Sunday.

A.: Well, you'll be a married woman soon and won't need to come here any more. But maybe I ought to tell my wife how I feel, but I don't know if that is the answer. The question that bothers me is what is the reason for my feeling so about her.

T.: It probably starts with your childhood, and your early feelings about your mother.

A.: I guess so, but let me try to figure it out. . . .

T.: Don't you want to examine it?

A.: But why was *I* punishing myself at the same time?

C.: Why does anyone want to punish himself?

A.: Why?

C.: Guilt!

A.: What am I guilty of?

T.: Couldn't it be that you create a kind of circular reaction? Look at it like this: one—you have hostility against your wife; two—you feel guilty about that, especially since you don't have the nerve to speak of it; three—you assume certain characteristic ways of upsetting her; four—you now begin to feel guilty about that too; and so, five—you punish yourself and her too by what I call the Samson complex.

A.: Samson complex?

T.: Yes, you destroy your enemies, but you destroy yourself too.

A.: I punish myself and her at the same time. I'll buy that, even though I don't see it yet.

SESSION 30

T.: I guess we can get started. Who wants the floor?

Z.: I don't have anything to say.

T.: How does it go with you?

Z.: Well, my mother met Jim, and she didn't seem to like him too much, but I expected that. He didn't seem to care for her either, and it didn't bother me. I could tell how they felt to each other, but I felt more on Jim's side than on my mother's.

B.: Bully for you.

Y.: I think we ought to have consideration for Z.'s mother, after all she should be considered too.

T.: Let us be fair about it, is that it?

Y.: Yes, let us not think of things being black and white; look at both sides.

T.: I think we all agree. Z. may be swinging, like a pendulum, one way and another, but all in all I think we all find that Z. is making progress. — — —

A.: I am not doing so well. Started waking up again. It gets me so mad. Especially since I did have a couple of good weeks.

T.: How would you explain it?

A.: Probably out to punish my wife some more. She went to visit her mother, and when she came back, it started all over again.

T.: Doesn't the answer seem obvious?

A.: Jealousy?

T.: Probably. You resented your wife-mother leaving you, and so you got even with her.

A.: I think you are right. Isn't it awful that my symptoms are of this kind?

C.: You can have mine in exchange if you want.

A.: No, thank you, I don't want to itch.

C.: This itching is killing me. I drew blood again. I practically go crazy with it.

A.: Maybe you, too, hate yourself?

C.: I sure think so when I start itching. I had to run to the toilet yesterday and give myself a real scratching. How the hell this got started I don't know.

T.: How about the area you scratch, could that be a clue?

C.: My rectum and the base of my penis. I guess you'd say that it was sexual.

T.: Wouldn't you?

C.: I don't have the slightest idea. I am getting pretty sick of it.

T.: Do you find any correlation between when you have to scratch and other events?

C.: No, I get the desire at the most awful and inconvenient times. But also when I am alone.

T.: Symbolically, you are hurting yourself. After all, you are attacking your body.

C.: Couldn't it be physical? I mean maybe it is nerves or something.

T.: You went to a dermatologist. He told you there was no evident reason for it. Why do you want to cling to a physical explanation?

C.: Because, damn it, it *is* a physical feeling. I got the damn itch right now. See how I squirm. I'd like to stick my hand in my pants and scratch the hell out of me.

T.: Why don't you?

C.: In front of the ladies?

T.: Why not?

C.: You are not serious?

T.: I am not telling you to do it, I am just wondering why you don't scratch yourself when you feel like it.

C.: For the simple reason I have some pride. I am not going to offend others.

T.: Would you be offending others?

C.: It is obvious.

T.: Is it?

C.: Now, what is the matter with you? Would you really suggest that I scratch myself in front of others?

T.: I am not suggesting that you do. I am only wondering why you don't.

C.: I told you. I have consideration for others. How would you feel if I did it right here and now?

X.: I certainly would object if a man did that in front of me anywhere else, but I'll tell you, Mr. C., if you want to scratch yourself here, go ahead as far as I am concerned. If it will do you anything of good, then I'd be glad to have you do it.

C.: Now ain't that the craziest thing? As though I'd do it in front of you.

Z.: I feel the same way. Scratch away.

Y.: And as the third female member of this group, since you saw fit to pick on us, I too will say, scratch away and have a good time.

C.: You are joking.

Z.: You fidget so on your chair scratching yourself anyway, that it would be even less abhorrent if you gave yourself an honest scratching.

C.: Christ, I feel like taking you on and doing it. But I haven't lost all sense of decency. What has this place done to you, anyway? How can you talk like that? I'll bet if I started to do it, you'd faint.

T.: Let us quiet down a bit; let us relax. I guess that C. feels pretty ashamed of his behavior and can't understand your attitudes. I must say that I am pretty surprised myself at how you women reacted, and I am proud of you. C. has been the least active of the group and seems to have made the least progress. He seems to view himself as some kind of loathsome monster.

C.: How do you know I am not?

T.: Are you?

C.: Not to my way of thinking!

T.: Is that a fact?

C.: Well. I don't know. I have done some things I am not proud of.

T.: With the parts you scratch?

C.: Yeah, but I'm not going to talk about it.

A.: Homosexual behavior?

C.: How can you talk so, before ladies?

A.: They ain't ladies, they are members of this group, and I think you are pretty silly to take such a protective attitude to them.

C.: Z. isn't even married.

A.: Z. can take care of herself, you don't have to protect her.

C.: Well, all right, you want it, I'll give it to you. I did have homosexual relations when I was in the Army. Now are you satisfied?

A.: I am only trying to help you. I don't want to pry.

C.: O.K. Now you all know, does that make you feel better?

T.: The question is whether it makes *you* feel better.

C.: No, it doesn't. I was bullied into it.

X.: That isn't true. You wanted to tell us and you got yourself all excited. You couldn't get it out until you got mad.

C.: Maybe that is right. But it isn't something to talk about. I couldn't even tell T. about it in individual therapy, although I was planning to.

T.: Do you itch now?

C.: It went away.

T.: How do you explain that?

C.: It comes and it goes. It'll come again.

T.: We're all pretty much excited by it. It is always a kind of a shock to express yourself, especially about something this sensitive. Now, what do you make out of it all?

C.: It must be happening when I think of it.

T.: What do you mean?

C.: Well, I must be reminded, and then I scratch.

T.: Like that was the sinful part and....

C.: I even thought of cutting it off. Crazy. It'd scare the hell out of me, but when I get the goddamn itch I'd do anything. You can't know what misery I have been in. You just can't imagine.

T.: Now, listen, C., it is all fairly simple. Did you have the scratching before you went into the Army?

C.: No.

T.: Why not?

C.: I guess I didn't catch whatever I had. I mean I used to think that I had caught something. But the doctors said I haven't. I got examined plenty of times, and they didn't find anything. Maybe it is like you say.

A.: Like my not sleeping.

T.: Certainly, it is a symptom. Look, A. wanted to punish himself, and he did it by not sleeping. Couldn't it be that you were saying: how can I get married since I have been such a bad guy? I am a homosexual; and I really ought to cut it off.

C.: I'll never do it. And I didn't think that way.

T.: Possibly not consciously. All you knew was that damn itch, but couldn't you have unconsciously said to yourself, I am a bad guy and I shouldn't get married. How can I get married when I scratch myself like this? And in this way you gain two things: you punish yourself, and you make it impossible to get married?

C.: Well, what I want to know is this: am I a homo?

T.: Don't you know?

C.: I don't think I am.

T.: Then you probably are not, but you aren't sure of yourself.

C.: You know what comes to my mind. Once, many years ago, my father said to me....

DISCUSSION

These several samples are presented to show how a group therapist who uses an analytic method might employ it in a group of this kind. It will be noted that he participates fully, not hesitating to ask questions, makes interpretations, and otherwise controls the group. One gets the experience of the group starting slowly and developing rapidly. The members fluctuate, reporting favorable and unfavorable reactions. Some are wordy, others are quiet. In general, the group as a whole seems to be developing well.

The therapist, Dr. T., is a psychologist who works for a university guidance center. The six members (A., B., C.—males; X., Y., Z.—females) applied for individual therapy but on being told that only group therapy was available, accepted the opportunity to join a group. The meeting place is a small room in the center. At the first session the therapist and the students are not acquainted with one another.

SESSION 1

T.: My name is Dr. T. I am glad to be here with you.— — —

A.: My name is A. I came for individual counseling but they told me that everybody was booked up, so I joined this group.

T.: I understand then that you were really interested in individual counseling, not group counseling.

A.: That's right.— — — — — — —

B.: Well, what are we supposed to do? — — —

T.: You asked a question and no one answered.

B.: I asked it of you.

T.: Oh, I am sorry, I didn't realize.

B.: I mean what are we supposed to do here, talk about our problems? — — —

T.: I am interested in understanding what you are saying. As I get it, you do wonder how we should operate, and then you ask me whether we ought to discuss our problems.

Z.: What I want to know is whether I have picked the right courses, should I continue in education? I wonder if maybe ... I shouldn't change my field and major in something else. I need vocational counseling, but I wonder if I came to the right place.

T.: You really want vocational counseling, and you appear to wonder whether this is the correct group for you.

171

B.: I wonder if I may say something. I don't know what the rules of this group are, whether we are supposed to advise each other, but I just wonder why the young lady...

Z.: My name is Z....

B.: ...why Miss Z. came here. Doesn't she know that there is a vocational counseling agency on the campus?

Z.: I went there, but I wasn't satisfied. I mean they couldn't tell me specifically whether or not I should be a teacher. I have doubts that this is really my field. I read some books on the subject, but they didn't help me.

T.: Mr....

B.: B.

T.: Mr. B. suggests to Miss Z. that she go to the proper place for vocational guidance, but Miss Z. reports she has gone but isn't satisfied. Is that about right? [Both nod.] — — — — — — — — — — — —

C.: I feel uncomfortable when no one talks.

T.: It is very uncomfortable. — — — —

C.: I mean, isn't there some procedure we ought to follow? Otherwise, we won't know what to do or what to say. I don't mean that we won't talk; but wouldn't it be more satisfactory all around if you told us how we should operate? For example, shouldn't you introduce us to each other?

X.: He couldn't introduce me because he doesn't know my name.

C.: He doesn't know my name either. It is C.— — —

T.: As I get C.'s message, he is suggesting that some kind of rules and regulations be drawn up, or perhaps more precisely that I should issue them to guide us.

C.: Well, are you going to tell us? — — — —

Y.: It doesn't look like it. I wonder why he doesn't. Can I ask you why?

T.: It appears to me that you two have a question. It goes somewhat as follows: how should we work in this group? Shouldn't the therapist tell us? If not, why not?

C.: I think you have put it correctly. Shouldn't we have some kind of understanding? Aren't there any recognized rules of procedure? Don't we work systematically at something? I would think that otherwise we would get nowhere.

T.: You seem to feel that rules are necessary. If we know how we should operate, then we can be more efficient.— — —

B.: Maybe you think we should establish our own rules? — — —

A.: Or maybe we can work without rules. I am somewhat uneasy about any restrictions. Maybe we should more or less speak when the spirit strikes us.

Z.: Maybe the therapist doesn't know. I'd ask him, but I don't think he would answer my question.

A.: Why don't you ask him? [Laughter.]

Z.: O.K., I will. Mr. Therapist, will you please tell us whether you know what you are doing? [Laughter.]

T.: I appreciate your question, but I really don't know if I can answer it. I could tell you about my background, my training, my intentions, and so forth, but I do not feel that would be of much help, and I don't feel inclined to do so.

Z.: Well, that is pretty clear.

A.: I think we are all somewhat suspicious and somewhat fearful, and nobody wants to start. I'd be glad to start off, but I don't like to take up everybody's time with my problems.

T.: I think I can understand your viewpoint. You feel that there is some hesitation in beginning on what you feel is the proper purpose of this group. You would like to break up the impasse, but the thought comes to you whether you ought to take up the time of the others with your own problems.

A.: That is it exactly. I should say that one of my major problems, if I may say something about myself, is that I tend to be impulsive. If they ask for a volunteer, up goes my hand. I am too ready to respond, and I make quick decisions. I have to learn more control, and this moment I feel that I am demonstrating my usual pattern by being the first one to talk about myself.

T.: This is an example of your usual impulsive behavior.

B.: I don't think that is so bad. I have just the opposite problem. In a group I ordinarily don't say much. Maybe in the group I can learn to be more like A. and A. can learn to be more like me. But I was wondering, some of the people in the group have not given their names or said anything so far. I'd like for them to introduce themselves.— —

T.: You present two ideas: first, wouldn't it be good if you and Mr. A. could exchange certain characteristics. You'd like to be more impulsive, and Mr. A. said he would like to be less impulsive. The second idea has to do with certain people in the room who have not spoken. You'd like to know who they are.

B.: I think I'd be more comfortable and . . . I think they would, too.

Y.: My name is Y. I have already spoken, but I think that if someone does not want to give his or her name, that is their privilege.

B.: I didn't mean to say that they ought to. All I said was that I thought I would feel more comfortable, and that they would too.

X.: My name is X. I am a student in the divinity school.

C.: My name is C. I am in the school of business, I think I said that.

Z.: I think I gave my name. It is Miss Z.— — — —

C.: Where do we go from here? I think Mr. A. was saying something.

A.: Yes, I was saying that I am too impulsive....

Comments. It may be seen from the above that a typical first session using nondirective, or group-centered, principles tends to be somewhat more confused and disorganized than an analtyic or therapist-directed session. Actually, first sessions in this mode are difficult to portray; they differ so much, one from another, since the therapist does almost no directing. It may be noted that the therapist sets limits on himself, rarely initiating any comments, rarely asking or answering questions, and being primarily interested in understanding the meaning of statements. He allows the group maximum latitude and makes no attempts to help the members come to an understanding of a *modus operandi.* The amount of material given above may occur within 10 or 15 minutes. We shall see in succeeding sessions how the group tends to organize and find its own method of expression and control.

SESSION 2

The members and the therapist enter the room and take seats. There is a long pause, the members looking at one another and at the therapist. When it becomes evident that the therapist will not initiate the discussion, A. speaks.

A.: I did a lot of thinking since last week. First, I wondered about this group. At first I was somewhat puzzled, and even a little angry, but as the session went on, I seemed to get the logic of it. Second, I thought a good deal about my impulsiveness, and it seemed to me it probably isn't wholly a bad thing. To be spontaneous isn't a crime. What counts is whether one really uses one's own spontaneity adequately.

T.: Last session you discussed your impulsivity and were pretty sure it was not too good, but today you seem to have changed your opinion.

A.: It's funny how I always felt this way, but now I don't know. Why I should pick on this I don't know. It doesn't seem like a very important thing. Actually, it is much more important for me to be able to stick to something. I mean it isn't impulsivity per se, but rather having a grasshopper mind. I am too distractible, can't settle down and study.

T.: Apparently, it isn't impulsiveness that bothers you, but rather the feeling that you are not able to stay with something.

B.: I have that too. I don't know how to study. But in my case, I start to become blue. I feel what is the use, and I get discouraged, and feel pretty miserable. I wonder if A. has something like that.

A.: No. I just get carried away with new thoughts. I don't have stability.

Y.: After all, you have a lot of things on your mind.

A.: Too darn much.

Y.: I think that isn't true only for you. I have this problem: I decide what I should do, make plans and all that, and then when I get set, bang—I do something else, and then I hate myself the next day.

T.: As I see it, Miss Y., you feel that A.'s problem is not unique to him.

Y.: Not at all. It must be common to all.

B.: I have the same thing. Sometimes instead of doing my homework, I go out and go to a movie or something, and then I remember that I should have been working and I get so angry with myself.

A.: But that isn't just what I mean. I mean that I am actually working on something and can't keep my mind on it. Sometimes I jump from one idea to another, and have all sorts of things all around. I get real upset at this.

T.: To be so grasshopper-minded really upsets you.

A.: Why do I do it? Why can't I stick to something? What is the meaning of it all?

T.: This is the question . . .

A.: And I can't find the answer.

Z.: You seem to be one of the active types of person, I mean very active.

A.: Manicky?

Z.: If you will. Maybe it is your constitution or something. I mean maybe you are just physically and mentally active.

A.: But it upsets me. It isn't natural.

B.: Maybe you feel you are different from others? All of us feel different from others, because we *are* different. I had a pretty hard time when I came to the big city after being brought up in a small town. I felt my differences.

Comments. It becomes evident that the nondirective group soon learns how to adjust and that they accept the therapist's role readily. As is true for other groups, the discussion begins at a fairly superficial level and gradually becomes more intense. In the beginning, the therapist usually has to carry out the major burden of the exchanges, but gradually, the members begin to participate more freely, as will be seen from a sample of a later session.

SESSION 10

X.: When I first entered this group I was frightened. I thought I never could participate. With me it has always been a question of sitting in the corner and being quiet. When I graduated from high school, in the yearbook they had about me, "still waters run deep." I don't know how deep I run, but I have been still. But I think I know why I have been still here, and why I am usually considered such a quiet person. I have never spoken about it to others, but I've always known what the reason was.— — —

T.: You are quiet, you know others see you as such, but you also know why you are quiet.

X.: Yes, and what it all is is a question of a kind of irrational fear. Do you want to know what it is? — — —

A.: I think I can say for myself that I am willing to listen to you and learn what is bothering you if it will help you.

X.: My mother committed suicide.

Z.: Oh, I am sorry to hear that.

X.: She cut her throat with a knife right in front of me. I was seven years old at the time.

Z.: What a dreadful experience!

X.: Of course, I was just a child, and I don't suppose I understood the significance of the act. I was scared of course, but I don't think it had any great effect on me. Nevertheless it did tend to make me serious. So, I have never been able to — — — [starts to cry] — It was — — — — — was — — — — — — — — — — — — — It was — — — — — — — — oh God! — — — — — — — — — — my fault. — — — — —

T.: Thinking about your mother's suicide upsets you because you think you are responsible for it.

X.: [Nods, still crying, holding a handkerchief to her eyes.] — — — — Yes, it was — — — — — — — — my fault — — — — — — she — — — killed — — — — — — — — — — — herself — — — — — — on account of — — — me.

T.: You are certain that it was really your fault.

X.: Because of me. Oh, I am sorry. I didn't want to break down. I am so sorry.

T.: You really didn't want to break down in front of us.— — — —

X.: It is crazy. I mean it wasn't my fault. It couldn't be. And yet I must think so. I swear it. I never said it. I mean I never said I was responsible for my mother's ... suicide, but I must have ... felt ... responsible. But it wasn't my fault. [Starts crying again.]

T.: This seems to be a statement that you never made before. But even though you feel responsible you seem to know that you are not.

C.: I think I understand X.'s position. Unconsciously she must have had the feeling that she was guilty of her mother's death, even though on the surface, in her sensible mind, she knew she wasn't guilty.

Z.: It must be an awful thing to carry around with you. I know that when one has guilt about something that one can verbalize it is pretty bad, but to have it underneath and not available to consciousness, that must be awful.

B.: I am glad that X. cried and got upset. I don't mean I like to see her upset, but I used to worry about her. God knows I have troubles of my own, but something about her used to bother me. She looked so prim and so quiet and so hopeless-looking. I figured she had some big tragedy.

X.: But why should I have this feeling? How can a seven-year-old girl come to this opinion?

T.: I believe that now you are questioning how you came to believe that you were responsible for your mother's death.

X.: I am still shaking inside. I always prided myself upon my control, and I want you to know that I am now perfectly rational. I guess when I cried it meant that I trusted you, because it would have been perfectly inconceivable that I should show any emotions at all.

Y.: You know X., I think it is becoming clearer to me. I hope I don't upset you, although I don't know if maybe it wouldn't be better for you to relax your guard and cry things out, rather than being so self-protective. But you stated at one time in the group—one of your few utterances, by the way—that you had few friends and never had a boy friend and never wanted one. Now, I am a girl too, and I didn't believe you, but now I can understand. You must have felt like a murderer all along and so didn't feel you could have friends, that people should like you.

X.: I want to explain my feelings right now. First, I have the impulse to crawl back in my shell and keep quiet. It feels good to talk about myself. I really enjoy it. Something just happened to me. I guess when I cried. But I could just shut up and say nothing. I don't know if I make sense. But now I feel good. Relieved.

T.: You are enjoying the experience. Somehow or other you feel free . . . good.

X.: Yes, free and good. And yet I have a lump of sadness deep in me, but it is sinking away. Could it be just that because I verbalized my guilt about my mother that I have this reaction? And yet there is terror behind my feeling. Let me explain it. Oh, I have to tell you. I am afraid the guilt will come out as soon as I am alone. I don't want to stop talking. I want you ... I want you all ... to hold me. Hold me physically. Protect me. Don't let me think bad things. Oh, am I crazy? Maybe I am. I can't stop talking. It's nonsense. Will I scream?

T.: You are upset right now. You are afraid that you will have fears, new guilts. You want us to crowd around you and hold you. Hold you physically.

X.: Isn't that just crazy?

C.: I don't think so. You suddenly become aware of how alone you are, and it is an expression of your desire to become part of the group. You are telling us you have confidence in us. I think something almost holy has happened here today. I am, for one, very happy you have been able to come out of that shell. And I hope you stay out. I want to suggest something to you. Maybe, after the session some of us can stay with you, just so you won't feel alone.

Z.: I'd stay with you overnight if you want.

X.: [Starts to cry.] — — — — — — —

T.: I assume the offers really please you and that is why you cry.

X.: Aren't I silly? I just feel ashamed. No, thank you. It won't be necessary, but I do appreciate it. I wish now we could go to someone else. I think I have taken too much time. It is really nothing. I have control of myself.

T.: You feel ashamed of yourself for breaking down, but now can control yourself. And you do appreciate how the others in the group want to help you.

X.: Very much. But the thought comes. If I could speak some more — — — — — I guess I can. How did I come to have such an opinion? And the thought comes — — — maybe my mother was insane? She had to be. No one commits murder or suicide if one is not insane. She must have said things that I can't remember, awful things one says to children, like, "It's all your fault. You're a bad girl. Wash your face. You're killing your mother." You know the kinds of crazy things mothers say to their children. And I must have developed a terrific guilt about myself which I brought out today — — — it really surprised me how I brought it out. It must mean that I had it in the back of my mind all the time.

Comments. In a nondirective session it is not uncommon for a member to be relatively passive and nonparticipating and then enter into the proceedings in a most dramatic manner. However, such reactions take time. The group has to cohere, and the members have to develop confidence. When a member enters a new plane of operation and opens up with intimate confidences, this has a sobering effect on the other members and sets a new level of operation for the group. A less intellectual type of discussion and a more emotional kind seems to emerge.

One may note that the therapist maintains throughout a constant attitude of wanting to accept without emotion the ideas of the members, and that he strives to achieve understanding. One may also note that the other members begin to operate more or less according to the manner of the therapist.

CHAPTER 14 *Family Counseling*

The most complex of the methods discussed is family counseling. The particular procedures and the interactions described below are in the spirit of the Adlerian centers developed by Dr. Rudolf Dreikurs.

A center is established and maintained by a committee of interested persons who raise funds, provide space and facilities, and serve to inform the public of the existence of the center. They also obtain the professional personnel for the centers.

The personnel ordinarily include (*a*) a counselor and possibly an associate counselor, (*b*) a receptionist, (*c*) a social worker, (*d*) a recorder, and (*e*) a playroom worker, who may have assistants. The receptionist serves to give information to visitors and new members. She asks each person to fill out an information sheet, and to register for every session. The social worker interviews new members, fills out a personal history blank, and schedules sessions. The recorder writes a summary of every session. The playroom worker observes children of the parents who are in the counseling room and gives oral reports to the counselor and members, besides writing a summary of the child's behavior for the records of the particular family.

Parents who wish to enroll in family counseling come to a center and, after getting some information from the receptionist, attend a meeting. Later, an appointment is made with the social worker, who gives further explanation of the purpose and philosophy of the family counseling and makes an appointment for a more complete history. Then, parents come with their children. The children wait in the playroom under the supervision of the playroom worker, who observes their behavior while the parents attend the sessions.

The counselor obtains information about the family from the following sources. First, he has a history of the family problem plus other information, possibly including a report on a home visit, from the social worker. Second, he obtains from the playroom worker a report of the behavior of the child or children of the family. Third, he interviews the children in the counseling room in front of the adult members, with the parents out of the room. And fourth, he interviews the parents in front of the other members.

While, from one point of view, the therapist does individual therapy in front of the group, the fact that other members contribute incidentally (with questions, suggestions, and objections) and the fact that members observe others and listen to the counselor's advice to others make this in fact a therapy of the group.

We shall follow Mr. and Mrs. X., who have come to the center for advice about their two children, Dan and Don. Mrs. X. came for the first time alone, on the advice of a neighbor. She was impressed with what she observed in the session and so requested an interview with the social worker. After the interview, she came with her husband and children. The children were put in the playroom, while the parents went into the counseling room. Here they found the counselor and recorder seated behind a table. To the left of the counselor was a piano bench, on which the children were to sit when they came from the playroom to be interviewed. The members sat in a series of semicircles about the therapist, with the parents to be counseled directly in front of the counselor. In the typical session, the counselor interviewed the parent or parents, then the playroom worker came in and gave a report on the children of the counseled parents, then the parents went out of the room while the children of the particular family were interviewed, then the parents came back into the counseling room after the children went back to the playroom, and then the counselor, after some discussion with the whole group and the parents, gave his opinions and advice. We shall now report the case of typical parents in such a center.

T.: And now we have Mr. and Mrs. X. Have you attended several sessions?

Mrs. X.: I have been here three times, and my husband was here twice.

T.: I see you have two children. Don is ten and Dan is seven. What is your problem?

Mrs. X. [taking out a piece of paper]: I wrote them down.

T.: Did you think you might forget them?

Mrs. X.: No, but I thought I might get nervous and forget some of them. Actually, we have so many problems that I feel pretty hopeless. Maybe I am not a good mother. I don't know why we have so many problems.

T.: Maybe you want to be too good a mother. Mothers are often so ambitious that they make many mistakes. But let me ask you, have you learned anything that can apply to your family from what you have heard up to now?

Mrs. X.: I have been impressed with the good you have been able to do, and I have heard a lot of things, but I didn't want to do anything until I talked with you.

T.: That is probably a good idea. But very soon you will have courage to experiment with new ways of dealing with your children. You must remember that our primary purpose is not to solve old problems but to give you an understanding of the best way to deal with new problems, or even more exactly, to operate in your family in such ways to prevent the occurrence of problems. But what have you got on your list?

Mrs. X.: Well, Dan, the older boy, is not doing well in school. He is not learning to read and has trouble keeping up with his work. He almost did not pass last year, and he is doing no better this time.

T.: Has the school tested him?

Mrs. X.: Yes, they say that his intelligence is normal but that he only reads at the second-grade level. I help him with his reading, and I make him study.

T.: Do you think that we can help with this kind of problem?

Mrs. X.: I really don't think so. But it is the problem that disturbs me most.

T.: Why?

Mrs. X.: Well, we want him to do well in school. As a matter of fact, his father and I want him to go to college and learn a profession.

T.: And he certainly cannot go to college if he can't read.

Mrs. X.: That is correct.

T.: Did either you or Mr. X. go to college?

Mrs. X.: No, neither of us went past high school, but we have hopes that our children will get a better education than we did.

T.: Your attitude is understandable, and your motives are commendable, but let me ask you, if Dan should not have the academic ability to go to college would you be seriously disappointed?

Mrs. X.: No, I would say no. I think it is more important that he and his brother be happy and successful in life.

T.: Not everybody can go to college, but if parents have great ambitions for their children, and if they are disappointed, then neither the parents nor the children can be happy. That is, if you love your mother, and your mother wants you to be a dancer, and you can't succeed, then you may feel unhappy that you don't give her what she wants.

Mrs. X.: I think I see what you mean. But all I want him to do is to keep up with his schoolwork. Why shouldn't he read?

T.: There may be many reasons. It may be that we can give you advice that may be of help in this problem. But Mr. X., you have been quiet, what do you say about this problem?

Mr. X.: I didn't get the chance to go to school much. I would like Dan to become a lawyer or an engineer, so he doesn't have to work with his hands like I do.

T.: Is that so bad?

Mr. X.: No, in fact I am proud of my work. I am a linoleum layer, but after all, if one has the ability, he should get his chance.

T.: And what do you think is the reason that Dan does not read?

Mr. X.: He is not serious. He plays too much. He looks at TV too much. He doesn't realize that it is necessary to study. I have to fight with him to study.

T.: You feel, then, that it is part of your problem. That is, as a parent you ought to supervise his studying.

Mr. X.: Of course, isn't that what parents ought to do? Should I let him play when he should be studying?

T.: Do you think you have been successful? I mean have your efforts done any good as far as you can see?

Mr. X.: Well, he studies when I watch him.

T.: Mrs. X., I suppose you also keep Dan occupied with his work.

Mrs. X.: Yes, I do. I tell him he ought to study.

T.: Do you think you have accomplished anything?

Mrs. X.: I am not sure. But if we didn't keep after him, he would never study.

T.: How can you tell?

Mrs. X.: Well, he would never pick up a book unless we told him to.

T.: I won't comment on this right now except to say that I disagree with both of you. I think your theories and your behavior are unsound. But let us leave this for the moment and ask about other problems. What else is on your list?

Mrs. X.: Fighting. Dan and Don are continually fighting.

T.: This disturbs you, no doubt.

Mrs. X.: They sometimes drive me crazy with their noise. And the neighbors complain.

T.: Why do they fight?

Mrs. X.: Over everything. A common reason is that Dan doesn't like Don to play with his toys.

T.: Do you think the boys like each other?

Mrs. X.: Oh yes, if another child hits one, the other defends him. It is only that they fight together.

T.: And what do you do?

Mrs. X.: I try to ignore them. Then I yell at them and tell them to stop.

T.: Do they?

Mrs. X.: When I yell loud enough!

T.: That is, when you really get upset.

Mrs. X.: I guess so.

T.: Do you do anything else?

Mrs. X.: Sometimes I try to find out who started it. And then I send him into his room.

T.: As punishment?

Mrs. X.: Yes.

T.: For how long?

Mrs. X.: Until I let him out.

T.: How long do you keep him in his room?

Mrs. X.: Until he asks me to let him out.

T.: Do you let him out as soon as he asks?

Mrs. X.: No, sometimes when I am angry I make him stay a long time.

T.: You ever have any trouble deciding who started it?

Mrs. X.: I usually send Dan out. I figure he is the older and should have more sense.

T.: Do you feel that the procedures you are using are successful?

Mrs. X.: No, but what else can I do? I have tried everything.

T.: Maybe, and then again, maybe not. We may give you some new ideas. But what do you say about the fighting, Mr. X.?

Mr. X.: They don't fight much when I am around. Besides it doesn't bother me too much. I think it is natural for kids to fight. It gives them courage.

T.: Why do you think they don't fight much when you are around?

Mr. X.: I guess—maybe it is wrong—but if they annoy me too much I will give them both a good healthy slap. That stops them!

T.: Are there any other problems?

Mrs. X.: We have an argument every night about going to bed. I start telling them to get ready about 7:30. I want them in bed by eight.

T.: Why?

Mrs. X.: They are very active. They need their sleep. But when I tell them, they don't seem to even hear me. So then, in 15 minutes, I tell them again. And then there is an argument. They want to watch a TV program. Finally, they get to bed about 8:30.

T.: Is this a usual routine?

Mrs. X.: It occurs almost every night.

T.: It must be unpleasant for you.

Mrs. X.: I am tired at the end of the day, and I can tell you that I do not look forward to it.

T.: I think that we certainly have a lot of problems. But Mr. X., can you tell me if you have any special problem?

MR. X.: Yes, it has to do with eating. Here's the way it is. I come home about 5:30. I wash up, and then my wife calls the children in. Sometimes she has to call them two or three times. Then I have to go out and get them. And then I have to argue with them about washing their hands.

T.: I think we have a great deal of information for the present. Let us not try too much in the first session. Now, Mr. and Mrs. X., we will call in the playroom worker and see what she has to say.

* * * *

T.: Mrs. B., what can you tell us about Dan and Don?

MRS. B.: They made an immediate good adjustment to the playroom. They play well with each other and with the other children. Dan is one of the oldest children in the room, and he acts as an organizer. They are both very active and sometimes boisterous, but they are not destructive.

T.: And how do the two boys behave with each other?

MRS. B.: Very nicely. They seem to respect each other. Dan is protective of Don. Actually, they do not give me much of a problem.

T.: Thank you, Mrs. B. I am certain that Mr. and Mrs. X. are glad to hear that they do not give you any trouble. And now, Mr. and Mrs. X., I'd like to ask you to go out of the room so that we can interview the boys.

* * * *

T.: Hello, are you Dan?

DAN: Yes.

T.: And then you are Don?

DON: Yes.

T.: How are things going?

BOTH: Fine.

T.: That is wonderful. Are you both in school?

BOTH: Yes.

T.: And what grade are you in, Dan?

DAN: Fifth.

T.: And how does it go in school?

DAN: Fine.

T.: Are you doing your work well?

DAN: Yes.

T.: Sometimes children have trouble with their schoolwork. Is there anything that gives you any trouble?

DAN: I am good in arithmetic.

T.: And how about reading?

DAN: I am not so good.

T.: Why?

DAN: I have trouble with the big words.

T.: Do you try to learn the big words?

DAN: Yes, my mother helps me to read.

T.: Why?

DAN: She wants me to do well in school.

T.: And you, Dan, do you want to do well, too?

DAN: Yes, I do. I try hard.

T.: Do you like to have your mother help you?

DAN: No.

T.: Why?

DAN: I don't know.

T.: Dan, why do you think your mother and your father bring you here?

DAN: I don't know.

T.: Don?

DON: I don't know.

T.: Shall I tell you?

BOTH: Yes.

T.: The reason is that things are not going so well at home. There is some unhappiness. Would you like things to go better?

BOTH: Yes.

T.: What bothers you, Dan and Don, at home? What isn't so good?

DAN: I don't know. Don takes my toys.

T.: Is that true, Don?

DON: Yes.

T.: What happens then?

DAN: I fight him. He should let my things alone.

T.: What do you say to that, Don?

DON: He takes my things, too.

T.: Well, fighting isn't the best way to solve problems. Maybe we can think of a better way. But let me come back to Dan. I think you like to have your mother help you with your schoolwork. Is that possible?

DAN: No, I need help because I am not doing so well with my reading.

T.: Now, listen Dan. I want to ask you something. Listen carefully, and think it over. Isn't it possible that you want your mother to pay attention to you and read to you?

DAN: No ... [hesitates and then breaks out into a big grin].

T.: You say no, but you smile. I think you really want her to give you a lot of attention. What do you think of that?

DAN: I don't know.

T.: Well, think it over. Now, boys, I have to tell you that we want to make things go better at home. All these people here come because they want to make *their* homes happier. Your father and your mother will change things, and I am sure you will be happier. Do you like coming here?

DAN: No.

DON: Yes.

T.: And now a last question. What would you like to be when you grow up.

DON: A policeman.

DAN: A doctor.

T.: Good. Now, boys, you can go back to the playroom.

* * * *

T.: Now Mr. and Mrs. X., we have listened to you, to the playroom report, and to the children. I'd like to start some discussion about your family problem. Actually, as I think you already know, all of the problems you have brought up are familiar ones to us. We have a good deal of experience in helping parents handle them. It is a question of learning better techniques. Psychologists have learned a good deal about human behavior. But let us see what your fellow mothers and fathers have to say. First, about the reading. What do you think these parents ought to do?

A.: I think they should send them to a reading specialist. Sometimes children can't learn to read by one method, and they do much better with another method.

B.: I'd get the children, I mean the older boy, some interesting children's books.

MRS. X.: I did that. I have gone with Dan to a book store and to a library and I let him pick his own books.

C.: I think that television is what keeps children from learning to read. I think the parents ought either to sell their TV set or let the children look at it only an hour or two at a time.

T.: Well, we have certain suggestions. What do you think of them?

MRS. X.: Well, about the specialist in reading. I was thinking of that. I even read about it in a book I got from the library. But it is very expensive. And maybe she is right about TV, but we would have more fights. I couldn't keep Dan from watching it while Don is looking at it.

T.: I have a much simpler suggestion, Mr. and Mrs. X.

MR. X.: What is it?

T.: I don't think you will like it. I am certain that Mrs. X will not like it.

MRS. X.: We came here to get help, and we will do whatever you say.

T.: Whatever I say?

MRS. X.: Well, doctor, it would be foolish to come here to get your advice and then not follow it.

T.: I am happy to hear you say that, and I hope you mean it. I'll now give you my first advice, in reference to the reading, and then I'll try to explain why you should follow it, then you tell me why you won't.

MRS. X.: I promise we will do whatever you say.

T.: Now, let us think about the problem of reading. We know that Dan is not doing well in school, especially with reading. Why should he do poorly in this subject and well in arithmetic, especially since arithmetic is usually more difficult and less interesting for children? Both are quite similar operations, reading symbols and doing mental work. And besides, from what we saw of Dan and what we heard from the mother with reference to intelligence tests, we know that Dan is at least average in his mental ability. Then, we must ask ourselves, if Dan is not reading well, what is the reason? He seems to like school. We got nothing from him or from the parents to make us think he doesn't like school. What then is the reason? And we actually got the reason right here in this room, when the parents were out.

Dan is exploiting the parents, especially the mother. He is making a sucker out of her. He is taking advantage of her. This is a means that he uses to keep her occupied with him. He is the older child. When he was the only child, he was the little king of the family, and then along came Don, and there was a new little king. And so, our little dethroned king has looked for new ways to get attention. Children are clever, and they soon discover ways to get their parents to give them special attention. One way is to learn what the parents want. In this family, the father and the mother are ambitious for their children. The mother worries about reading. As long as Dan does poorly, his mother gives him attention. So why should Dan do well? If he read well, then his mother would no longer have any reason to give him special attention. How do we know this? When I asked Dan if this was the reason, he denied it, but he showed what we call the "recognition reflex," that is to say, even though with words he denied this was the reason, he did involuntarily demonstrate that this was the true reason by a grin which he could not suppress. In other words, Dan wants attention, and in order to get attention he does not read. He is not consciously aware of why he does this, but nevertheless I am of the opinion that this is his reason.

Now in this work we usually take the simple and direct way of dealing with problems. If rapid, simple, inexpensive solutions are not the right answer, then we try others. And now here, Mr. and Mrs. X., is my first suggestion to you, about reading.

Do not help Dan any longer with his reading. Do not ask him how he is doing in school. No longer make a fuss over his report card. Take the attitude that school is Dan's problem, not yours. Do you think you can do that?

Mrs. X.: I didn't expect you to say this. I don't know. . . .

T.: It is my opinion that any interference on your part with Dan's school-work will have exactly the opposite effect from what you intend. You actually prevent him from reading by giving him help. Now, I ask you whether you are willing to go along with me and absolutely refrain from showing any interest in his work.

Mrs. X.: But if he asks me?

T.: Tell him he can do it alone, and that it is not your problem, that he has to take it up with his teacher.

Mrs. X.: Won't he think that I am rejecting him?

T.: I am sure you are not rejecting him, and also that he will not think so. You must realize and accept the fact that your help does not help Dan. He must learn to stand on his own feet. Now, do you think you can do this?

Mrs. X.: Yes. I will not help Dan any more. Even if he should ask me to.

T.: Mr. X.?

Mr. X.: I will do the same. I won't ask him any more about school.

T.: That is fine. I am certain that you will be surprised how things go. Keep in touch with the teacher, but don't let the children know you have called. Give Dan several months. If this does not work, then we will try something else. Now, what was the second problem? Ah, yes, the fighting.

Once again, I have to advise you not to interfere. This is a long story. The children fight when the mother, who gets upset, is in the house, but rarely when the father is in the house. Can it be that the basic motive of the children is to get attention from the mother? Can it be that Dan, who I believe is so interested in his mother's attention that he does not learn to read, provokes fights to get more attention? This is a good hypothesis. But there is more to it than that. The mother becomes the judge. She tries to decide who is the guilty one. It is usually Dan. How does Dan feel if he is misjudged? Maybe he did start the fight, but maybe Don provoked him and Don is actually more guilty. How does he feel when he is unjustifiably punished? And how long does Dan stay in his room? Until the mother decides that the punishment is sufficient. All this is not good. It divides the two children. It may create resentment. It gives the mother more work. And yet, what can be done? It is obvious that what she is doing does not work, because the fighting continues. Do we then take the father's attitude that fighting is all right? Do we see an answer?

I think there is a simple and obvious solution to this problem. What do you think?

E.: I would get boxing gloves and tell them to fight it out.

T.: A ten-year-old with a seven-year-old?

E.: Well, if the mother acts as the referee.

T.: And if they want to fight ten times a day, then there would be ten boxing matches every day?

E.: Well, they can fight only at night.

T.: And if they start fighting when they are not supposed to, or if they do not want to fight when you want them to?

E.: Well, if they fight when they are not supposed to, then I'd punish both of them.

T.: How?

E.: I would make them go to their rooms and stay there.

Mrs. X.: I have only one room for both of them.

E.: Well, I'd separate them until they promised to stop fighting.

T.: I am afraid your solution is not good. After all, what we want is not supervised fights between unequals, but rather a cessation of fights. We want brothers to cooperate, not fight.

F.: Maybe if the mother says, "Well, you want a fight, then I'll give you a fight!" And she should beat both of them.

T.: More fighting! In a year or two Dan will be bigger than his mother. No, I don't like that. Are there any other suggestions? Well, let me give one.

A family should be a cooperative affair. Everyone should respect the rights of others. Do the boys have a right to fight? I don't think so, when their fighting disturbs others. Do I have a right to fight with my wife? Yes, when we are alone. But would you like it if we were guests in your family, and every time we came, we fought? Would you keep inviting us if we fought every time? I am sure you would not. You would feel that you too have rights, and that we had no right to disturb you. You would say in effect, fight all you want, but don't do it in my house. And that is exactly the attitude I would suggest that Mr. and Mrs. X. take. If you believe that Dan and Don have the right to fight if they want to, but that they have no right to fight when they disturb you, we can now suggest a solution. Can you see it, Mrs. X. or Mr. X.?

Mr. X.: Tell, I mean order, them to fight outside the house?

T.: Exactly. You are catching on Mr. X. As soon as they fight, open the door and tell them to fight outside, in the halls, in the yard, in the street, but not in the house. Can you do that?

Mrs. X.: Why didn't I think of that myself?

T.: Well, we don't have time now to take care of the other problems. Maybe you will find the solutions yourself. If you come here you may hear similar cases and will understand what to do. The social worker will schedule you again, we will then see how you are doing, and we shall help you some more. Do you have any questions? I am certain you will help your kids and also help yourselves. I think we must now go on.

SECOND SESSION WITH MR. AND MRS. X.

T.: How do things go?

Mrs. X.: Much better.

T.: What happened?

Mrs. X.: Well, like you said, I no longer help Dan. Was I surprised! He kept asking me to help him. I told him school was his problem. He told me I didn't care if he passed or failed.

T.: And how did you respond?

Mrs. X.: I told him I was very anxious that he should do well, but that he should ask his teacher. I called her up, incidentally, and I don't know if I told you before that she had asked me to help him. I told her what you said. I don't think she was impressed, but she said that if I didn't want to help him that was all right with her, but unless he improved, he would not be promoted.

T.: And what did you say?

Mrs. X.: I told her that things were not getting better with my helping Dan, and that I would like to try letting Dan alone, like you said.

T.: Notice any improvement?

Mrs. X.: Well, I don't know. I don't ask Dan any more, and he studies by himself now.

T.: Without your asking him? I see from the recorder's report of the first session that you felt he would not study unless you urged him to.

Mrs. X.: I guess I was wrong.

T.: Most parents don't have enough confidence in their children. If we give them responsibility, then we are often surprised how sensible and resourceful they are. Keep up the good work. Isn't it easier for you?

Mrs. X.: Yes, it is much better for me. I am not a teacher, and I would get upset when I tried to help him to read.

T.: Keep out of it. You have enough to do. You have your own life to lead. We want parents and children to work cooperatively, but we do not approve of children making servants out of their parents. It may seem hard to do, especially if we have fallen into bad habits, but it is best in the long run. And how about fighting?

Mrs. X.: It stopped.

T.: You mean those two scrappers of yours no longer fight? Is that possible?

Mrs. X.: When they started, I sent them out. And would you believe it, as soon as they were out of the house, they stopped.

T.: I not only believe it, but I expect it. The two boys do not hate each other. They only fight to get your attention. Did it take long to stop the fighting?

Mrs. X.: Well, one morning, it was a Sunday morning, they were in their pajamas and started fighting over the Sunday newspaper. It had to do with who was going to see the comics, and my husband pushed them right out of the house in their pajamas. That was the last fight. [Laughter.]

T.: Well, I want to congratulate you, Mr. X. Do you think things are better now at home?

Mr. X.: Much better. Once in a while they start fussing, and I open the door and send them out. That is only once in a while.

T.: Good, now you told us about two other problems. Have you done anything about them?

Mrs. X.: They still won't go to bed when they are told.

T.: Do you now have more confidence in yourself and in your children to follow some more advice on this matter?

Mrs. X.: We will do just what you say.

T.: No matter how foolish it sounds?

Mrs. X.: It won't sound foolish.

T.: And about the feeding, do you still call them, and they don't come?

Mrs. X.: Yes, and they won't wash their hands, and they have poor manners at the table.

T.: Now come, Mr. and Mrs. X. You are both intelligent people, you have come to this center for 7 weeks and have seen a number of problems handled, can't you think of a solution that will be natural and workable? Do you really have to ask me for an answer? Can't you figure out a good solution on your own?

Mr. X.: I'd like to know what to do about both problems.

T.: Well, let us get the playroom worker's report and see the children now....

*   *   *   *

T.: Well, we have heard the playroom worker's report, and we find that there is no essential change. They still play well and give no trouble. The children also seem happy, and although Dan misses his mother's help, he has a more cheerful and more optimistic attitude about his capacity. So now let us go to the two specific problems. Keep in mind, Mr. and Mrs. X., that we want to have you learn our philosophy. But what opinions do we have about the sleeping problem?

F.: I think the parents ought to have a talk with the children, tell them that they have to have sleep and that they must go to bed by a certain time.

T.: And if the children will not actually do what they agree to do?

F.: Then the parents should send them to bed.

T.: So we come back to what they are now doing.

F.: Well, what else can you do if children won't go to bed?

Mrs. X.: They are worse when we have visitors.

T.: How do you feel when you start fighting with your children in front of company?

Mrs. X.: I get so mad, I'd like to hit them. They seem to act worse when there is company.

G.: Why not let the children go to bed when they want to? That is what I do with my own children.

Mrs. X.: Oh, they would love that. They would never go to bed.

T.: Are you sure?

Mrs. X.: Is this a serious suggestion? Would they ever go to bed, Herman?

Mr. X.: I can't see that.

T.: I think that Mr. G.'s suggestion is sound. Tell the kids that from now on they go to bed whenever they want to.

Mrs. X.: But how can they get up to go to school?

T.: Why not?

Mrs. X.: They won't have enough sleep. They will get rings around their eyes. They won't be able to stay awake in school. Their health may be impaired.

T.: Do you want to keep doing things the way you have been doing?

Mrs. X.: I'd like to ask Mr. G. how old his child is.

G.: I have three children. The youngest is four, the next is seven, and the oldest is eight. We always let them decide their own sleeping time.

Mrs. X.: And when do they go to bed?

G.: The youngest goes about seven, the oldest about nine. Sometimes they go earlier, sometimes later.

Mrs. X.: That is marvelous. I don't think my children would go.

T.: Would you be willing to try it?

Mrs. X.: How should I do it?

T.: Easiest thing in the world. Just don't say anything and see what happens.

Mrs. X.: And if they are not in bed by ten?

T.: Why ten?

Mrs. X.: Well, that is the time we usually retire.

T.: Go to bed, then.

Mrs. X.: And let them stay up?

T.: If they want to.

Mr. X.: Somehow that doesn't sound right to me. But if you say so, we'll do it. Just go to bed without saying anything to them. Not even ask them to clean their teeth?

T.: You go to bed at ten. That's all.

Mr. and Mrs. X.: Just like that?

T.: Just like that. Let me explain a bit. Your primary job as parents is to permit your children to grow up to be self-sufficient adults. You certainly will not help them if you continually assume responsibilities that rightfully belong to children. A child has the right to learn to take care of himself. A child is very eager to learn. He wants to do the right thing. He has to learn limits. If parents assume all responsibilities, when then do they learn?

Mr. X.: Well, we will try it.

T.: Now, let me give you advice about the feeding problem. Do you eat at the same time every night?

Mr. X.: Just about.

T.: From now on, no longer call them, no longer tell them to wash their hands. Eat at your regular time. If they do not come, eat without them. If they come to the table to eat, do not let them sit down unless they are presentable. And if they come too late, do not let them have their supper. And, of course, do not allow them to eat.

H.: Why, that is awful! Are you seriously suggesting to a father and mother that they do not feed their children? Have you no heart? Would you do that to your own child?

I.: Isn't it dangerous? Wouldn't a child get a headache if he didn't have his supper?

J.: Don't you think that you could talk with the children about it?

T.: I see we have touched a lot of feelings. What have I suggested? Nothing more than happens to all of us as adults. We eat when we are hungry. If we are in a boarding house or in the Army, when they feed everybody else, we eat. No special exceptions are made continuously. Isn't that so? Children all like to eat. Now, we can use this natural desire to get children to conform, not to arbitrary standards but to common requirements of social living. I must suggest that you tell your children the rules of the house from now on and if they come dirty to the table, they do not eat, because you do not want to eat with pigs. If they don't come when the regular hour arrives, you eat without them, and if they come too late, clean up and give them nothing.

THIRD SESSION WITH MR. AND MRS. X.

T.: How does it go? We have not see you for 2 weeks.

Mrs. X.: We had quite a time, but things are so much better. I have to tell you this. We had some neighbors over a couple of nights ago, and when Dan and Don went to bed without our telling them to, these neighbors said they wished their children were so good. When I heard this, I almost cried. [Laughter.]

T.: Dan and Don went to bed without being told? How did that come about?

Mrs. X.: We did just what you said. They went wild when I told them. At ten that first night they were going strong. I don't know how we were able to do it, but we went to bed. I could hear them at twelve. It was after midnight that Dan went to bed. Then I fell asleep. I woke up about two, and I got up and found Don asleep on the floor of the kitchen. He had his toy gun and a flashlight. He told us the next day that he was going to guard the house against burglars. I was going to pick him up and undress him and put him to bed, but then I thought maybe I ought just to put a blanket around him. I went to the bedroom, and then I lay down to think it over, and then I heard Don get up and go to bed. He fell asleep with his clothes on.

T.: Did they get up the next morning?

Mrs. X.: They did. It didn't seem to hurt them. But that next night Don went to bed about eleven, and Dan went to bed about twelve again. They had a hard time getting up the next morning. I was beginning to worry, and I must say I began to wonder whether I was doing the right thing. I called up the social worker and told her shouldn't I make them go to bed early, but she told me to follow your advice. They looked awful. It almost broke my heart to see poor Dan. He looked so bad.

T.: Rings around his eyes?

Mrs. X.: He looked pretty tired. But you know what happened? They both went to bed right after supper the next night. At 6:30. [Laughter.]

T.: And after that?

Mrs. X.: We don't have trouble with them any more. They now go to bed about nine.

T.: And this was, if I remember, about the same time they used to go before with all the fighting.

Mrs. X.: Yes, that is true.

T.: Are things better now? No helping in schoolwork, no ...

Mrs. X.: His teacher tells me he is doing much better in reading.

T.: And without your helping him? And with no sleep?

Mrs. X.: Things are so much better, but I think his father ought to tell you about eating.

Mr. X.: Well, I told my wife we should not put into operation your suggestion about the meals until we settled the sleeping question, so we waited until the fourth day, when they started to go to bed early and on their own. I told them that from then on, we would not call them. That night they came without being called.

T.: Did this surprise you?

Mr. X.: I have been so surprised that I don't know what will surprise me now. And they have to pass inspection before they can eat. Dirty hands and face, no dinner. But after 3 days, they didn't come until about seven. We had eaten, my wife washed the dishes, and they came in famished. No food I told them, and I wouldn't even let them in the kitchen. Give me some bread, give me a glass of milk or a cracker, they cried. I had to keep them out, because I think their mother couldn't have done it. They cried and yelled and called us bad parents, and they finally went to bed hungry. It was pretty bad. But I must say one thing, they haven't missed another meal. I had a talk with them the next day, and I think they weren't resentful. I mean they saw that we had a point too.

T.: I think you parents have done wonderfully well. It may seem cruel, and it may seem hard to not feed one's own children, but I am certain that in the long run the family will be able to operate more happily, and as a matter of fact it does run somewhat better right now. Now the parents are no longer the children's servants. The children meet their own responsibilities, they do not disturb the parents with their fighting, they go to bed when it is their bedtime, and they eat in a proper fashion and on time. But now we have to suggest to the parents that they do something equally important. That is, they must allow themselves to play with their children. I strongly suggest that they look for opportunities for the whole family to engage in play. Fill in some of the time that you have saved in arguing and fighting with pleasure. This will help create the feeling in the children that the family is a happy institution and will teach them cooperation.

Now, do you have further problems in the family?

Mr. X.: Well, Don has difficulty. . . .

Comments. The above transcript of real family problems indicates the typical approach in Adlerian family counseling. As may be seen, the counselor is very active and controls the situation, but nevertheless the whole personnel work together as a team. Periodically, the staff of recorder, playroom workers, receptionist, social worker, and counselor meet to discuss cases and to evaluate themselves.

There is, of course, considerable flexibility in the use of the method. At times, the counselor may lecture extensively; at other times he may invite and have considerable group participation; at times, the interchanges are mostly between himself and the parent or parents whose problem is under discussion. Interviews with children are usually short, taking on the average some five minutes, but on occasion they may be much longer. Scheduling usually follows a 4-week cycle, but at times the intervals are shortened or lengthened. The final step of counseling usually consists of the establishment of a family council, which meets in the homes periodically, with rotating chairmen, every member being chairman in turn. The purpose of the family council is to provide a time and place for the settling of problems in an atmosphere of democratic harmony.

CHAPTER 15 *Psychodramatic Group Therapy*

Probably the most difficult of methods to illustrate through description is psychodrama, since a good deal of its essence is found in action rather than in talk. It would be appropriate, although somewhat unusual, to use a dramatic procedure in depicting the method, thereby creating a greater sense of participation.

Psychodramatic group therapy is one of the many versions of psychodrama, and it combines some of the characteristics of circular discussional interview groups, as in analytic group therapy, with the classic psychodrama of Moreno. It may be carried out in any protected place, using members as auxiliary egos. The particular version used by the writer will be described. The description begins with the arrival of Mr. Yablonsky, a social worker, at the office of Dr. T., the therapist.

OFFICE MEETING

T.: Good afternoon, Mr. Yablonsky, I am glad to see you. Won't you have a seat?

Y.: Thank you, Dr. T. This is my first time in a prison.

T.: How do you find it?

Y.: Well, frankly, I don't know what I expected. I imagined that I'd see scar-faced men slinking about under guns.

T.: I guess that is the stereotype of prisons. Actually, probably there is little difference in the appearance of men in prisons, in the Army, in industry, or anywhere else. The difference, if there is a difference, is inside. And that is what we are concerned with, helping people to obtain a greater understanding of themselves, and new attitudes.

Y.: You mean attitudes to property and the rights of people?

T.: No, I wouldn't say so. I think those attitudes differ, on the whole, very little from those of people in general. This is my own opinion, you understand, but I think of men who go to prison as distorted in more fundamental respects: they have less self-confidence, are more suspicious, and in general have a sense of inadequacy, which I am afraid being in an institution contributes to. And that, of course, is the reason for group therapy.

Y.: Do they really cooperate?

T.: What do you mean?

Y.: Well, somehow or other I have the feeling that they would not really be honest about therapy. Like you said, I would expect them to be suspicious.

T.: Aren't other people who enter group therapy initially suspicious?

Y.: Yes, but I should think that these people would be even more suspicious.

T.: You may be right; it is hard to tell; but you will have the opportunity to decide for yourself.

Y.: I want to thank you for the opportunity to visit and observe your group.

T.: We allow no visitors.

Y.: No visitors? But I thought you agreed that I could come and observe.

T.: Yes, but still we do not allow visitors.

Y.: I am afraid I do not understand.

T.: Let me explain. It is a matter of semantics; and it all comes to the same thing. Our group is group-centered, which is to say that all major decisions are made by the group as a whole, except those I reserve for myself, about which more later. One of our earliest decisions was whether or not to permit visitors. We discussed it thoroughly and considered the pros and cons, and finally, the decision was made to not permit visitors. After all, we are a serious group, we take up serious matters, and the intrusion of any nonparticipating member might well affect the attitudes of members. I think that you, for example, might resent having people come and watch and listen while you unburden your heart.

Y.: I am certainly in accordance with that: I can understand that, and yet you said I might come in.

T.: But only as a member, not as a visitor. That is, as a real member, even though your tenure may be only one session. As a member you have responsibilities as well as privileges. You will be expected to keep the code of the group, that is, not reveal any information you obtain, to participate with equal status with others. You will be accepted as a member by the others.

Y.: Did you assume responsibility for inviting me?

T.: Yes, but the responsibility was given to me by the other members. They told me that any person I invite to become a member, whether the person is an inmate or a free person, will be acceptable to them.

I try, of course to use discretion in the selection of new members. In your case, the group feels that as a professional person, who may learn in this manner, you have a right to participate.

Y.: It makes sense, and I appreciate the invitation. Now I have a number of questions.

T.: Shoot away.

Y.: How many are in the group?

T.: I find the optimal size is 12. At the present time we have, including you and me, 15 people.

Y.: How do members come in?

T.: I make all final selections for admissions. Members may refer themselves. That is to say, they hear about the group, and they ask for admission. Or other members may suggest new members. Or other members of the staff may suggest members. In any case, any applicant comes to see me. I explain how the group works. If the individual is interested, I tell him that he must agree to come for *at least* three successive sessions, and then at the end of the third session he has to decide whether or not he wishes to become a full-fledged member.

Y.: Why do you ask for this?

T.: As you indicated earlier, people are suspicious, and they are also fearful. Some men, when they see what we do, feel that they can not possibly participate, and they want to withdraw. That is, the very first session may create an unfavorable impression, and the individual, even though he might be helped by the group if he stayed, might leave and thus lose an opportunity for self-improvement. There is another reason for asking for three meetings. It has to do with publicity. If a lot of people came just one time, and if they were not impressed with what we were doing, they would go out and give a distorted picture of what goes on. If they report after three sessions, then that is another matter.

Y.: Why three sessions, why not two or four?

T.: Well, there is a good reason for three sessions. Actually, to understand our group, you have to know that there are three independent cycles: a daily cycle, a 3-week individual therapeutic cycle, and an 8-week group cycle.

Y.: Sounds complicated.

T.: It isn't. None of these cycles came about through planning: they just happened. But let me explain them to you. First, the daily cycle. As soon as we start, the first order of the group is business. That is to say, I'll introduce you to the rest of the members, and the rest of the members to you. If there are any announcements, this is the time I make them, at the very beginning. That is, announcements of changes in hours, whether a person who has attended three meetings is now present for the fourth meeting and is now a full member, etc. So, that is the first event.

The second event is recapitulation. The subject or subjects of the previous week's psychodrama now tell the group about their introspections and reactions to the previous week's session, and the group as a whole discusses the previous session.

The third event is the preparation for the psychodrama. We give the floor to a subject who has asked for it the week before, and he talks about himself, usually with reference to a problem, and the group discusses the problem and, with the help of the therapist, sets up the drama.

The fourth event is the drama itself. The subject picks members to act as auxiliary egos, playing the roles of significant people in his environment, and they, under the coaching of the therapist, interact with him. The drama is ended by the therapist. I'll explain why later. And then, usually, we have another psychodrama, usually a short one, or some special event.

The fifth event, and this takes usually only a few seconds, is volunteering for the next session. That is to say, I ask who will come up next week, and we ordinarily get two volunteers to be the psychodrama subjects for the next session.

The sixth event, which occurs when we have a new member, is the sociodrama, which is a prepared situation, a kind of icebreaker for the new member, giving him experience in role playing. This is usually a humorous situation, and it serves to counteract the seriousness and intensity of the psychodramas.

The seventh and final event, which occurs when we have new members, is the evaluation of the group by the new member. I ask the visitor or new member to tell what he thought of the group. And that ends a typical session.

Y.: I see that it is a logical sequence. You have to keep an eye on the clock, don't you?

T.: Yes, it requires some judgment on my part to keep things going so we can do everything. It is part of the central idea of the method to operate in a rapid manner. We are strictly business. There is never any slack time. A member keeps working for an hour and a half. A lot of time pressure is generated.

Y.: You said that there was another cycle. I think you called it an individual cycle.

T.: Yes, the cycle for any subject has five phases which go over 3 weeks. First, the individual volunteers to come up the next session. This requires a personal decision. Then during the period between the first and the second week, the individual keeps thinking about what to bring up—he examines his conscience as it were; then on the second week we have the psychodrama; then he has another week of thinking about what happened; and then on the third week he discusses his reactions in the recapitulation, and there is a common discussion of the problem of the week before and of his reactions. This completes a therapeutic cycle.

Y.: And then you said there was a group cycle.

T.: The typical meeting that I discussed with its seven aspects occurs for 7 weeks in a row. The eighth session is completely different. We have no program; we do no therapy.

Y.: What occurs?

T.: Nothing. It is a social hour. We have coffee or soft drinks. We sit in a circle and talk or not, depending on our mood. I am no more than any other member in the group. I assume no responsibilities, although I may participate if I feel like it.

Y.: What goes on in this last session?

T.: We call it, somewhat inelegantly, the bull session, and we cut up whatever comes to mind. For example, we may review some of the highlights of the previous seven sessions. This is the session when any member may evaluate what he got out of the sessions, and where he may criticize any member, the therapist, the group, the procedures. Here we discuss ourselves and plan new procedures. We evaluate any new method we may have tried out. In short, we operate in an extremely informal, unstructured, permissive manner.

Y.: Would you call it a nondirective session?

T.: Yes, that would be a good name for it. It is nondirected. It is a period for relaxation, for winding up loose ends, for getting gripes off the chest, for personal evaluations, and for whatever else anyone may want to do. It is a period of good fellowship. The main reason for this session is to obtain a breather from the tension and excitement of the regular sessions. This also brings the members closer together. They can see each other as social individuals rather than as patients.

Y.: I get the impression that your procedure makes use of contrasting methods. I mean there seem to be in operation two distinct types of procedures.

T.: How do you mean this?

Y.: Well, of course, I am depending on your description rather than on personal observations. First, I note considerable rigidity with respect to form. I am referring to the cycles. And yet one session out of eight is formless. Then, I assume from what you have said that during a good part of the sessions, when you use psychodrama, you have a great deal of emotionality stirred up. Is that right?

T.: Oh, yes, we may have people acting quite violently.

Y.: And then, you balance this emotionality with rational discussions during the period of recapitulation. And then, you begin in a quite authoritarian manner. I mean you decide who is to come in. You decide when one phase goes to another in the sessions, and you "coach" or direct the action, and yet I assume that in the recapitulation every person has the right to say what he wishes, and in the bull sessions you assume the role of another member.

T.: Very well put. You are quite right. I play many parts. However, I'd like to make one point clear. The authority I assume has been given to me by the members of the group. I have brought this up several times in the bull sessions, and the consensus is that I am the director or the facilitator. I have been given certain administrative privileges which I exercise at the discretion of the members. For example, I do not give any interpretations or advice. Every man's opinion is as good as the next man's, and mine is no better than anyone else's. It is now a quarter to three, and we begin at three sharp. We end at 4:30 sharp. Are there any other further questions?

Y.: I'll probably have some more after I participate. Have you any suggestions for my behavior?

T.: No, about the only thing I'd suggest is that you do not sit next to me. I do not like to create the impression that visitors are to be too closely identified with me. I would suggest that you take a seat in the circle, some distance from me.

Y.: That sounds reasonable. And what is the icebreaker you will want me to participate in?

T.: Well, I can't tell you that. But if you have a little anxiety about it, that is all to the good. You will enjoy it, I am sure.

Y.: Can you tell me anything about your members?

T.: Yes. They are, of course, all convicts. We had, incidentally, an interesting experience. One of the staff attended several sessions, and he later indicated an interest in becoming a permanent member of the group. I had to tell him that this was probably not a good idea. I don't know whether I should have let him join in with us, but it was my decision, or rather I advised him that it would not be wise. I'd say that our members are representative of the institution as a whole. They may be a bit older and a bit more intelligent, but all levels of ages and intelligence, all kinds of crimes, all types of personality, etc., are represented. Actually, the person who decides whether he belongs is the individual himself. A new member comes in, looks around, and then comes to a decision whether he belongs to the group. There is a self-selection, and I think that only the more serious and the more intelligent tend to remain. But we must go now. It's almost time to begin.

THE SESSION

As Dr. T. and Mr. Y. come into the therapy room, there are several members already seated on chairs arranged in a circle. In the room there is a table and an easy chair, as well as a screen. Dr. T. and Mr. Y. sit down, and by three o'clock, there are 15 people in the room.

T.: It is three o'clock, and I think we are all here. Today we have a new member, Mr. Y., who is a social worker and who is interested in what we are doing because he is thinking of starting group work with youths in a social agency. I told him that he was invited by the group as a whole, and I have given him an explanation of how we work. I would now like to introduce the various members of this psychodrama group. To your right is Mr. A. Mr. A. has been in this group for about three months. Next to him is the next to the oldest member of the group. I am the only one who has been in longer than he. Mr. B., how long have you been in this group?

B.: I think that it is just about a year. I guess I am due to go out soon.

Y.: Why do you say that?

B.: Well, I actually should have gotten out some time ago, but I felt that I could be of help to the group.

T.: A member may leave whenever he wishes. Usually we discuss the question in the bull session. There was a great deal of feeling that Mr. B. is of help to others, especially since he is a very sensitive auxiliary ego.

B.: You ought to see me portraying grandmothers!

T.: And next to Mr. B. is Mr. C., who is the next oldest member. He has been with us about nine months, I'd say.

Y.: What is the average length of stay?

B.: I'd say it is about four months for those who stay three sessions.

Y.: Isn't that rather short?

T.: Perhaps. I think there is a feeling that if one is to get anything out of these sessions, one usually gets it quickly. Besides, we try to make room for new people. We always have a waiting list. And next to Mr. C. is Mr. D. He is the newest member of the group. Today is his second session.

Y.: Might I ask Mr. D. about his reactions to the group?

D.: Well, if I'd have done what I wanted to do, I wouldn't have come to this meeting.

Y.: And why is that?

D.: I came because I promised Dr. T. to come at least three sessions, but I decided that this group is not for me. I can't act, and I think this won't do me any good.

Y.: Have you really settled this in your mind?

D.: No, I have an open mind. I wonder about the other members being in it. I have never seen anything like it. But I just don't think this is what I need.

T.: You know that we are here to help people. This method is not suitable, perhaps, for everybody, but after you have taken in three sessions, then you can decide better. But I appreciate your coming again even though you do feel it will not help you. We want you in only if you think you can participate fully and frankly. Now, next to Mr. D. is Mr. E. . . . [Introductions go on.]

T.: And now we come to our recapitulation. Mr. E., you were the subject for the psychodrama last session, and you have the floor.

E.: Well, you fellows gave me a rough time. When I left the room I was pretty upset. It was all so real. I felt like I was back at home. I was almost crying. So, when I went back to my cell, I kept thinking about it. And then the realization came that perhaps I didn't hate my brother so much. I began to see that he couldn't help himself, and that if he had been cruel to me, I, in turn, had not been too good to him. I even thought that I ought to write to him to tell him how I felt about him, and why I changed. I have been thinking about it a great deal. It is funny how one can keep hating someone for so long. But I think I don't hate Jim so much any more. Besides, there is no point to it. I think I ought to forgive and forget. Sounds silly, don't it?

T.: You feel that you have changed, to some extent, your attitude toward your brother. Would you now like to hear the opinions of the other members?

E.: Yes, I'd be very much interested.

T.: As you know, we ask every member to give his reactions to your psychodrama of the last session and to your remarks made today, and so I'd like to ask each of you in turn to comment on your impressions.

A.: I think that a lot of people have hatred in them for things that people did to them. So, E. isn't so different. I have hatreds in me that go way back. There is one teacher I'd like to get, and I haven't seen him for 25 years.

B.: I got the impression that E. really likes his brother, and that he is only carrying on an old grudge. He sort of established a pattern of hating him.

C.: I don't think that E. has changed his attitude. I bet if he met him now, he'd still want to kill him. He is just saying he changed his opinion because he thinks he is expected to change it. In other words, I doubt that he really has changed.

D.: I don't have any opinion.

T.: You were here last session. It was your first time. I am sure you must have come to some opinion.

D.: No, I really didn't.

T.: Let me explain why I am asking you to comment. You see, this is group therapy. If you stay in the group, and if eventually you bring up some problem, then you would want others to tell you what they really think. In that manner you would be helped by knowing how others see you. Now, you can help E. by telling him what you think.

D.: Well . . . I must say that I was pretty much upset. What kind of a guy is E. anyway, wanting to kill his brother? I don't think that E. is right. I can't understand it. I got upset by him, too.

F.: Well, I think that E. never really hated his brother, otherwise he wouldn't have changed his opinion. Maybe he really hated himself and wanted to punish the brother.

G.: There is a lot of hatred in the world. Most children hate their fathers. E. did not have a father, and his older brother played the part of the father. Maybe he had a kind of father hatred.

H.: Sometimes a person knows he should change his attitude, but he doesn't want to lose face. I mean, I think that E. knew all along that he shouldn't hate his brother, but he needed an opportunity to say it right. I mean that when he enacted actually killing his brother, he realized that he had the wrong idea.

I.: I get a different feeling about it. He hates his brother, but now that he has killed him, even in imagination, he has gotten rid of his hatred, and it is all gone. Like if you don't like somebody and you play a dirty trick, then you feel you got even. I think he got even by play acting. It was real enough to him. I mean he really did kill him—in his own mind.

J.: Maybe E. never really hated his brother. He just is upset by his past experiences and blamed his brother, but now he realizes that his brother wasn't guilty.

K.: I don't know what to say. But I think E. feels he got a load off his mind.

L.: That's how I feel. He is free of hatred, and he feels better. He even looks better.

M.: I think he really has gone through something. I think the fact that he was able to talk about his hatred dissipated it.

T.: Well, Mr. E., you have heard a number of opinions, what do you say to them?

E.: Well, I think I can agree with most of them. I don't know now whether I really hated Jim, but I sure thought I did. I feel a bit foolish about it. How I used to think of hurting him! But I feel better about it. It is stupid going around hating people. I am going to write to him and tell him about it. I sort of want his ... forgiveness. I mean I understand him now better.

T.: Well, now we can have some discussion, if there is any. . . .

J.: I think there is little to say. E. had hatred, now he doesn't have it any more, and now he can go on to other problems. I didn't have the feeling that it was real hatred.

D.: But who knows what real hatred is? If you think you hate somebody, then, by God, you hate him. I don't see this "real hatred" part of it.

J.: I mean if you really hate a guy, you aren't going to change your attitude just by talking it over!

B.: I still think that he was carrying along a childish attitude, and now that he is growing up in his mind, he understands how foolish it was.

T.: Well, I think we should cut off discussion at this point and proceed to the psychodrama. Mr. K., it is your turn. The floor is yours.

K.: Well, thanks. I have a very embarrassing problem to bring up. I am probably the most miserable guy in this place, and after I tell you what it is I am sure all of you will think I am a rat. How one could do what I have done is beyond me. It's killing me. I can't sleep. But I'll give you the whole dirty story, and see if you can tell me what to do.

You see I got married when I was young. I was only eighteen, and my wife was sixteen. We had two kids. Joe, my son, is now eighteen, and my daughter Lillian is seventeen. We lived in the South, and we had a fairly good life. I never really was very much in love with my wife. She was a very good woman, not too flashy, sensible, and a good housekeeper, a good mother, and a good wife. Well, anyway, I was married to her for fifteen years when I met another woman. You see my job was a traveling one, and I don't want to create a wrong impression. I went around with a lot of women. I had all sorts of affairs: waitresses, check girls, B girls, and that sort of thing. None of them ever meant anything to me, you know what I mean. I never said anything to my wife, and I think she had an idea, but she just kept it inside her. And I made out I was a good husband, and I guess I was.

And then, it all happened. I fell in love. Funny thing, I was thirty-three, had two kids, but it was the first time I really fell in love. My wife had been more like a sister to me. I had known her all my life, but I really went big for this other woman. She had everything that I had ever wanted in a woman. She had looks, she had class, she had style. She could tell stories, she was amusing, and boy—how she could make love. I had never experienced anything like it. And the funny part—she was crazy over me. She had been married before, she told me, but her husband had never really given her the thrill I gave her. And so I told her about my wife, Helen, and we had something in common. Well, anyway, I kept seeing her. We went together for about 3 months. We were living together in another city, but finally she told me that I would have to make up my mind. I had met a lot of her friends, and they were real nice people. So, I went back home and asked my wife for a divorce. She cried, and I felt like a heel, but she agreed. I left the house, not even seeing the kids, and so she filed for divorce. The divorce came through, and I married Lil, the other woman.

About this time the war came on, and I started a business, making a part for an airplane, and before you knew it, I was making $10,000 a month. I was hiring several hundred people at one time. You have to understand that before the war, I used to make about five-six thousand, and now I was in the $100,000-a-year class. And when I was married to Helen, I watched every penny, but now I learned how to spend. Go to a hotel, get the best suite, pay for everything by check, what the hell, I had a smart manager, and he was sending me more than a thousand dollars a week. All I had to do was to spend it, and I sure had a girl with me who knew how to have a good time. We had a baby, but that didn't bother her much. She had another child with her mother. So we got a nursemaid and gave the town a good painting. It was wild and delirious. And then the bubble broke. The war was over. But we kept living at the same pace, and before you knew it, we were broke. Lil couldn't stop spending. I tried to make money, but I couldn't. I overdrew on the bank. Then I was in a mix-up, Lil started to raise hell, I passed more checks, and before you knew it, I was in prison.

As soon as I got in prison, Lil divorced me. And so there I was, twice married, and twice divorced. And so I did my time and finally came out. When I got out I didn't know which way to go. I tried to find work and became a salesman, living from hotel room to hotel room, and then one day, I remembered it was my son's birthday, and so I impulsively got on a plane. At the airport I called my first wife and told her I wanted to come back. I came home, and the family was there. I cried when I saw her and told her it was a big mistake. The kids were fine, and they suggested we get married again. I begged Helen to take me back, and she did. So, we got married again. And, having learned my lesson, I settled down. But I had gotten a taste of the good life, and before you know it I got into more trouble. I just violated my parole. Nothing serious, but here I am again. And now comes the hard part of it all. After not hearing from Lil for 3 years, she suddenly wrote to me, telling me about our son, what a big boy he was getting to be, sending me photographs of her and the kid, and telling me she was now doing fine, and that she had thought the whole thing over and wanted me to come back to her when I came out. She told me that she had kept some of the money and that she had bought a house, would I forgive her and take her back? Well, then I realized how much I loved her. The old feeling came back, and so I wrote to her, and she came to visit me, but I didn't tell her I had remarried Helen.

And now, that is my problem. I am in love with Lil, she *was* my wife, we *do* have a child, and I was *much* happier with her. She is exciting, glamorous, and now she wants me and wants us to settle down. But I remarried Helen, and I have given her a rough time, but I don't love her. And she expects me back. Suppose the two of them should come here and meet? And here I am trapped in this place. I have about six months to go. And I have to write letters to both, telling them both that I love them, and I feel like a dirty heel. What am I to do? I can't hurt Helen again. I owe it to my two children not to upset them any more. I hardly know the other child that Lil has. But Helen is dull and not exciting; life is gay and wonderful with Lil. But I want to tell you it is all killing me, trying to decide what to do. Should I tell Lil? Should I tell Helen? To whom should I go? What is the best thing? I can't keep up writing to two women like this, telling one I love her one night and then telling another I love her on the next night. And that is my problem.

T.: Could you think of how we might be able to dramatize the story?

K.: I don't know, I am all confused.

F.: I think that we could set up a situation where one of the women comes to see K., and then while we are having that visit, the other woman comes.

T.: How does that sound to you, K.?

K.: My God, the one thing I fear the most!

T.: Should we do it?

K.: If you want. Oh, what a mess that would be!

T.: Who are in the drama, and where will it be?

K.: In the visiting room. And there should be Helen, Joe, and Jane. Then in comes Lil with her kid.

T.: Who should take the parts?

K.: I don't know. Anyone.

T.: How about some volunteers? There is Helen, the first and present wife.

A.: I'll take her role.

T.: Then there is Joe, Helen's son. He is about eighteen.

C.: I'll be Joe.

T.: Then there is Jane, Helen's daughter.

Y.: I'd like to try that.

T.: Good, Mr. Y., I am sure you will make a fine girl! And now, who'll take the difficult part of Lil, the second wife?

B.: That is my role.

T.: Tell the various people now, K., about themselves.

K.: Well, Helen, you have been married to me about twenty years. About five years ago I divorced you and remarried. Then I went to prison. About a year ago I persuaded you to remarry me. I have hurt you a lot. You care for me, and you are hoping that when I come back I'll settle down. You are a person who has a lot of dignity, but I have been pretty irresponsible. You, Joe, like me a lot, and you love your mother, and you don't want me or anybody else to hurt her. And you, Jane, you are very close to your mother, but you are a bit suspicious of me.

T.: And Lil, how about her?

K.: Well, she is . . .

T.: No, tell Lil to her face what kind of person she is.

K.: You are touchy. You fly off the handle. When you get excited, you don't care what you say. You are sort of easy to get excited. You like good times. You are impatient. You don't have fears.

T.: Everybody know his part? Good! Will you go out, K., and a "guard" will come to bring you in to have a visit. You will find Helen, Joe, and Jane there. [K. goes out of the room.]

T.: Now, let me suggest the following: Helen, you say very little, just cry a lot. Joe, you try to be manly and brave about seeing your father in prison. Jane, I think you will comfort your mother, and you should have an attitude of protection for your mother. And then, at the signal, Lil, you come in. Be really excited when you find out what is going on. I think our job is to make the situation as realistic as possible. And now, for the rest of you, try to watch K. carefully, notice his reactions, and try to figure out how he feels. Ready, J., will you go and tell K. that he has a visit? Ready now, let us make this one sing!

Psychodrama

The group has opened up. Seated in the center are the auxiliary egos playing the parts of Helen, Joe, and Jane. In comes K., led by the "guard."

J.: There is your family, K. They sure are a nice family.

HELEN [running to K. and putting her arms about him]: Oh, Ken!

K. [nervously]: Take it easy, Helen. Now, don't cry, don't get upset.

HELEN: Oh, I can't stand it. Seeing you here surrounded by bars... like a wild animal. I can't stand it. [Cries.]

K.: Don't cry, Helen. Don't cry. [Jane leads mother to seat and comforts her. Throughout the rest of the drama, Helen cries and Jane sits by her.]

JOE: Hello, Dad. How do you feel?

K.: Gee, you sure are growing up. My, are you on the football team?

JOE: No, I went in for basketball. I think it is a faster game. How are you, Dad?

K.: Good. Helen. Please, stop crying, it upsets me. [Helen cries louder.]

JANE: What do you expect, anyway? Do you want her to laugh? What do you think people say about you, anyway?

K.: Oh, get her to stop crying. This is a hell of a visit! Joe, tell me, how is fishing? Did you get any trout this year?

JOE: Well, I didn't go fishing much.

K.: Well, we'll do more when I get out. I'll be out in...

J.: I am sorry to interrupt you, K., but you have another visitor....

LIL: Darling! [Runs in and throws arms about K.] Oh, my darling, how changed you look. Oh, my poor dear, you have lost weight. Tell me about yourself. It is almost 2 years I haven't seen you. But things are going to be different. But Ken, who are these people?

K.: This... this... this is my family, my wife, Helen. [Helen begins to sob loudly.] Oh, for Christ's sake, Helen, you knew... please STOP it!

JANE: Don't yell at my mother. You ought to be ashamed of yourself.

JOE: Are you the woman who stole my father? You have some nerve coming here.

JANE: You dirty bitch! You broke up my mother's marriage.

K.: Stop it. Stop. For God's sake, give me...

JOE: Why don't you leave him alone?

LIL: What the hell is going on here? I married him. I have a child. He is the father of my child. He is free. He's not married to your mother. Why doesn't she leave him alone? He loves me, don't you?

K.: God! Helen, stop your crying. I'll explain everything. I am glad...

JANE: Women like you ought to go to prison. You drove my father to prison, you broke my mother's heart.

LIL: I like that. Ken, make her stop saying such things about me.

[The room is in an uproar, everyone is trying to shout down everyone else. Helen cries loudly all the time.]

K.: Quiet. QUIET. I am glad this happened. I feared it. For Christ's sake, shut up, Helen. I'll explain everything, everything. Will you please...

T. [slapping hands twice]: That is all. You may leave the room now, K. Let us go on to the next psychodrama.

[A new situation is taken up by F., and a new drama takes place.]

T.: Well, we have had our two psychodramas, and I'd like to ask at this time for volunteers for the next session.

J.: I'll come up next week.

T.: Well, can we have another? Some of the people have not come up for a long time.

M.: Well, maybe I ought to volunteer.

T.: That gives us our cast for next week. And now, let us go on to our icebreaker. Last week, when D. was here for the first time he participated in the sociodrama. How would you like, D., to take the role of the bartender this time, and let Mr. Y. be the customer?

D.: Well, all right. I don't know how I will do.

T.: And who'll take the role of the other customer?

L.: I'll do that. I got a new angle.

T.: Are you ready, Mr. Y.? You did very well in your role as Jane, but how would you like to experience our little icebreaker?

Y.: I'm game for anything. What is it like?

T.: It is simple. This table is a bar. You come to it to have a drink. You are a bit lonely, and you try to get into conversation with the bartender and the other person. Now, they may take various attitudes, but the whole point of it is that it is a test, to see how well you can react to a difficult situation. Try to make friends if you can. O.K., let us get into places.

[D. goes behind the bar, L. is a customer. Mr. Y. comes in. The bartender comes over.]

D.: What'll you have?

Y.: Give me a whisky.

D.: I got lots of whisky. What kind do you want?

Y.: How about Four Roses?

D.: Don't you want something good?

Y.: What's wrong with Four Roses?

D.: Nothing, but we got more expensive drinks.

Y.: Four Roses will be good enough for me.

D.: Well, if that is what you want, I'll give it to you. [Goes through motions of pouring a drink.]

Y.: Nice place you have.

D.: Lousy clientele. You should see the bums that come in here.

Y.: Who is he? [Points towards L.]

D.: None of my business. And none of yours.

Y.: That is a hell of a way. No wonder you don't have a good clientele. You have to treat your customers nicely.

D.: You mind your business, I'll mind mine. If you don't watch out, I'll throw you out of the joint. Who in hell do you think you are anyway?

Y.: Oh, nuts. I'll buy that guy a drink. Say, what do you want to drink?

L.: None of your f-----g business.

Y. [looking disconcerted]: I only asked you if you would have a drink with me.

L.: I don't drink with homosexuals. Just keep away from me, or I'll punch you in the nose.

Y.: Oh, all right, I'll drink alone.

[L. comes over and looks Y. right in the face. Y. stares back.]

L.: Say, Dan, look who this crumb is. It's Schlett.

D.: Who's Schlett?

L.: You know the bastard, the one who borrowed 10 bucks from you and never paid it back.

Y.: My name is not Schlett, or whatever you called me. My name is Yablonsky.

L.: A likely story. Look at him, Dan, don't you recognize him?

D.: Yeah, that's him. Where is my 10 bucks? Come on, cough it up, or you'll feel sorry. [Comes over the bar.] Well, do I get my money, or do you get your lumps?

Y.: It's a mistake. You got me confused with someone else.

L.: No, and you know what you did to Anna, the poor girl, aren't you ashamed of yourself, why you bastard, you got your nerve coming back here!

Y.: Honest . . .

T. [slapping hands twice]: Well, that's that. I hope that it wasn't too real, Mr. Y., but this is a situation we have used on and off for a long time; everyone in the room has gone through it. How did you find it?

Y.: Well, it was really interesting. For a time I thought that maybe I was really Schlett. It was quite an experience. I think that D. has a lot of potentialities for acting. He scared me.

D.: I enjoyed it. Last week I was just as scared as you was when I was in your place.

T.: Well, now it is almost time to conclude. Mr. Y., we usually ask new members to give us their first impression. What impressed you in this group? What suggestions would you give? And most important, what criticisms might you have?

Y.: I have no criticisms. It was quite an experience that I went through.

I think you are doing something very interesting and very important. I would like to come again next week, so that I can get a little more experience, and then maybe I can tell you some more.

T.: Thank you. And this ends this session. See you next week.

Discussion

T.: Well, Mr. Y., now that we are back in my office, maybe you would like to ask further questions.

Y.: I'd like to say it was quite an emotional experience. What will happen to Mr. K.? I think he went through quite a scene with his two wives.

T.: We feel that the real therapy occurs now, right after the session. A man is now alone with his conscience. That is when he really thinks.

Y.: Why do you send people out after their psychodrama?

T.: Because they can have an opportunity to meditate on their problems alone. We came to the conclusion empirically that it was the best way.

Y.: Would it be all right for me to come the next session?

T.: Of course. I guess we'll have to separate now. I have to fill out some reports before I leave. I'll see you next week at a quarter of three in this office.

NEXT SESSION

T.: We have Mr. Y. with us again. If we have no other business, we can go on with the recapitulation. How did it go, K.?

K.: You pulled a dirty trick on me, bringing in the two wives. But I have settled the problem. I wrote to Lil and told her the whole truth. I said that I still liked her, but that I had remarried Helen and that it was off between us. And I asked her not to write to me any more. After all, when I was in trouble she divorced me. Sure, she has glamour, but can I trust her? How do I know how many men she has gone with since she left me? She left her other husband in the lurch, too, and she left me. So I figured, why should I be a sucker and get into more trouble? And then I got to thinking about what a nice person Helen was, and what a dog I would be to go through it all over again. So, like I said, I settled the whole thing. I wrote to Lil, and I am sure I did the right thing. So that is all there is to it. But I sure felt rotten when I left this room last week. I did a lot of thinking, you can be sure.

T.: Well, you may be interested in hearing some other opinions. How about it?

A.: I guess you never really loved Lil. You were just excited by her. A glamour girl. Sort of something you never had.

B.: All she wanted was your money.

C.: But how come she writes when she knows he's in here? Maybe she thought it over?

D.: I think he did the right thing.

E.: How come he fell for her all over again? I think it is a hard decision.

F.: I'll bet that if he gets out, he will go and see this Lil anyway. She seems to have a fatal attraction for him.

G.: No, he must have come to his senses. The other woman will only give him more trouble. I think he has a pretty good wife, and he should stick to her.

H.: Anyway, K. is settled. I am surprised he didn't think of writing to her before.

I.: Well, as I see it, someday a guy has to wake up, and today K. worked himself up to the point where he opened his eyes.

[The session goes on.]

THE BULL SESSION

The group meets in the same place, and the members take seats.

M.: I think we had a pretty good set of sessions.

K.: It did me a lot of good. I feel much better since I wrote to Lil and told her to get off my back.

L.: Ha, ha, that is one way of putting it.

D.: Say, doctor, when does one know when he ought to get out of the group?

T.: Is that a problem for you?

D.: Well, not yet it ain't. I wanted to get out as soon as I got in, but now that I decided to stay in I wonder about how one knows when he ought to get out.

J.: What we usually do is discuss it here and give our opinions.

D.: Well, what do you think?

J.: About what?

D.: About me. Should I be in this group or not? I got things I can hardly dream of talking about.

M.: Are they more personal than what I talked about?

D.: I wouldn't say that, but after all you and I are different. I can't talk in front of others like some of you can.

E.: Well, I am going to quit the group today. I think I got out of it what I wanted. But I am asking also for the opinions of others.

D.: How long have you been coming here?

E.: About six months. I could stay, but I'd like to know what others think.

F.: I'd say you ought to stay a bit longer. I wouldn't run out too soon if I were you.

G.: D. asked about whether others have trouble. I wanted to get out when I first came in, and I want to tell you that it was the smartest thing I ever did to stay in. You don't know how much good it did me. Where else can you talk about anything and nobody will criticize you or tell you what you ought to do?

D.: Well, if somebody doesn't tell you, how do you learn?

G.: From your own good sense. You listen to others, and then you make up your own mind.

D.: But if you ain't got no mind?

G.: You got as good a mind as anybody. What are you trying to do, run yourself down?

D.: No, but maybe this won't do me any good.

E.: It isn't doing you no harm, is it?

D.: No. I guess I'll stick. I just wanted to know what you fellows thought.

T.: Do you mean to say you weren't really sure whether you wanted to leave or not, but wanted to know the opinions of others?

D.: Sure. What's wrong with that? What do you think, do you think that I can get anything out of it?

T.: What do you think?

D.: I am not sure, but I'm willing to give it a chance. After all, what have I got to lose?

E.: I'd like to ask about the free association we tried out.

M.: What was that? I think I missed that session.

E.: I got up in the middle of the room, closed my eyes, and said all the words I could think of in 10 minutes, and everybody listened, and then they tried to analyze what was in my mind.

J.: You got a mind?

E.: So it turned out. I felt that the guesses were pretty good.

F.: I think there isn't much to that. I like the psychodramas better.

M.: Dr. T. I'd like to ask this. Do you think that people really get benefit from these sessions? How do we know we won't go out and steal after we go out?

T.: You may steal, but it will be a different person who will steal. If your stealing has neurotic reasons, then if we remove the neurosis we remove the motivation to steal. Is that sufficient?

B.: I used to pass checks for emotional reasons. I sure hope that I'll stop that kind of silly behavior. People sure do silly things.

J.: Well, anyway, some day some of us learn before it is too late.

Discussion

The interview between Dr. T. and Mr. Y., the two parts of two psychodramatic sessions, and the part of the bull session should have created an impression of psychodramatic group therapy. As may have been evident from the nature of the interchanges, considerable emotionalism is developed in the sessions; this frees the members of inhibitions and enables them to make substantial progress. This loss of inhibitions, combined with the rational aspects of the group, the discussions and mutual supports, enables individuals to gain new perspectives about themselves and others.

Bibliography

1. Abrahams, J. Preliminary report of an experience in the group psycho-therapy of schizophrenics. Amer. J. Psychiat., 104: 613–617, 1948.
2. ——— Group psychotherapy: implications for direction and supervision of mentally ill patients. In Theresa Muller, Mental health in nursing. Washington, D.C.: Catholic University, 1950. Pp. 77–83.
3. ——— and L. W. McCorkle. Group psychotherapy of military offenders. Amer. J. Sociol., 51: 455–464, 1946.
4. ——— Group psychotherapy at an army rehabilitation center. Dis. nerv. Syst., 8: 50–62, 1947.
5. Abrahamsen, D. Evaluation of the treatment of criminals. In P. H. Hoch, Failures in psychiatric treatment. New York: Grune & Stratton, 1948. Pp. 58–77.
6. Ackerman, N. W. Group therapy from the viewpoint of a psychiatrist. Amer. J. Orthopsychiat., 13: 678–687, 1943.
7. ——— Group psychotherapy with veterans. Ment. Hyg., N.Y., 30: 559–570, 1946.
8. ——— Round table conference: group psychotherapy and the treatment of minority problems. Group Psychother., 4: 74–76, 1951.
9. ——— Some structural problems in the relation of psychoanalysis and group psychotherapy. Int. J. Group Psychother., 4: 131–145, 1954.
10. Alexander, F., and T. M. French. Psychoanalytic therapies: principles and applications New York: Ronald, 1946.
11. Alexander, G. H. Psychotherapy and psychotherapist: new orientations. Psychosom. Med., 2: 304–310, 1940.
12. Allison, S. G. Non-directive group therapy of alcoholics in a state hospital. Quart. J. Stud. Alcohol., 13: 596–601, 1952.
13. Allport, G. Personality: a psychological interpretation. New York: Holt, 1937.
14. Altshuler, I. M. One year's experience with group psychotherapy. Ment. Hyg., N.Y., 24: 190–196, 1940.
15. ——— The organism-as-a-whole and music therapy. Sociometry, 8: 465–470, 1945.
16. Amster, Fannie. Collective psychotherapy of mothers of emotionally disturbed children. Amer. J. Orthopsychiat., 14: 44–51, 1944.
17. Atterbury, G. P. Psychodrama as an instrument for diagnostic testing. Sociometry, 8: 79–81, 1945.
18. Axline, Virginia. Play therapy. New York: Houghton Mifflin, 1947.
19. Bach, G. R. Intensive group psychotherapy. New York: Ronald, 1954.

20. Backus, O. L., and Harriet M. Dunn. Intensive group therapy in speech rehabilitation. Speech Disord., 12: 39–60, 1947.
21. Baehr, G. O. The comparative effectiveness of individual psychotherapy, group psychotherapy and a combination of these methods. J. consult. Psychol., 18: 179–183, 1954.
22. Bales, R. F. The therapeutic role of Alcoholics Anonymous as seen by a sociologist. Quart. J. Stud. Alcohol., 5: 267–278, 1944.
23. Barnes, R. H., E. W. Busse, and H. Dinken. The alleviation of emotional problems in multiple sclerosis by group psychotherapy. Group Psychother., 6: 193–201, 1954.
24. Barton, W. B. Convalescent reconditioning program for neuropsychiatric casualties in the United States Army. Res. Publ. Ass. nerv. ment. Dis., 25: 271–284, 1946.
25. Baruch, Dorothy W. Description of a project in group therapy. J. consult. Psychol., 9: 271–280, 1945.
26. ——— and H. Miller. Group and individual psychotherapy as an adjunct in the treatment of allergy. J. consult. Psychol., 10: 281–284, 1946.
27. ——— The use of spontaneous drawings in group therapy. Amer. J. Psychother., 5: 45–58, 1951.
28. Bauer, I. L., and S. Gurovitz. Group therapy with parents of schizophrenic children. Int. J. Group Psychother., 2: 344–357, 1952.
29. Beasley, Jane. Group therapy in the field of speech correction. J. except. Child., 17: 102–107, 1951.
30. Becker, M. The effects of activity group therapy on sibling rivalry. J. soc. Casewk, 29: 217–221, 1948.
31. Bell, J. E. Projective techniques. New York: Longmans, 1948.
32. Bender, Lauretta. Group activities on a children's ward as methods of psychotherapy. Amer. J. Psychiat., 93: 151–173, 1937.
33. ——— and A. G. Woltman. The use of puppet shows as a psychotherapeutic measure for behavior problem children. Amer. J. Orthopsychiat., 6: 341–354, 1936.
34. Berl, Mildred E. The relationships of group psychotherapy to remedial reading. Group Psychother., 4: 60–62, 1951.
35. Berlien, I. C. Rehabilitation center: psychiatry and group therapy. J. crim. Law Criminol., 36: 249–255, 1945.
36. Bettleheim, B., and Emmy Sylvester. Therapeutic influence of the group on the individual. Amer. J. Orthopsychiat., 17: 684–692, 1947.
37. Bettis, M. C. A method of group therapy. Dis. nerv. Syst., 8: 235–246, 1947.
38. Bice, H. V., and Margaret Holden. Group counseling with mothers of children with cerebral palsy. J. soc. Casewk., 30: 104–109, 1949.
39. Bierer, J. Psychotherapy in mental hospital practice. J. ment. Sci., 86: 928–947, 1940.
40. ——— Group psychotherapy. Brit. med. J., 1: 414–417, 1942.
41. ——— A new form of group therapy. Ment. Hlth, London, 5: 23–26, 1944.
42. ——— Modern social and group therapy. In N. G. Harris (editor), Modern trends in psychological medicine. New York: Hoeber, 1948. Pp. 289–310.
43. ——— (editor). Therapeutic social clubs. London: Lewis, 1948.
44. Bion, W. R. The leaderless group project. Bull. Menninger Clin., 10: 77–81, 1946.
45. ——— Experiences in groups. Hum. Relat., (1) 1: 314–320, 1948; (2) 1:

487–496, 1948; (3) 2: 13–22, 1949; (4) 2: 295–304, 1949; (5) 3: 3–14, 1950; (6) 3: 395–402, 1950; (7) 4: 221–227, 1951.

46. ———— and J. Rickman. Intra-group tensions: their study as a task of the group. Lancet, ii: 678–681, 1943.

47. Bixby, F. L., and L. W. McCorkle. Guided group interaction in correctional work. Amer. sociol. Rev., 16: 455–460, 1951.

48. Blackman, N. W. Experiences with a library club in the group treatment of schizophrenics. Occup. Ther. Rehabil., 19: 293–305, 1940.

49. ———— Ward therapy: a new method of group psychotherapy. Psychiat. Quart., 16: 660–667, 1942.

50. ———— Group psychotherapy with aphasics. J. nerv. ment. Dis., 111: 154–163, 1950.

51. Boisen, A. T. The service of worship in a mental hospital: its therapeutic significance. J. clin. Pastoral Wk., 1: 19–25, 1948.

52. Borgatta, E. F. Research: pure and applied. Group Psychother., 8: 263–277, 1955.

53. Boring, R. O., and H. L. Deabler. A simplified psychodramatic approach in group therapy. J. clin. Psychol., 7: 371–375, 1951.

54. Brancale, R. Psychotherapy of the adult criminal. J. crim. Psychopathol., 4: 472–483, 1943.

55. Brody, M. W., and S. I. Harrison. Group psychotherapy with male stutterers. Int. J. Group Psychother., 4: 154–162, 1954.

56. Bromberg, W., and G. Franklin. The treatment of sexual deviates with group psychodrama. Group Psychother., 4: 274–289, 1952.

57. Buchmueller, A. D., and Margaret C-L. Gildea. A group therapy project with parents of behavior problem children in public schools. Amer. J. Psychiat., 106: 46–52, 1949.

58. Buck, Alice E., and T. Grygier. A new attempt in psychotherapy with juvenile delinquents. Amer. J. Psychother., 6: 711–724, 1952.

59. Buck, Betsy. Psychodrama of drug addiction. Group Psychother., 4: 310–321, 1952.

60. Buck, R. W. The class method in the treatment of essential hypertension. Ann. intern. Med., 11: 514–518, 1937.

61. Buckley, C. F. The Emmanuel movement and its affinities. Alienist neurol., 31: 70–79, 1910.

62. Burchard, E. M. L., J. J. Michaels, and B. Kotkov. Criterion for the evaluation of group psychotherapy. Psychosom. Med., 10: 257–274, 1948.

63. Burlingham, Susan. Therapeutic effects of a playgroup for pre-school children. Amer. J. Orthopsychiat., 8: 627–638, 1938.

64. Burrow, T. The group method of analysis. Psychoanal. Rev., 14: 268–280, 1927.

65. ———— The basis of group analysis. Brit. J. med. Psychol., 8: 198–206, 1928.

66. ———— The biology of human conflict. New York: Macmillan, 1937.

67. Camus, J., and P. Pagniez. Isolement et psychothérapie. Paris: Alcan, 1904.

68. Carmichael, D. M. Potential of group practices in mental hospitals. Int. J. Group Psychother., 3: 309–314, 1953.

69. Case, Mary E. The forgotten ones. Smith Coll. Stud. soc. Wk., 21: 199–231, 1951.

70. Cavanagh, J. R., and S. Gerstein. Group psychotherapy in a naval disciplinary barracks: preliminary report. Nav. med. Bull., Wash., 49: 645–654, 1949.

71. Chappell, M. H., J. J. Stefano, J. S. Rogerson, and H. S. Pike. Value of group psychological procedures in the treatment of peptic ulcers. Amer. J. dig. Dis. Nut., 3: 813–817, 1937.

72. Cholden, L. Group therapy with the blind. Group Psychother., 6: 21–29, 1953.

73. Clarke, E. K. Group therapy in rehabilitation. Fed. Prob., 16(4): 28–32, 1952.

74. Clinard, M. The group approach to social reintegration. Amer. sociol. Rev., 14: 257–262, 1949.

75. Coffey, H. S. Group psychotherapy. In L. A. Pennington and I. A. Berge (editors), An introduction to clinical psychology. New York: Ronald, 1954.

76. ———, M. Freedman, T. Leary, and A. Ossorio. Social implications of the group therapy situation. J. soc. Issues, 6(1): 44–61, 1950.

77. Cohen, R. R. Factors in adjustment to army life. War Med., 5: 83–89, 1944.

78. ——— Visual aids in group psychotherapy: puppetry. Group Psychother., 8: 311–314, 1945.

79. ——— Military group psychotherapy. Ment. Hyg., N.Y., 31: 94–102, 1947.

80. Coleman, J. C. Group therapy with parents of mentally deficient children. Amer. J. ment. Def., 57: 700–704, 1952.

81. Cope, J. R. The church studies its emerging function. J. soc. Issues, 6(1): 5–13, 1950.

82. Corbin, Maria L. Group speech therapy for motor aphasia and dysarthria. J. Speech, Hearing Disord., 16: 21–34, 1951.

83. Corsini, R. J. The method of psychodrama in prison. Group Psychother., 3: 321–326, 1951.

84. ——— Psychodramatic treatment of a pedophile. Group Psychother., 4: 166–171, 1951.

85. ——— Immediate therapy. Group Psychother., 4: 322–330, 1952.

86. ——— The "behind-your-back" technique in group psychotherapy and psychodrama. Group Psychother., 6: 102–109, 1953.

87. ——— Group psychotherapy with a hostile group. Group Psychother., 6: 168–173, 1954.

88. ——— Towards a definition of group psychotherapy. Ment. Hyg., N.Y., 39: 647–656, 1955.

89. ——— and W. H. Lundin. Group psychotherapy in the mid-west. Group Psychother., 8: 316–320, 1955.

90. ——— and Bina Rosenberg. Mechanisms of group psychotherapy. J. abnorm. soc. Psychol., 51: 406–411, 1955.

91. Cotton, J. M. The psychiatric treatment program at Welch Convalescent Hospital. Res. Publ. Ass. nerv. ment. Dis., 25: 316–321, 1946.

92. ——— Group psychotherapy: an appraisal. In P. Hoch, Failures in psychiatric treatment. New York: Grune & Stratton, 1948. Pp. 121–128.

93. Cotzin, M. Group psychotherapy with mentally defective problem boys. Amer. J. ment. Def., 53: 268–283, 1948.

94. Curran, F. J. The drama as a therapeutic measure in adolescents. Amer. J. Orthopsychiat., 9: 215–231, 1939.

95. ——— and P. Schilder. A constructive approach to the problems of childhood and adolescence. J. crim. Psychopathol., 2: 125–142; 305–320, 1940.

96. Cypreansen, Lucile. Group therapy for adult stutterers. J. Speech hearing Disord., 13: 313–319, 1948.
97. Davidoff, E., and G. Buckland. Reaction of a juvenile delinquent group to story and drama techniques. Psychiat. Quart., 13: 245–258, 1939.
98. Day, M., E. Day, and R. Hermann. Group therapy of patients with multiple sclerosis. Arch. neurol. Psychiat., 68: 193–196, 1953.
99. DeFries, Zira, and Sue Browder. Group psychotherapy with epileptic children and their mothers. Arch. neurol. Psychiat., 67: 826–827, 1952.
100. Déjérine, J., and E. Gauckler. The psychoneuroses and their treatment by psychotherapy. Translated by S. E. Jelliffe. Philadelphia: Lippincott, 1913.
101. Deutsch, A. A., and J. Zimmerman. Group psychotherapy as adjunct treatment of epileptic patients. Amer. J. Psychiat., 104: 783–785, 1948.
102. Dreikurs, R. Challenge of parenthood. New York: Duell, Sloan & Pearce, 1948.
103. ———— Techniques and dynamics of multiple psychotherapy. Psychiat. Quart., 24: 788–799, 1950.
104. ———— The unique social climate experienced in group psychotherapy. Group Psychother., 3: 292–299, 1951.
105. ———— Family group therapy in the Chicago Community Child Guidance Centers. Ment. Hyg., N.Y., 35: 291–301, 1951.
105a.———— General Review. In Comptes rendus des séances. Premier congrès mondial de psychiatrie. Paris: Hermann, 1952. Pp. 223–239.
106. ———— Individual psychology. In A. A. Roback, Present-day psychology. New York: Philosophical Library, 1955. Pp. 711–731.
107. ———— and R. J. Corsini. Twenty years of group psychotherapy. Amer. J. Psychiat., 110: 567–575, 1954.
108. Dreikurs, Sadie. Psychological techniques applied in a group situation. Indiv. Psychol. Bull., 4: 110–125, 1945.
109. Durkin, Helen. Group dynamics and group therapy. Int. J. Group Psychother., 4: 56–64, 1954.
110. Dynes, J. B. and F. J. Hamilton. Group psychotherapy of psychiatric war casualties. U.S. Naval med. Bull., 44: 549–597, 1945.
111. Ebaugh, F. G. Group therapy. Neuropsychiatry, 1: 19–32, 1951.
112. Eliasberg, W. G. Group treatment of homosexuals on probation. Group Psychother., 7: 218–226, 1954.
113. Ellis, A. American sexual tragedy. New York: Twayne, 1954.
114. Emerson, W. R. P. The hygienic and dietetic treatment of delicate children. Bost. med. surg. J., 163: 326–328, 1910.
115. Eyesenck, H. The effects of psychotherapy: an evaluation. J. consult. Psychol., 16: 319–324, 1952.
116. Feifel, H., and A. D. Schwartz. Group psychotherapy with acutely disturbed psychotic patients. J. consult. Psychol., 17: 113–121, 1953.
117. Fenton, N. The potential treatability of prison inmates of different custodial levels. Proc. Amer. Prison Ass., 279–285, 1951.
118. Fidler, J. W. The concepts of levels in group therapy with psychotics. Int. J. Group Psychother., 1: 51–54, 1951.
119. Fiedler, F. E. A comparison of therapeutic relationships in psychoanalytic, non-directive and Adlerian therapies. J. consult. Psychol., 14: 436–445, 1950.

120. Fisher, Louise, and I. Wolfson. Group therapy of mental defectives. Amer. J. ment. Def., 57: 463–476, 1953.

121. Fleming, Louise, and W. U. Snyder. Social and personal changes following non-directive group play therapy. Amer. J. Orthopsychiat., 17: 101–116, 1947.

122. Flesch, R. Why can't Johnny read? New York: Harpers, 1955.

123. Foulkes, S. H. Principles and practice of group therapy. Bull. Menninger Clin., 10: 85–89, 1946.

124. ———— An introduction to group analytic psychotherapy. London: Heinemann, 1948.

125. Franks, T. W. A note on role playing in an industrial setting. Group Psychother., 5: 59–63, 1952.

126. Freeman, R. V., and A. Schwartz. A motivation center: a new concept in total neuropsychiatric hospital care. Amer. J. Psychiat., 110: 139–142, 1953.

127. Freud, S. Group psychology and analysis of the ego. London: International Psychoanalytic Press, 1922.

128. ———— Collected Papers: Volume II. New York: International Psychoanalytic Library, 1924.

129. Friedman, J. H., and L. Gerhart. The question box method of group therapy. Ment. Hyg., N.Y., 31: 246–256, 1947.

130. Fuller, Justin K. Extension of group therapy to parolees. Prison World, July–Aug.: 8–11, 1952.

131. Furst, W. Homogeneous versus heterogeneous groups. Int. J. Group Psychother., 1: 120–123, 1951.

132. Geller, J. J. A program of group psychotherapy in the treatment of chronic mental illness. Psychiat. Quart., 23: 425–438, 1949.

133. ———— Current status of group psychotherapy: Practice in the state hospitals for mental disease. Group Psychother., 3: 231–240, 1950.

134. ———— Concerning the size of therapy groups. Int. J. Group Psychother., 1: 118–120, 1951.

135. Gersten, C. Group therapy with institutionalized juvenile delinquents. J. genet. Psychol., 80: 35–64, 1952.

136. Gerstenlauer, C. Group therapy with institutionalized male juvenile delinquents. Ph.D. thesis, New York University, 1950.

137. Glatzer, Henriette, and Helen Durkin. The role of the therapists in group relationships. Nerv. Child, 4: 243–251, 1945.

138. Goldfarb, W. Principles of group psychother., Amer. J. Psychother., 7: 418–432, 1953.

139. Gordon, G., and K. Bowman. The auxiliary treatment of psychotic women —group therapy for their husbands. Calif. Med., 78: 303–308, 1953.

140. Gordon, T. Some theoretical notions regarding changes during group psychotherapy. Group Psychother., 4: 172–178, 1951.

141. Gorer, G. The revolutionary ideas of the Marquis de Sade. London: Wishart, 1934.

142. Gorlow, L., E. L. Hoch, and E. Telschow. The nature of non-directive group psychotherapy. New York: Columbia University Press, 1952.

143. Grant, Marjorie. The group approach for weight control. Group Psychother., 4: 156–165, 1951.

144. Greenblatt, M. Altruism in the psychotherapeutic relation. In P. A. Sorokin, Explorations in altruistic love and behavior. Boston: Beacon Press, 1950. Pp. 188–193.

145. Grunwald, Bronia. The application of Adlerian principles in a classroom. Amer. J. Indiv. Psychol., 10: 131–141, 1951.

146. Grunwald, Hannah. The case of Jean Case. Int. J. Group Psychother., 1: 64–77, 1951.

147. Gula, M. Boys' House—the use of a group. Ment. Hyg., N.Y., 28: 430–437, 1944.

148. Haas, R. B. Action counseling and process analysis: a psychodramatic approach. Sociatry, 1: 256–285, 1947.

149. ——— Psychodramatic retraining of stutterers. Sociatry, 1: 293–295, 1947.

150. Hadden, S. B. Group psychotherapy. Trans., Amer. Neurol. Ass., 69: 132–135, 1943.

151. ——— Group psychotherapy: a superior method of treating larger numbers of neurotic patients. Amer. J. Psychiat., 101: 68–72, 1944.

152. ——— Group therapy in prisons. Proc. Amer. Prison Ass., 178–183, 1948.

153. ——— Group psychotherapy in general hospitals. Int. J. Group Psychother., 1: 31–36, 1951.

154. ——— Dynamics of group psychotherapy (abstract). Arch. neurol. Psychiat., 65: 125, 1951.

155. ——— Historic background of group psychotherapy. Int. J. Group Psychother., 5: 162–168, 1955.

156. Harms, E. Group therapy—farce, fashion or sociologically sound? Nerv. Child, 4: 186–195, 1945.

157. Harris, H. I. Efficient psychotherapy for the large outpatient clinic. New Eng. J. Med., 221: 1–15, 1939.

158. Harrow, Gertrude S. Psychodrama group therapy. Group Psychother., 5: 120–172, 1952.

159. Hawkey, L. The use of puppets in child psychotherapy. Brit. J. med. Psychol., 24: 206–214, 1951.

160. Hill, B. An experiment in treating seriously disturbed juvenile delinquent boys. Psychiat. Quart. Suppl., 27: 105–119, 1953.

161. Hinckley, R. G., and Lydia Hermann. Group treatment in psychotherapy: a report of experience. Minneapolis, Minn.: University of Minnesota Press, 1951.

162. Hobbs, N. Group psychotherapy in preventative mental hygiene. Teachers Coll. Rec., 50: 170–178, 1948.

163. ——— Insight in short-term psychotherapy (abstract). Amer. Psychol., 4: 273, 1949.

164. ——— Group-centered psychotherapy. In C. R. Rogers, Client centered psychotherapy. Boston: Houghton Mifflin, 1951.

165. ——— Client-centered psychotherapy. In J. L. McCary and D. E. Sheer, Six approaches to psychotherapy. New York: Dryden, 1955.

166. ——— and G. R. Pascal. A method for the quantitative analysis of group psychotherapy (abstract). Amer. Psychol., 1: 297, 1946.

167. Honig, P. Psychodrama and the stutterer. Sociometry, 9: 175–176, 1946.

168. Horney, Karen. Self analysis. New York: Norton, 1942.

169. Hulse, W. Group psychotherapy with soldiers and veterans. Milit. Surg., 103: 116–121, 1948.

170. ——— The therapeutic management of group tension. Amer. J. Orthopsychiat., 20: 834–838, 1950.

171. ——— International aspects of group psychotherapy. Int. J. Group Psychother., 1: 172–177, 1951.

172. Hulse, W. Group psychotherapy at the 4th International Congress on Mental Health, Mexico City, Dec. 11–19, 1951. Int. J. Group Psychother., 2: 270–272, 1952.
173. Illing, H. The prisoner in the group. Group, 13(4): 3–8, 1951.
174. Jackson, E. N. The therapeutic function in preaching. Pastoral Psychol., 1: 36–39, 1950.
175. Jacobson, J. R. Group therapy in the elementary schools. Psychiat. Quart., 19: 3–16, 1945.
176. ———— and Katherine W. Wright. Review of a year of group psychotherapy. Psychiat. Quart., 16: 744–764, 1942.
177. ———— Review of a year of group psychotherapy. Elgin St. Hosp. Papers, 5: 26–42, 1944.
178. Jacques, E. Some principles of organization of a social therapeutic institution. J. soc. Issues, 3(2): 4–10, 1947.
179. Janet, P. Psychological healing. New York: Macmillan, 1925.
180. Janney, H. M., and C. E. Bemis. Efficient use of the prison psychiatrist. Prison World, Jan.–Feb.: 4, 1954.
181. Joel, W., and D. Shapiro. Some principles and procedures for group psychotherapy. J. Psychol., 29: 77–88, 1950.
182. Johnson, P. E. Introduction. In J. H. Pratt and P. E. Johnson, A 20 year experiment in group therapy. Boston: New England Medical Center, 1950.
183. Johnston, M. Experiment with narcotic addicts. Amer. J. Psychother., 5: 24–31, 1951.
184. Jones, F. D., and H. N. Peters. An experimental evaluation of group psychotherapy. J. abnorm. soc. Psychol., 47: 345–353, 1952.
185. Jones, M. Group psychotherapy. Brit. med. J., 2: 276–278, 1942.
186. ———— Group treatment with particular reference to group projective methods. Amer. J. Psychiat., 101: 293–299, 1944.
187. ———— Emotional catharsis and re-education in the neuroses with the help of group methods. Brit. J. med. Psychol., 21: 104–110, 1948.
188. Kadis, A., and Sophie Lazarfeld. The group as a psychotherapeutic factor in counseling work. Nerv. Child, 4: 228–235, 1945.
189. Kafka, H. Impromptu express. Impromptu, 1: 9–10, 1931.
190. Kahn, Jane, A. D. Buchmueller, and Margaret Gildea. Group therapy for parents of behavior problem children in public schools: failure of the method in a Negro school. Amer. J. Psychiat., 108: 351–357, 1951.
191. Kahn, Shirley, W., and R. A. Prestwood. Group therapy of parents as an adjunct to the treatment of schizophrenic patients. Psychiat., 17: 177–186, 1954.
192. Karpman, B. Principles and aims of criminal psychopathology. J. crim. Psychopathol., 1: 187–218, 1940.
193. Kelley, D. M. The use of general semantics and Korzybskian principles as an extensional method of group psychotherapy in traumatic neuroses. J. nerv. ment. Dis., 114: 189–220, 1951.
194. Kelman, H. Group therapy. Amer. J. Psychoanal., 8: 144–153, 1948.
195. Kennedy, M. L. The organization and administration of a group treatment program. J. correct. Educ., 3: 14–19, 1951.
196. Kew, C. E., and C. J. Kew. Group psychotherapy in a church setting. Pastoral Psychol., 1(5): 36–39, 1950.
197. Kiernan, J. G. Limitations of the Emmanuel movement. Amer. J. clin. Med., 16: 1088–1090, 1909.

198. King, M. R. Trends in medical correctional work. Newsletter of the Medical Correctional Association, p. 1 ff., 1953.
199. Klapman, J. W. Group psychotherapy: theory and practice. New York: Grune & Stratton, 1946.
200. ——— Didactic group psychotherapy. Dis. nerv. Syst., 11: 35–41, 1950.
201. ——— Social adjustment. Chicago: Resurgo Association, 1950.
202. ——— Group psychotherapy: social activities as an adjunct to treatment. Group Psychother., 3: 327–338, 1951.
203. ——— Psychiatric social club therapy. Group Psychother., 6: 43–49, 1953.
204. Klein, H. S. Psychogenic factors on dermatitis and their treatment by group therapy. Brit. J. med. Psychol., 22: 32–52. 1949.
205. Kline, N. S. Psychodrama for mental hospitals. J. clin. Psychopathol., 8: 817–825, 1947.
206. ——— Some hazards in groups psychotherapy. Int. J. Group Psychother., 2: 111–115, 1952.
207. ——— and A. Dreyfus. Group psychotherapy in Veteran Administration hospitals. Amer. J. Psychiat., 104: 618–622, 1948.
208. Klopfer, W. G. The efficacy of group therapy as indicated by group Rorschach records. Rorsch. Res. Exch., 9: 207–209, 1945.
209. Kolodney, E. Group treatment of mothers as a supplement to child psychotherapy. Ment. Hyg., N.Y., 28: 437–444, 1944.
210. Konopka, Gisela. Group therapy in overcoming social and cultural tensions. Amer. J. Orthopsychiat., 17: 693–699, 1947.
211. ——— Therapeutic group work with children. Minneapolis: Minn.: University of Minnesota Press, 1949.
212. ——— Group work in the institution: a modern challenge. New York: Whiteside, 1954.
213. Kotkov, B. Techniques and explanatory concepts of short-term group psychotherapy. J. Psychol., 28: 369–381, 1949.
214. ——— A bibliography for the student of group therapy. J. clin. Psychol., 6: 77–91, 1950.
215. ——— Group psychotherapy with wayward girls. Dis. nerv. Syst., 14: 308–312, 1953.
216. ——— Experiences with group psychotherapy with obese. Psychosom. Med., 15: 243–251, 1953.
217. Landsman, W. D., and T. Sheldon. J. consult. Psychol., 14: 210–215, 1950.
218. Lassner, R. Playwriting and acting as diagnostic therapeutic techniques with delinquents. J. clin. Psychol., 3: 349–356, 1947.
219. ——— Psychodrama in prison. Group Psychother., 3: 77–91, 1950.
220. Laughlin, H. P. A group approach to management improvement. Int. J. Group Psychother., 4: 165–171, 1954.
221. Lawlor, G. W. Psychodrama in group therapy. Sociometry, 9: 275–281, 1946.
222. Lazell, E. W. The group treatment of dementia praecox. Psychoanal. Rev., 8: 168–179, 1921.
223. Lenert, Marguerite, H. Eight original monodramas for speech personality therapy and development (abstract). Speech Monogr., 4: 211, 1947.
224. Lerner, A. An exploratory approach in group counseling with male alcoholic inmates in a city jail. Quart. J. Stud. Alcohol., 14: 427–467, 1953.
225. ——— An experiment in group counseling with male alcoholic inmates. Fed. Prob., Sept.: 37–39, 1953.

226. Leslie, R. C. Pastoral group psychotherapy. J. pastor. Counseling, 6 (Spring): 56–61, 1951.

227. Levy, M. M. Outdoor group therapy with adolescent boys. Psychiat., 13: 333–347, 1950.

228. Lewin, K., R. Lippitt, and R. White. Patterns of aggressive behavior in experimentally created social climates. J. soc. Psychol., 10: 271–299, 1939.

229. Linden, M. E. Group psychotherapy with institutionalized senile women. Int. J. Group Psychother., 3: 150–170, 1953.

230. Lindner, R. Rebel without a cause. New York: Grune & Stratton, 1944.

231. Lipkin, S. Notes on group psychotherapy. J. nerv. ment. Dis., 107: 459–479, 1948.

232. Lipnitzky, S. J. Psychotherapy in an institution for mentally defective patients. Lost & Found, 3: 5–6, 1940.

233. Lippitt, Rosemary, and Catherine Clancy. Psychodrama in the kindergarten and nursery schools. Group Psychother., 7: 262–290, 1954.

234. Lipschutz, D. M. Group psychotherapy as an auxiliary aid in psychoanalysis. Int. J. Group Psychother., 2: 316–323, 1952.

235. ——— Psychoanalytic group therapy. Amer. J. Orthopsychiat., 22: 718–737, 1952.

236. Little, Marion L. Psychiatric and psychological group therapy: I. The Elem. Sch., J., 46: 369–374, 1946.

237. Loeffler, F. J., and H. M. Weinstein. The co-therapist method: special problems and advantages. Group Psychother., 6: 189–192, 1954.

238. Loeser, L., W. Furst, I. S. Ross, and Thea Bry. Group psychotherapy in private practice. Amer. J. Psychother., 3: 213–233, 1949.

239. Low, A. A. Group psychotherapy. Illin. Psychiat. J. 1: 3–4, 1941.

240. ——— Mental health through will-training. Boston: Christopher, 1952.

241. Lowrey, L. G. (chairman). Group therapy: special section meeting. Amer. J. Orthopsychiat., 13: 648–691, 1943.

242. ——— Group therapy for mothers. Amer. J. Orthopsychiat., 14: 589–592, 1944.

243. Luchins, A. S. A course in group psychotherapy: method, content and results. J. clin. Psychol., 2: 231–239, 1946.

244. ——— Methods of studying the progress and outcomes of a group psychotherapy program. J. consult. Psychol., 11: 173–183, 1947.

245. ——— Restructuring social perceptions; a group psychotherapy technique. J. consult. Psychol., 14: 446–451, 1950.

246. Lundin, W. H., and B. M. Aronov. The use of co-therapists in group psychotherapy. J. consult. Psychol., 16: 76–80, 1952.

247. Marsh, L. C. Group treatment of the psychoses by the psychological equivalent of the revival. Ment. Hyg., N.Y., 15: 328–349, 1931.

248. ——— An experiment in the group treatment of patients at Worcester St. Hospital. Ment. Hyg., N.Y., 17: 396–416, 1933.

249. ——— Group therapy and the psychiatric clinic. J. nerv. ment. Dis., 81: 381–393, 1935.

250. McCann, W. H. The round-table technique in group psychotherapy. Group Psychother., 5: 233–239, 1953.

251. ——— and A. A. Almada. Round-table psychotherapy: a technique in group psychotherapy. J. consult. Psychol., 14: 421–435, 1950.

252. McCarthy, R. G. Group therapy in an out-patient clinic for the treatment of alcoholism. Quart. J. Stud. Alcohol., 7: 98–109, 1946.

253. —— Group therapy in alcoholism. Quart. J. Stud. Alcohol., 10: 63–108, 217–250, 479–500, 1949; 11: 119–140, 309–330, 630–653, 1950.

254. McCorkle, L. W. Group therapy in correctional institutions. Fed. Prob., 13(2): 34–37, 1949.

255. —— Group therapy in the treatment of offenders. Fed. Prob., 16: 22–27, 1952.

256. —— The present status of group therapy in U.S. correctional institutions. Int. J. Group Psychother., 3: 79–87, 1953.

257. —— Guided group interaction in a correctional setting. Int. J. Group Psychother., 4: 199–203, 1954.

258. Meals, D. W., and J. Summerskill. A technique for dealing with hostility in activity therapy. J. clin. Psychol., 7: 376–378, 1951.

259. Mehlman, B. Group play therapy with mentally retarded children. J. abnorm. soc. Psychol., 48: 53–60, 1953.

260. Meier, C. A. Advances in group and individual psychotherapy. Proceedings of the International Conference on Medical Psychotherapy. London: Lewis, 1948.

261. Meiers, J. I. Origins and development of group psychotherapy. Sociometry, 8: 499–534, 1945.

262. —— Thoughts of recent advances in group psychotherapy. Group Psychother., 3: 241–245, 1951.

263. Miller, H., and Dorothy W. Baruch. Psychological dynamics in allergic patients as shown in group and individual psychotherapy. J. consult. Psychol., 12: 111–115, 1948.

264. Mitchell, S. D. and A. Zanker. The use of music in group therapy. J. ment. Sci., 94: 737–748, 1948.

265. Moreno, J. L. Application of the group method to classification. New York: National Committee on Prisons and Prison Labor, 1932.

266. —— A case of paranoia treated through psychodrama. Sociometry, 7: 312–327, 1944.

267. —— Open letter to group therapists. Sociatry, 1: 16–30, 1947.

268. —— Psychodrama of an adolescent. Sociatry, 2: 7–26, 1948.

269. —— The ascendancy of group psychotherapy and the declining influence of psychoanalysis. Group Psychother., 3: 121–125, 1950.

270. —— Who shall survive? New York: Beacon House, 1952.

271. —— Sociodrama of a family conflict. Group Psychother., 5: 20–37, 1952.

272. —— Psychodramatic frustration test. Group Psychother., 6: 137–167, 1954.

273. Moreno, Zerka T. Psychodrama in the crib. Group Psychother., 7: 291–302, 1954.

274. Moss, E. P. A vacation experiment with a group of psychoanalytic patients. Psychoanal. Rev., 32: 219–224, 1945.

275. Mueller, E. E. Group therapy with alcoholics in a hospital setting. Dis. nerv. Syst., 10: 298–303, 1949.

276. Mullan, H. Some essentials in group psychotherapy. Group Psychother., 5: 68–69, 1952.

277. Newburger, H. M., and G. Schauer. Sociometric evaluation of group psychotherapy. Group Psychother., 6: 7–20, 1953.

278. Nicholson, W. H. Emotional factors in obesity. Amer. J. med Sci., 211: 443–447, 1946.

279. O'Brien H. P. The use of group methods in correctional treatment. Proc. Amer. Prison Ass., 80: 263–268, 1950.

280. Papanek, E. Treatment by group work. Amer. J. Orthopsychiat., 15: 223–229, 1945.

281. Paster, S. Group psychotherapy in an army general hospital. Ment. Hyg., N.Y., 28: 529–536, 1944.

282. Peck, H. B., R. D. Rabinovitch, and J. B. Cramer. A treatment program for parents of schizophrenic children. Amer. J. Orthopsychiat., 19: 592–598, 1949.

283. Pederson-Krag, Geraldine. Unconscious factors in group therapy. Psychiat. Quart., 15: 180–189, 1946.

284. Pepinsky, H. B. and Pauline N. Pepinsky. Implications of social dynamics for methods of therapy with college students (abstract). Amer. Psychol., 2: 292–293, 1947.

285. Peters, H. N., and F. D. Jones. Evaluation of group psychotherapy by means of performance tests. J. consult. Psychol., 15: 363–367, 1951.

286. Pfeffer, A. A., P. Friedland, and S. B. Wortis. Group psychotherapy with alcoholics. Quart. J. Stud. Alcohol., 10: 198–216, 1949.

287. Plowitz, P. E. Psychiatric service and group therapy in the rehabilitation of offenders. J. correct. Educ., 2: 78–80, 1950.

288. Pohlmann, K. E. Group techniques in rehabilitative counseling. J. Rehabilit., 17(4): 7–9, 1951.

289. Polansky, N. A., S. C. Miller, and R. B. White. Some reservations regarding group psychotherapy in inpatient psychiatric treatment. Group Psychother., 8: 254–262, 1955.

290. Powdermaker, Florence, and J. D. Frank. Group psychotherapy. Cambridge, Mass.: Harvard University Press, 1953.

291. Powell, J. W. Group reading in mental hospitals. Psychiat., 13: 213–226, 1950.

292. Prados, M. The use of pictorial images in group therapy. Amer. J. Psychother., 5: 196–214, 1951.

293. ———— The use of films in psychotherapy. Amer. J. Orthopsychiat., 21: 36–46, 1951.

294. Pratt, J. H. The home sanitarium treatment of consumption. Bost. med. surg. J., 154: 210–216, 1906.

295. ———— The home sanitarium treatment of consumption. Johns Hopkins Hosp. Bull., 17: 140–144, 1906.

296. ———— The organization of tuberculosis classes. Med. Communic., Mass. med. Soc., 20: 475–492, 1907.

297. ———— The class method of treating consumption in the homes of the poor. J. Amer. med. Ass., 49: 755–759, 1907.

298. ———— Results obtained in the treatment of pulmonary tuberculosis by the class method. Brit. med. J., 2: 1070–1071, 1908.

299. ———— The class method in the homes of tuberculars and what it has accomplished. Trans. Amer. climat. Ass., 27: 87–118, 1911.

300. ———— The tuberculosis class. Proc., New York Conference Hosp. Soc. Serv. Ass. N.Y.C., 4: 49, 1917.

301. ———— The principles of class treatment and their application to various chronic diseases. Hosp. soc. Serv., 6: 401–411, 1922.

302. ———— The influence of emotions in the causation and cure of psychoneuroses. Int. Clinics, 4: 1–16, 1934.

303. ———— The group method in the treatment of psychosomatic disorders. Sociometry, 8: 323–331, 1945.
304. ———— The use of Déjérine's methods in the treatment of the common neuroses. Boston: New England Medical Center, 15: 1–9, 1953.
305. ———— and P. E. Johnson (editors). A 20-year experiment in group therapy. Boston: New England Medical Center, 1950.
306. Randall, G. C., and W. C. Rogers. Group therapy for epileptics. Amer. J. Psychiat., 107: 422–427, 1950.
307. Redl, F. Group emotion and leadership. Psychiat., 5: 573–596, 1942.
308. ———— Diagnostic group work. Amer. J. Orthopsychiat., 14: 53–67, 1944.
309. ———— Resistance in therapy groups. Hum. Relat., 1: 307–313, 1948.
310. Redwin, Eleanore. The behind-your-back technique in marriage counseling. Group Psychother., 8: 40–46, 1955.
311. Reider, N., D. Olinger, and J. Lyle. Amateur dramatics as a therapeutic agent in a psychiatric hospital. Bull. Menninger Clin., 3: 20–28, 1939.
312. Reik, T. Listening with the third ear. New York: Farrar, Strauss, 1948.
313. Renouvier, P. Group psychotherapy in the United States. Sociatry, 2: 75–83, 1948.
314. Rew, K. G. The patients' evaluation of group therapy. Milit. Surg., 105: 389–399, 1949.
315. Riesman, D. The lonely crowd. New Haven, Conn.: Yale University Press, 1950.
316. Rogers, C. R. Counseling and psychotherapy. Boston: Houghton Mifflin, 1942.
317. ———— Client-centered psychotherapy. Boston: Houghton Mifflin, 1951.
318. Rome, H. P. Comments on Hadden's paper. Trans. Amer. neurol. Ass., 69: 136, 1943.
319. ———— Audio-visual aids in psychiatry. Hosp. Corps Quart., 18: 37–38, 1945.
320. ———— Military group psychotherapy. Amer. J. Psychiat., 101: 494–497, 1945.
321. Rosenthal, L. Group psychotherapy in a child guidance clinic. Soc. Casewk., 8: 337–342, 1951.
322. ———— Counter-transference in activity group therapy. Int. J. Group Psychother., 3: 431–440, 1953.
323. Ross, T. A. The common neuroses and their treatment by psychotherapy. London: Arnold, 1924.
324. Ross, W. D. Group psychotherapy with patients' relatives. Amer. J. Psychiat., 104: 623–636, 1948.
325. Rubin, H. E., and E. Katz. Auroratone films for the treatment of psychotic depression in an Army general hospital. J. clin. Psychol., 2: 333–340, 1946.
326. Ruesch, J., and G. Bateson. Communication, the social matrix of psychiatry. New York: Norton, 1951.
327. Ruskin, I. W. Analytic group psychotherapy for husbands and wives. Calif. Med., 77: 140–145, 1953.
328. Sacks, J. M., and S. Berger. Group therapy techniques with hospitalized chronic schizophrenic patients. J. consult. Psychol., 18: 297–302, 1954.
329. Sanderson, H. Basic concepts in vocational guidance. New York: McGraw-Hill, 1954.
330. Sarbin, T. R. Spontaneity training of the feebleminded. Sociatry, 7: 389–393, 1945.

331. Sarlin, C. N., and M. A. Berezin. Group psychotherapy on a modified analytic basis. J. nerv. ment. Dis., 104: 611–667, 1946.

332. Scheidlinger, S. Group therapy—its place in psychotherapy. J. soc. Casewk., 29: 299–304, 1948.

333. Schiffer, M. Trips as a treatment tool in activity group therapy. Int. J. Group Psychother., 2: 139–149, 1952.

334. Schilder, P. The analysis of ideologies as a psychotherapeutic method, especially in group treatment. Amer. J. Psychiat., 93: 605–615, 1937.

335. ——— Introductory remarks on groups. J. soc. Psychol., 12: 83–100, 1940.

336. Schmidhoffer, E. Mechanical group therapy. Science, 115: 120–123, 1952.

337. Schulman, I. The dynamics of certain reactions of delinquents to group psychotherapy. Int. J. Group Psychother., 2: 334–343, 1952.

338. Schwartz, E., and J. Goodman. Group therapy of obesity in elderly diabetics. Geriatrics, 7: 280–283, 1953.

339. Schwartz, L. A. Group psychotherapy in the war neuroses. Amer. J. Psychiat., 101: 498–500, 1945.

340. Sears, R. Leadership among patients in group therapy. Int. J. Group Psychother., 3: 191–197, 1953.

341. Seguin, C. A. Un experimento con psicoterapie colectiva. Rev. Neuro-Psychiat., Lima, 10: 378–379, 1947.

342. Seidler, Regine. School guidance clinics in Vienna. J. Indiv. Psychol., 2: 75–78, 1936.

343. Shaskan, D. A. Must individual and group psychotherapy be opposed? Amer. J. Orthopsychiat., 17: 290–297, 1947.

344. ——— Evolution and trends in group psychotherapy. Amer. J. Orthopsychiat., 18: 447–454, 1948.

345. ———, Dorothy Conrad, and J. D. Grant. Prediction of behavior in group psychotherapy from Rorschach protocols. Group Psychother., 3: 218–230, 1951.

346. ——— and Miriam Jolesch. War and group psychotherapy. Amer. J. Orthopsychiat., 14: 571–577, 1944.

347. ——— and H. Lindt. The theme of the aggressive mother during group therapy: analysis of a group interview. Psychoanal. Rev., 35: 295–300, 1948.

348. ———, R. Plank, and H. Blum. The function of the group. Psychoanal. Rev., 36: 385–388, 1949.

349. Sheldon, W. H. Variety of delinquent youths. New York: Harper, 1949.

350. Shor, J. A modified psychodramatic technique for rehabilitation of military psychoneurotics. Sociatry, 1: 414–420, 1948.

351. Silver, A. Group psychotherapy with senile psychotic patients. Geriatrics, 5: 147–150, 1950.

352. Simmel, E. War neuroses. In S. Lorand, Psychoanalysis today. New York: International Universities Press, 1949. Pp. 227–248.

353. Simon, B., J. D. Holzberg, A. Solomon, and C. H. Saxe. Group therapy from the viewpoint of the patient. J. nerv. ment. Dis., 105: 156–170, 1947.

354. Slavson, S. R. An introduction to group therapy. New York: Commonwealth Fund, 1943.

355. ——— The field and objectives of group therapy. In B. Glueck, Current therapies of personality disorders. New York: Grune & Stratton, 1946. Pp. 166–193.

356. ——— Differential dynamics of activity and interview group therapy. Amer. J. Orthopsychiat., 17: 293–302, 1947.

357. —— The group in child guidance. In E. Harms, Handbook of child guidance. New York: Child Care Publications, 1947. Pp. 402–412.

358. —— Advances in group psychotherapy. Int. Congress Ment. Health, Proc., 1948, 24–26.

359. —— The practice of group therapy. New York: International Universities Press, 1951.

360. ——, E. Hallowitz, and L. Rosenthal. In E. A. Spiegel (editor), Progress in neurology and psychiatry. New York: Grune & Stratton, 1952. Pp. 521–539.

361. Smith D. S., and Mary E. Hawthorne. Psychiatric rehabilitation: a follow-up study of 200 cases. Nav. med. Bull., Wash., 49: 655–669, 1949.

362. Smith, Marion, R., J. E. Bryant, and Doris Twitchell-Allen. Sociometric changes in a group of adult female psychotics following an extensive socializing program. Group Psychother., 4: 145–155, 1951.

363. Snowden, E. N. Mass psychotherapy. Lancet, 11: 759–770, 1940.

364. Solby, B. The psychodramatic approach to marriage problems. Amer. sociol. Rev., 6: 523–530, 1941.

365. Solomon, A. P., and T. L. Fentress. A critical study of analytically oriented group psychotherapy utilizing the techniques of dramatization of the psychodynamics. Occup. Ther. Rehabilit., 26: 23–46, 1947.

366. Solomon, A., F. J. Loeffler, and G. H. Frank. An analysis of cotherapists' interaction in group psychotherapy. Int. J. Group Psychother., 3: 171–180, 1953.

367. Solomon, J. C., and P. L. Axelrod. Group psychotherapy for withdrawn adolescent children. Amer. J. Dis. Child., 68: 86–101, 1944.

368. Somers, M. R., and P. S. Pouppirt. Discussion groups as an adjunct to psychotherapy. Calif. west. Med., 53: 79–82, 1940.

369. Sommers, Vita S. An experiment in group psychotherapy with members of mixed minority groups. Int. J. Group Psychother., 3: 254–269, 1953.

370. Speroff, B. J. Rotational role-playing used to develop executives. Personnel J., 33: 49–50, 1954.

371. Spitz, R. A., and Katherine M. Wolf. Anaclitic depression: an inquiry into the genesis of psychiatric conditions in early childhood, II. Psychoanal. Stud. Child, 2: 313–342, 1946.

372. Spotnitz, H. Group therapy as a specialized technique. In G. Bychowski and J. Louise Despert (editors), Specialized techniques in psychotherapy. New York: Basic Books, 1952. Pp. 85–101.

373. —— and Betty Gabriel. Resistance in analytic group therapy: a study of the group therapeutic process in children and mothers. Quart. J. child Behavior, 2: 71–85, 1950.

374. Stahl, G. R. A statistical report of industry's experience with role playing. Group Psychother., 6: 202–215, 1954.

375. Standish, C. T. and E. V. Semrad. Group psychotherapy with psychotics. J. psychiat. soc. Wk., 20: 143–150, 1951.

376. Stein, M. I. Visual aids in group psychotherapy for veterans with psychosomatic complaints. J. consult. Psychol., 4: 206–211, 1948.

377. Sternbach, O. The dynamics of psychotherapy in the group. J. child Psychiat., 1: 91–112, 1947.

378. Stone, A., and Lena Levine. Group therapy in sexual maladjustment. Amer. J. Psychiat., 107: 195–202, 1950.

379. Stoute, A. Implementation of group interpersonal relationships through psychotherapy. J. Psychol., 30: 145–156, 1950.

380. Strauss, E. B. Comments on J. Bierer's paper. Proc. Royal Soc. Med. 37: 209, 1944.

381. Sutherland, J. D. Notes on psychoanalytic group therapy: therapy and training. Psychiat., 15: 111–117, 1952.

382. Symonds, P. M. Role playing as a diagnostic procedure in the selection of leaders. Sociatry, 1: 43–50, 1947.

383. Talland, G. A., and D. H. Clark. Evaluation of topics in therapy group discussions. J. clin. Psychol., 10: 131–137, 1954.

384. Taylar, E., C. A. Stickland, and C. S. Lindsay. Social clubs in the treatment of defectives. In J. Bierer, Therapeutic social clubs. London: Lewis, 1948.

385. Taylor, F. K. The therapeutic factors of group analytic treatment. J. ment. Sci., 96: 976–997, 1950.

386. ——— On some principles of group therapy. Brit. J. med. Psychol., 25: 128–134, 1952.

387. Teirich, H. R. Was ist Gruppenpsychotherapie?, Psychother. med. Psychol., 1951. 1: 26–30, 1951.

388. ——— Group psychotherapy in Austria. Group Psychother., 4: 107–111, 1951.

389. ——— The use of video methods in group psychotherapy. Group Psychother., 8: 47–48, 1955.

390. Thorpe, J. J. and B. Smith. Operational sequences in group therapy with young offenders. Int. J. Group Psychother., 2: 24–33, 1952.

391. ——— Phases in group development in the treatment of drug addiction. Int. J. Group Psychother., 3: 66–78, 1953.

392. Toeman, Z. Audience reactions to therapeutic films. Sociometry, 8: 493–497, 1945.

393. Torrance, P. Psychodramatic methods in the college. Sociatry, 2: 368–375, 1948.

394. Turnbloom, Martha, and J. S. Myers. A group discussion program with families of aphasic patients. J. Speech Hearing Disord. 17: 393–396, 1952.

395. Van Emde Boas, C. Group therapy with anorgastic women. Int. J. Sexol., 4: 1–6, 1950.

396. War Department. Technical Bull. No. 103, p. 7, 1944.

397. Weeks, H. A. Preliminary evaluation of the Highfields project. Amer. Sociol. Rev., 18: 280–287, 1953.

398. Weingold, J. T., and R. P. Hormuth. Group guidance of parents of mentally retarded children. J. clin. Psychol., 8: 118–124, 1953.

399. Wender, H. B. Experiences in group psychotherapy with insulin-treated patients. Psychiat. Quart., 24: 314–323, 1950.

400. Wender, L. The dynamics of group psychotherapy and its application. J. nerv. ment. Dis., 84: 54–60, 1936.

401. ——— Group psychotherapy: a study of its application. Psychiat. Quart., 14: 708–718, 1940.

402. ——— Group psychotherapy. Sociometry, 8: 346–349, 1945.

403. ——— Group psychotherapy within the psychiatric hospital. In B. Glueck, Current therapies of personality disorders. New York: Grune & Stratton, 1946. Pp. 46–58.

404. ——— Reflections on group psychotherapy. Quart. Rev. Psychiat. Neurol., 6: 246–248, 1951.

405. ——— Current trends in group psychotherapy. Amer. J. Psychother., 5: 381–404, 1951.

406. —— Selection of patients for group psychotherapy. Int. J. Group Psychother., 1: 55–58, 1951.

407. —— and A. Stein. Group psychotherapy as aid to outpatient treatment in a psychiatric hospital. Psychiat. Quart., 23: 415–424, 1949.

408. Wendland, L. V. A therapeutic group with husbands and wives of poliomyelitis patients. Group Psychother., 8: 25–32, 1955.

409. Whitaker, C. A., J. Warkentin, and Nan Johnson. A philosophical basis for brief psychotherapy. Psychiat. Quart., 23: 439–443, 1949.

410. Willner, G. P. Preliminary report of the introduction of group psychotherapy on a chronic ward in a mental hospital. Psychiat. Quart. Suppl., 26: 86–92, 1952.

411. Wineman, D. Group therapy and casework with ego disturbed children. J. soc. Casewk., 30: 110–113, 1949.

412. Wittenberg, R. Psychiatric concepts in group work. Amer. J. Orthopsychiat., 14: 76–83, 1944.

413. Wolf, A. The psychoanalysis of groups: I. Amer. J. Psychother., 3: 213–232, 1949.

414. ——, N. Locke, M. Rosenbaum, E. Hillpern, W. Goldfarb, Asya Kadis, S. J. Obers, I. L. Milberg, and R. G. Abell. The psychoanalysis of groups: the analysts' objections. Int. J. Group Psychother., 2: 221–231, 1952.

415. Worcester, E., S. McComb, and I. H. Coriat. Religion and medicine. New York: Moffat, 1908.

416. Wright, Katherine W. Group therapy in extramural clinics. Psychiat. Quart., 20: 322–331, 1946.

417. Yablonsky, L. Preparing parolees for essential social roles. Group Psychother., 8: 38–39, 1955.

418. Yonge, K. A., and N. O'Connor. Measurable effects of group psychotherapy with defective delinquents. J. ment. Sci., 100: 944–952, 1954.

419. Zimet, C. N., and H. J. Fine. Personality changes with a group therapeutic experience in a human relations seminar. J. abnorm. soc. Psychol., 51: 68–73, 1955.

Visual Aids

The films listed below and on the following pages can be used to illustrate and supplement much of the material in this book. Both motion pictures and filmstrips are included, the character of each being indicated by the abbreviations "MP" and "FS." Immediately following this identification is the name of the producer and, if different, the primary distributor of the film, then the date of its production. Abbreviations used for the names of producers and distributors are identified in the list of sources at the end of the section. Unless otherwise indicated, the motion pictures are 16-mm sound black-and-white films and the filmstrips are 35-mm black-and-white and silent. The length of motion pictures is given in minutes (min), that of filmstrips in frames (fr).

Most of the films in this list can be borrowed or rented from state and local film libraries listed in "A Directory of 3,300 16mm Film Libraries," compiled by the U.S. Office of Education and available for 70 cents from the Superintendent of Documents, Government Printing Office, Washington 25.

This list is selective, and readers, if interested in locating additional films, should consult the following references:

"Educational Film Guide" and "Filmstrip Guide." H. W. Wilson Co., New York.

"Mental Health Motion Pictures." National Institute of Mental Health, Bethesda, Md.

"Psychological Cinema Register." Pennsylvania State University, University Park, Pa.

"Films in Psychiatry, Psychology, and Mental Health." Health Education Council, New York.

Special attention is called to a series of films entitled *Mental Mechanisms,* produced by the Canadian National Film Board for the Department of Public Health of Canada and designed specifically for use in group psychotherapy under professional leadership. The films in this

237

series, distributed in the United States by the Text-Film Department of the McGraw-Hill Book Company, Inc., are:

The Feeling of Rejection (1947, 23 min). Documentary-dramatic study of a young woman whose feelings of rejection are manifested in maladustment and physical illnesses. Through flashbacks, traces her feelings of rejection to childhood origins and shows her beginning to understand her problem through psychiatric help.

The Feeling of Hostility (1948, 27 min). Documentary-dramatic study of Clare, a young woman apparently successful in her profession but a failure in personal relationships. Through flashbacks, traces her hostility to childhood experiences and shows how psychiatric treatment helps her direct her hostility into constructive efforts.

Feelings of Depression (1950, 30 min). Dramatized case study of how and why feelings of depression shadow the business and home life of John, a conscientious young married man. Explains how psychiatry could help him understand himself and the reasons for his feelings.

Overdependency (1949, 32 min). Dramatized story of a young married man whose inability to face the ordinary problems of life, including vague physical ailments and vocational maladjustment, stems from a childhood too dependent upon his mother and sister.

Breakdown (1951, 40 min). Case study of a young woman who has a schizophrenic breakdown. Follows the course of her treatment from a mental health clinic to a state hospital and concludes with her discharge from this institution to complete her rehabilitation as a member of her family.

To Serve the Mind (1954, 25 min). Case study of a doctor who suffers a schizophrenic breakdown; shows the various forms of treatment that gradually lead to his recovery and return to work.

OTHER FILMS

Activity Group Therapy (MP; Col U 1950; 50 min). Film record of a group of emotionally disturbed and socially maladjusted boys undergoing activity group therapy. Shows the gradual improvement in personalities and the role of the therapist.

Activity for Schizophrenia (MP; USVA, 1950; 25 min). Shows how therapists under the guidance of psychiatrists establish interpersonal relationships through intensified physical activities and motivate patients from lower levels of activity to more socialized levels.

Alcoholism (MP; EBF, 1952; 22 min). Attempts to show that the roots of alcoholism are embedded in personality difficulties. Contains sequences portraying group psychotherapy used by Alcoholics Anonymous.

Animal Studies in the Social Modification of Organically Motivated Behavior (MP; PCR, 1938; 12 min silent). Using rats as experimental animals, demonstrates how social situations pattern behavior.

Belonging to the Group (MP; EBF, 1952; 16 min color or b&w). Explains the meaning of the idea of respect and its essential relation to living in a democracy, the origin and development of some barriers to respect, and ways of eliminating such barriers.

Client-centered Therapy, Parts 1 and 2 (MP; PCR, 1952; 30 min each). Documentary record of interviews between Dr. Carl R. Rogers and clients. Part I covers the initial interview with a female graduate student perturbed about her social isolation. Part 2 records the 32d session in the case of a middle-aged mother who is experiencing conflict with her husband and daughter.

Counseling Adolescents (MP-FS series; McGraw, 1955). Three motion pictures and follow-up filmstrips, correlated with Williamson, "Counseling Adolescents."

A Counselor's Day (11 min). Portrays the activities of a student counselor, his techniques before and during counseling of individuals, and his relationships with adolescents in curricular and extracurricular activities. (Follow-up filmstrip, 29 fr.)

Diagnosis and Planning Adjustments in Counseling (18 min). As a companion to *Using Analytical Tools,* this film explains and illustrates the successive steps in counseling—searching for the cause, easing anxieties and strain, planning courses of action, and making new adjustments. (Follow-up filmstrip, 23 fr.)

Using Analytical Tools (14 min). Portrays a counselor analyzing a typical student problem and the various tools which he uses—cumulative record, test data, anecdotal records, and other information on the student's physical, emotional, and scholastic growth. (Follow-up filmstrip, 24 fr.)

Experiment (MP; GM, 1947; 12 min). Humorous explanation of how to influence people by gentle persuasion. Live-action photography and cartoon animation.

Experimental Studies in Social Climates of Groups (MP; Iowa U, 1940, rev. 1953; 31 min). Shows behavior of groups of boys organized in clubs run on democratic principles, as an autocracy, and as a laissez-faire group. Shows responses when groups are changed from one type to another.

Introduction to Psychodrama (MP; TFP, 1951; 25 min). Didactic demonstration of the functions of a therapeutic theater and various psychodramatic techniques, supplemented by an explanatory narrative. Psychiatric consultant: J. L. Moreno, M.D.

The Lonely Night (MP; MHFB, 1954; 62 min). Story of a young woman's journey out of the dark hours of emotional disturbance. Shows the process of psychiatric treatment candidly and completely and the kind of family life that can help build emotional strength.

Mental Hospital (MP; IFB, 1953; 20 min). Day-to-day story of the treatment received by a mental patient from the time of his admission to the hospital until he is discharged. Sponsored by Oklahoma State Department of Health.

Mind and Medicine (MP; AMA, 1955; 46 min). Kinescope of a program originally produced for closed-circuit television explaining the problems of mental illness and the latest techniques being used, including a report on the "open ward" system and "therapeutic communities" in Belgium and England. Produced by Smith, Kline & French Laboratories in cooperation with the American Psychiatric Association and the American Medical Association.

Nurse's Day with the Mentally Ill (MP; PCR, 1954; 22 min color or b&w). Shows typical activities of a student nurse in a modern psychiatric hospital. Includes many examples of spontaneous behavior of the mentally ill. Showings restricted to professional audiences.

Our Invisible Committees (MP; NEA, 1951; 25 min). Explores the point of view that one of the important obstacles to group thought and decision making is the conflict of social pressures operating within individuals during a meeting. Presents a case study of such a group.

Out of True (MP; BIS/IFB, 1951; 41 min). Story of a typical case of mental illness, followed through to its conclusion. Centers upon Molly Slade, who lives with her husband, two children, and mother-in-law in a crowded block of flats, and shows how she recovers through expert psychiatric treatment and returns to her family.

A Positive Approach to the Psychiatric Patient (MP; USVA, 1955; 30 min). Shows the treatment in Veterans Administration hospitals for psychiatric patients who have emerged from acute episodes of mental illness but who are not yet well enough to leave the hospital. Uses a hospital ward unit as the focal setting and stresses the roles of the nurse, aide, and physician.

Psychotherapeutic Interviewing (MP series; USVA, 1950–1952). Series of 6 films:

An Approach to Understanding Dynamics (34 min). Depicts an interview between a patient and a psychiatrist; analyzes the dynamics of the interview; and explains the patient's reactions to certain experiences and the meaning of these reactions to the psychiatrist.

A Clinical Picture of Anxiety Hysteria (26 min). Illustrates psychotherapeutic interviewing principles and techniques through an unrehearsed interview between a psychiatrist and a patient suffering from anxiety hysteria.

A Clinical Picture of Claustrophobia (31 min). Illustrates psychotherapeutic interviewing principles and techniques through an unrehearsed interview between a psychiatrist and a patient suffering from claustrophobia.

Nonverbal Communication (27 min). Discusses the recognition of clues of nonverbal communication and the manner in which these clues can be used in an interview situation to obtain information and to further therapy. Illustrates the various points through pictures, with subtitles, of actual unrehearsed interview situations.

Psychotherapeutic Interviewing: Introduction (11 min). Explains basic principles of the doctor-patient relationship and the structure and goals of the psychotherapeutic interview.

Psychotherapeutic Interviewing: Method of Procedure (32 min). Depicts an interview between a patient and a psychiatrist; analyzes the principles and methods employed in the interview; and emphasizes the importance of the doctor-patient relationship, planning in terms of goals, focusing upon relevant topics, and minimal activity on the part of the doctor.

Role Playing in Guidance (MP; Calif U, 1953; 14 min). Shows how a teacher uses a role-playing technique in counseling a young boy. The method shown is halfway between "advice-giving" therapy and "deep-level" therapy. Based on "Action Counseling, a Psychodramatic Approach" by Robert B. Haas.

Role Playing in Human Relations Training (MP; NEA, 1949; 25 min). Portrays skills required in role playing and the uses of role playing in the study of human relationships.

Room for Discussion (MP; EBF, 1952; 25 min). Examines the nature and function of discussion in its personal and group aspects.

Social Process (MP; EBF, 1952; 20 min). Professor Harold D. Lasswell conducting a seminar on the patterns of behavior common to all cultures and explaining the concept that "man seeks values through institutions using resources."

Someone Who Cares (MP; Ind U, 1955; 22 min). Points out the too frequent overcrowding and monotony in mental hospitals and gives examples of the contributions being made by citizen volunteers who bring program services such as games, music, and parties to the mental patients.

Unity of Personality (MP; PCR, 1946; 18 min silent). Shows consistency of expressive movements of five individuals with very different personalities, via films made with their knowledge. Shows and explains similarities of expressive behavior characteristics which relate to the "unity of personality."

What Do You Think? (MP series; CNFB/McGraw, 1953). Seven films,

6 minutes each, dramatizing problem situations, leaving discussion and resolution to the audience:

Getting What You're After

Having Your Say

Honest Truth

Majority Vote

One Man's Opinion

Public's Business

Who's Running Things?

Working and Playing to Health (MP; MHFB/IFB, 1954; 35 min). Shows programs of therapy for the patients of a mental hospital and explains how and why such techniques are used to help bring patients back to health. Sponsored by the Illinois Department of Public Welfare.

PRIMARY SOURCES OF FILMS

AMA—American Medical Association, 535 N. Dearborn St., Chicago 10

BIS—British Information Services, 30 Rockefeller Plaza, New York 20

CALIF U—University of California, Berkeley, Calif.

CNFB—National Film Board of Canada, 630 Fifth Ave., New York 20

Col U—Columbia University Press, Center for Mass Communication, 413 W. 117 St., New York 27

EBF—Encyclopaedia Britannica Films, Inc., 1150 Wilmette Ave., Wilmette, Ill.

GM—General Motors Corp., 3044 W. Grand Blvd., Detroit 2, and 405 Montgomery St., San Francisco 4

IFB—International Film Bureau, 57 E. Jackson Blvd., Chicago 4

Ind U—Indiana University, Bloomington, Ind.

Iowa U—State University of Iowa, Iowa City, Iowa

McGraw—McGraw-Hill Book Company, Inc., Text-Film Dept., 330 W. 42 St., New York 36

MHFB—Mental Health Film Board, Inc., 166 E. 38 St., New York 16

NEA—National Education Association, 1201 16 St., NW., Washington 6

PCR—Psychological Cinema Register, Pennsylvania State University, University Park, Pa.

TFP—Therapeutic Film Productions, Inc., P.O. Box 311, Beacon, N.Y.

USVA—U.S. Veterans Administration, Central Film Library, Washington 25

Author Index

243

Subject Index

248

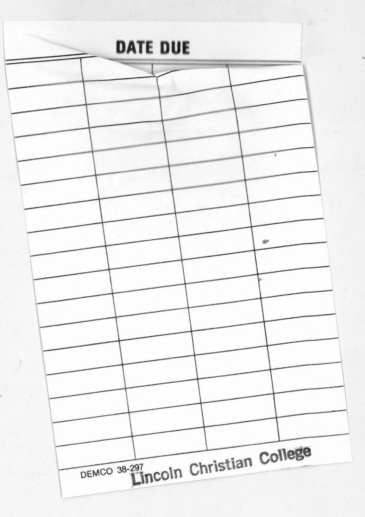